Sufficient Reason

Sufficient Reason

VOLITIONAL PRAGMATISM AND THE
MEANING OF ECONOMIC INSTITUTIONS

Daniel W. Bromley

PRINCETON UNIVERSITY PRESS
PRINCETON AND OXFORD

Copyright © 2006 Princeton University Press
Published by Princeton University Press, 41 William Street,
Princeton, New Jersey 08540
In the United Kingdom: Princeton University Press,
3 Market Place, Woodstock, Oxfordshire OX20 ISY

Library of Congress Cataloging-in-Publication Data

Bromley, Daniel W., 1940–
Sufficient reason : volitional pragmatism and the meaning of
economic institutions / Daniel W. Bromley.
p. cm.
Includes bibliographical reference and index.
ISBN-13: 978-0-691-12419-3 (hardcover 13 digit : alk. paper)
ISBN-10: 0-691-12419-1 (hardcover 10 digit : alk. paper)
1. Economics—Philosophy. 2. Institutional economics.
3. Economic policy. I. Title.

HB72.B75 2006
330.15′52-dc22   2005017807

British Library Cataloging-in-Publication Data is available

This book has been composed in Sabon

Printed on acid-free paper. ∞

pup.princeton.edu

Printed in the United States of America

10 9 8 7 6 5 4 3 2 1

Contents

vi • Contents

Acknowledgments

THE SEEDS for this work were planted in June 1998 at a conference in Oslo, Norway, sponsored by the Norwegian School of Management. Approximately twenty of us were invited to Oslo to commemorate the centenary of Thorstein Veblen's classic paper "Why Is Economics Not an Evolutionary Science?" which appeared in the *Quarterly Journal of Economics*. At this conference I first offered an early treatment of final cause and sufficient reason in connection with institutional change. The term "sufficient reason" came from Veblen's 1909 paper "The Limitations of Marginal Utility," published in the *Journal of Political Economy*. The stimulating discussions on this pleasant occasion provided the necessary inspiration and motivation for me to elaborate the early thoughts, and thus to work out the general themes developed here. I am grateful to my longtime friend and frequent collaborator Arild Vatn for the opportunity to participate in this conference. And I am especially grateful for the many hours we have spent together discussing economics, institutions, and the challenge of making economic advice pertinent to public policy.

Over the intervening six years I have benefited from a number of invited lectures at universities too numerous to list. Most everything I presented in one way or another related to the core ideas that I was developing for this book. In that sense, my debt of gratitude extends to all who listened, challenged, and struggled with the concepts and ideas presented here. At times my audiences were intrigued but skeptical. Yet with very few exceptions they were receptive and open to the idea of understanding institutions and institutional change from the perspective of volitional pragmatism. All who listened and commented have strengthened this final product. On those few occasions when I was told, with aggressive conviction, that I was "wrong"—an indictment suited to the answer to a problem of addition or subtraction but certainly not to a new way of formulating a theory of human action and economic institutions—I was reminded of the superadhesive qualities of what it is that some economists are quite certain they know. Ironically, those with the most assured convictions were usually the very same people eager to denounce others for choice and action predicated on habit instead of "rational analysis." I was reminded again just how durable are those habits of mind of such interest to Veblen. As Nietzsche warns us, firm convictions—not lies—stand as the more serious impediment to truth. More elegantly, the French philosopher Charles Renouvier observed that: "A proprement parler, il n'y a pas de certitude; il y a seulement des hommes certains" (Properly speaking, there is no certainty; there are only people who are certain [Renouvier 1859, p. 390]).

For the past three or four years I have used drafts of the book in my graduate course on Institutional Economics at the University of Wisconsin–Madison. I am indebted to the students in those classes for helping me to refine the material and the presentation so that it might be more accessible and coherent.

Finally, three people warrant special mention. My longtime assistant Mary Johnson continues to keep the days well organized and pleasant—all the while maintaining a cheerful and reassuring countenance. My good friend Juha Hiedanpää of the University of Turku, Finland, participated in a course on Institutional Economics I taught in Uppsala, Sweden, in the summer of 1999. There he spotted my nascent pragmatism and generously provided a marvelous (and ever-expanding) reading list that continues to enrich and refine my understanding of a wide range of the literature in philosophy. I am indeed grateful for this special friendship.

My wife, Joyce Elizabeth, has provided countless hours of insightful discourse as we share the best part of every day—our morning walks. Before sunrise, through spring rain, summer heat, and winter snow we "hit the road" each day for an hour during which we discuss a wide variety of topics. And in all of that she has helped me to craft a better book. More importantly, she has helped me to find a better life.

Preface

A BOOK I published in 1989 entitled *Economic Interests and Institutions: The Conceptual Foundations of Public Policy* (Blackwell) is the logical precursor of this current effort. That early work continues to bring satisfaction and recognition in some quarters, but it was not an entirely successful project. Institutional economists regarded it as too orthodox, and orthodox economists (whatever that may mean) regarded it as too institutional. My purpose at the time was to clarify the concept (and content) of economic institutions and to show how we might use rather standard welfare theory to assess institutions and institutional change. However, I insisted that the proper assessment was not in terms of the circular concept of efficiency but rather in broader terms. The legislature and the courts continually address the need for new institutional arrangements—driven by the recognition that the economy is always in the process of becoming. I suggested that the proper way to view institutions is as the legal foundations of the economy. This approach is consistent with the ideas of John R. Commons, but especially his *Legal Foundations of Capitalism* (1924). My model of institutional change was based on Commons's ideas of prospective volition and "reasonable valuing."

In that book I advanced the proposition that a major motivation of much institutional change could be thought of as reallocating economic opportunity. Of course, new technology animates institutional change, and new relative prices certainly animate institutional change. But I rejected the traditional dichotomy that institutional change was either in the interest of efficiency or merely redistributive. I argued that societies undertake many institutional changes with the specific intent of reallocating economic opportunity: laws to prohibit child labor, laws to protect the environment, laws to keep children in school until a particular age, laws to prohibit discrimination on the basis of gender or race or religion, and laws to enhance the safety of the workplace. I insisted that it is incoherent to view these institutional changes as being motivated by standard efficiency arguments for the simple reason that welfare economics teaches us that *any* institutional setup will conduce to efficiency if it is accompanied by competitive markets. The question worth asking therefore concerns the reasons for both the existing as well as the new structure of working rules and entitlements (institutions)—and that is a question that cannot be answered using standard efficiency arguments. Nor did it seem correct to consider new institutional arrangements as merely redistributing income to those now protected by these new rules and entitlements.

While most readers seemed to like the idea of "reallocating economic opportunity," they were troubled about how to tell when institutional change was really for the purpose of reallocating economic opportunity, and when institutional change was really mere rent seeking. How could I tell the difference, and how could I instruct others to spot the difference in other instances of institutional change? In other words, how could we be sure about which category of institutional change we had in our sights? In the years since that book appeared, I struggled for an answer to this problem. And then one morning I realized that the question itself was flawed. The question was flawed because it invoked two quite arbitrary categories—categories that seemed to recapitulate by another name the flawed dichotomy between achieving efficiency and effecting a redistribution of income. And it was flawed because it presumed that there was a way to be sure about the "really" part. More fundamentally, the dichotomy I had created was itself incoherent. The epiphany came somewhere in the middle of reading Richard Rorty, Hans Joas, Robert Brandom, Friedrich Nietzsche, Richard Bernstein, Stanley Fish, Willard Van Orman Quine, Joseph Raz, Pierre Bourdieu, Ludwig Wittgenstein, Charles Sanders Peirce, William James, and John Dewey. Now, having come to grips with this literature, I realize that back in 1989 (and long before that) I was a pragmatist without yet realizing it. I had been making most of the right moves but without the benefit of a structured set of language and concepts. I had failed to offer sufficient reasons for my approach.

There was also a strong methodological focus to the 1989 book in which I challenged the standard presumption that economics was a value-free science. I sought to put to rest the tired debates about positive and normative economics by insisting that objectivity resided not in the science but in the scientist. That is, could a scientist use the best practices of the day to advance an argument that would find agreement among other equally proficient members of the same discipline? If so, that scientist could be considered "objective." Here too, I was making the right moves but without the benefit of the right language and concepts. Again, I had failed to offer sufficient reasons for my approach.

I have now reconsidered my earlier ideas about economic institutions and institutional change. What follows is pragmatism all the way down.

Sufficient Reason

Prelude

IT MAY BE supposed that the most fundamental of human needs concerns food, water, and staying warm. This supposition would be mistaken. The most fundamental human need concerns what to believe. Believing is precedential to eating and drinking (and staying warm) for the simple reason that even the seemingly basic acts of eating and drinking require a concept about surviving and thereby experiencing the future. This attribution of value to the future is what renders survival a conceptual rather than a physical matter. Without the *idea* of the future, and without the attribution of value to the future, eating is not an obvious or compelling activity. Eating requires the will to live.

With the future driving actions in the present, believing becomes the predicate for all action. What should I eat? What should I drink? How might I stay warm? From this one may further suppose that believing is an individual enterprise. This supposition, too, would be mistaken.

As social beings, we tend toward—indeed, we are defined by—social beliefs. The essence of socialization is precisely the stabilization of beliefs. And stabilized beliefs define for us what is normal, natural, correct, right. It could not be otherwise.

And from this spare beginning, one can begin to make out the ground beneath the social arrangements—the institutions—that define our very being as social creatures.

CHAPTER ONE

Prospective Volition

> While the content of knowledge is what *has* happened, what
> is taken as finished and hence settled and sure, the *reference*
> of knowledge is future or prospective. For knowledge fur-
> nishes the means of understanding or giving meaning to what
> is still going on and what is to be done.
> —John Dewey, *Democracy and Education* (1916)

SUFFICIENT REASONS

At midnight on September 2, 1967, the Swedish government undertook
a profound institutional change: it altered the side of the road on which
automobiles were to be driven. We might suppose that Sunday, September
3 was a day of some considerable adjustment for drivers in Sweden, and
it seems probable that the following months were interesting times on
Sweden's roads. Why would the government of Sweden undertake such
a disruptive institutional change? Why does it matter on which side of
the road a people drive, as long as they all do it on the same side? How
much did it cost to change all the highway signs? What possible benefits
motivated this change? How could those benefits be measured against the
known—and presumably large—costs of the change? Was a benefit cost
study undertaken prior to this massive institutional change? In the absence of such study, how can we be sure that economic efficiency and
social welfare have not suffered? In the absence of this evidence, how can
we possibly know if the Swedes, in 1967, acted rationally? Surely, some
rent-seeking sign makers managed to gain control of the machinery of
state with the intent of garnering large contracts to produce millions of
new signs. Or, perhaps Swedish politicians and civic leaders saw a future
that they imagined would be better if they brought their driving institutions in line with those of their neighbors?

In 1973, approximately a decade after the publication of Rachel Carson's book *Silent Spring*, the pesticide DDT (dichloro-diphenyl-trichloro-
ethane) was banned in the United States for all but emergency uses. Since
the end of World War II, DDT had been used to control mosquitoes in
order to combat malaria, yellow fever, and typhus—among other diseases. Carson's book documented the extent to which DDT, by entering
the food chain, was the probable cause of reproductive problems. The

serious decline of the bald eagle (America's national symbol) in the United States was blamed on DDT, and this controversy was apparently an important stimulus to eventual passage of the Endangered Species Act. Many other nations have also banned DDT or placed it under strict control. Was the banning of DDT preceded by a careful benefit-cost study to prove that the ban would be socially beneficial? If not, how can we be certain that the ban of this powerful chemical was socially preferred? How can the U.S. economy remain competitive with the rest of the world if the government is able, quite arbitrarily, to impose regulations in the absence of benefit-cost analysis? Perhaps something else was at work here? Was DDT banned because of some sense that, regardless of how the benefits and costs might look to a Paretian economist, the larger issue of human safety—and environmental integrity—was absolutely compelling?

In 1819 the British social reformer Robert Owen successfully persuaded Parliament to enact a law prohibiting the employment in cotton mills of children less than nine years of age, and limiting the workday for all employees less than sixteen years of age to twelve hours per day. In 1825 and 1831 the law was extended so that all those under eighteen years of age were limited to twelve-hour workdays, and they could not be made to work nights until they reached the age of twenty-one. These measures were so aggressively fought by the millowners that Parliament was persuaded to refuse inspections and monitoring of compliance with the act. In 1844, under pressure from industrialists, the minimum age for entering factory work was pushed back down to eight years of age. Finally, in a series of acts between 1847 and 1853 the workday of women and children was set at twelve hours (6 a.m. to 6 p.m.) with ninety minutes for meals. In 1875 Lord Sandon's Education Act became law requiring that all children must be in school until they reach the age of twelve (Checkland 1964). How is a dedicated welfare economist to look upon these changes? Are these examples of "inefficient institutions"? Did these institutional changes reduce the rate of Britain's economic growth? Were these social reforms accompanied by a complete welfare analysis proving that the benefits of these institutional changes exceeded the costs of change? If not, how can we be sure that efficiency and social welfare did not suffer as women and children were suddenly constrained in the number of hours they might (be made to) work in the factories? How could it possibly happen that politics was allowed to interfere in the market in such an arbitrary fashion? Isn't this but another example of inefficient policies that redistribute income (welfare) away from the owners of factories and toward workers?

In November 2004 the British Parliament outlawed fox hunting with hounds—long regarded as the quintessential defining trait of proper recreation among the rural gentry in England and Wales. The issue had been fought over for at least two decades. Arguments were advanced about the economic impacts on the rural economy. Claims were made that as many as eight thousand people would be put out of work—including saddlers, blacksmiths, grooms, stablehands, and employees of pubs and lodging establishments. In addition, it was alleged that the countryside would soon be overrun with foxes wreaking havoc on all manner of living creatures. How can we explain this dramatic break with England's long and durable institutional tradition? Is nothing sacred? Were welfare economists invited in to offer estimates of the economic value of fox hunting, or to produce estimates of the economic impacts of foxes with and without hunting? Were studies undertaken to determine the willingness to pay on the part of others to see the regal splendor of fine horses and finer riders coursing through verdant hills in hot pursuit of their beagle hounds and the pesky fox? What about the "passive use value" of those who, though never themselves intending to hunt, conjured great value (utility?) merely knowing that somewhere, on a particular Sunday, imperial England was still alive and well—even if its empire had disappeared?

In 1872 Yellowstone National Park in the western United States was created. This park, the first of many areas to be set aside for preservation, covered almost nine thousand square kilometers in Wyoming and part of Montana. Following this action, Yosemite National Park in California and Grand Canyon National Park in Arizona were soon added to the nation's park system. And that system continues to expand slowly as new ideas emerge about particular ecological settings and circumstances. To the best of my knowledge, there was no proper welfare analysis undertaken to make sure that the private and social benefits of these actions exceeded the private and social costs. How can we be sure that efficiency did not thereby suffer, and that social welfare in the United States has not subsequently been permanently undermined by these actions? Are we to conclude that these massive land grabs by the government of the United States placed the American economy on an inefficient growth trajectory from which it will never recover?

These examples highlight the obvious problem facing those who imagine that prescriptive economic analysis offers essential and meaningful advice in the formulation of public policy. When Paretian economists lament the lack of welfare analysis of public actions, are they suggesting that legislation to limit the workday of women and children at the height of the Industrial Revolution was "inefficient"? When Paretian economists insist that important public actions must be subjected to a welfare analysis, are they suggesting that the creation of America's system of national parks was a mistake because they were not consulted to ascertain whether those actions were efficient (Arrow et al. 1996)? When development economists lament the absence of efficient institutions in some nations, do they mean to suggest that Norway and Sweden are somehow deficient because they do not resemble the United States in their institutional structures? Can it be that we have reached the point where it is possible to suggest that the main problem with India is that it is not more like Germany? And that the answer for Somalia is that it must become more like the Netherlands? If the teleology of growth is so compelling, then development economists from the United States need only say, "Become like us." Indeed, the Washington Consensus of the past few years—epitomized by American attitudes toward free trade and open capital markets, and the policies of the World Bank and the International Monetary Fund—seems to have consisted of little else (Stiglitz 2002; Taylor 1997). The financial crisis in Southeast Asia at the end of the twentieth century is what might have been predicted from the convergence of massive inflows of foreign capital into a region of the world without the requisite institutional infrastructure. That missing infrastructure, often dismissed as "regulations," would provide the necessary architecture and institutional scaffolding to make sure that fragile nations were not overwhelmed by massive and quite rapid inflows and outflows of capital.

Not surprisingly, these examples of institutional change reveal that democratic nation-states manage to find sufficient reasons for new policies (new institutions)—and those reasons stand despite the absence of monetary evaluations from Paretian economists. Does optimality and social welfare suffer accordingly?

REASONS VERSUS CAUSES

Public policy is concerned with debating reasons for collective action, and those reasons necessarily are found to reside in the circumstances of the future. The standard Paretian approach tends to evaluate public policy choices using decision rules predicated on individualistic utility maximization. But it seems worthy of notice that this approach to public policy employs methods whose failures precipitate the new-felt need for institutional change. That is, public policy—collective action—issues arise precisely because of the clear failure of atomistic maximizing behavior to yield aggregate outcomes that are considered to be socially redeeming. Does it not seem odd to use as a truth rule for collective action intended to correct existing problems the very same analytical algorithm that produced the particular circumstances suddenly found unacceptable?

In addition to using a flawed prescriptive rule for collective action, traditional economic approaches to policy analysis fail on other grounds as well. When considering individual choice, it is generally understood that we must assess the alternative states to be occupied by the individual in the future. John flips the light switch because he desires that the front yard be lighted. This desire for a future state (a particular outcome) is the reason for the choice, while the cause is that he flipped the light switch. The flipping of the switch is merely a necessary though quite uninteresting step in a process that starts with reason, entails a causal sequence, and ends with a desired outcome. The prospector rises early and digs hard well into the evening because of the prospect of finding gold. That is the reason he works hard. Notice that we need not introduce the notion that the utility of actors is thereby enhanced by their choice. It is quite enough to admit that the actors have sufficient reason for their actions. Our task is to understand those reasons. The economist may well insist that the actors' utility is thereby increased, but this embellishment of the reason for the action is unnecessary. To say that an action increases the actor's utility is neither necessary nor sufficient for us to explain a particular action. Quite obviously the individual imagines (and desires) being better off, or the action under consideration would not have been taken. But the pertinent idea in the mind of the prospector is that if he digs in a particular place, the chances are good that he will find gold. Indeed, he has convinced himself that he is digging in the most efficacious place—otherwise we might expect to find him digging elsewhere.

We see that individual actions are both explained and justified in terms of the future states they are expected to bring about, whether it be a nicely lighted front yard or a leather pouch bulging with valuable gold nuggets. Both individuals—John of the porch light and the prospector—are acting with the future clearly in mind. Notice that their reasons run from the future back to the present and not the other way around. This conceptualization of the choice problem requires us to comprehend that the imagined purposes of the future drive choice in the present. This vision of the choice problem entails the concept of final cause in which the "final cause of an occurrence is an event in the future for the sake of which the occurrence takes place. . . . things are explained by the purposes they serve" (Russell 1945, p. 67).

The gold prospector digs early and diligently (an occurrence in the present) for the prospect of an event in the future (finding gold). The prospect of gold in the future explains the digging in the present. The enhanced appearance of John's front yard in the future—and the future begins the minute he flips the switch—explains the flipping of the switch in the present. We see that plausible outcomes in the future motivate and therefore explain choices. Humans act with an eye to the future, not to the past, and not to the present. We are not pushed by the circumstances of the past or the present, but rather we are moved by the desire to alter future states we might occupy. Or, perhaps, we are moved by the realization that if we do not act now, the future will be worse than the present.

The first step in the quest for new public policy is not that current and future outcomes are found to be economically inefficient. Rather, existing settings and outcomes lead to questions about why those particular circumstances exist. Why is the health system so horrible? Why are highways not safer? Why are rivers fouled by pollution? From these challenges to the status quo will arise consideration of new institutional arrangements that might deliver improved outcomes for individuals in society. Perhaps newly published information about the effects of DDT will induce some individuals to question whether the future will be well served by the existing institutional arrangements that allow DDT to be used as a pesticide. The matter might be put: "If it is true that DDT causes particular environmental problems, as the evidence seems to suggest, then do we wish to continue down that path?" Notice that the pertinent question is not a matter of whether efficiency will suffer. Nor is it an issue of determining whether there is a bona fide "market failure" in our midst. Rather, the question concerns whether we want that particular future to be realized.

When reformers such as Robert Owen pressured the British Parliament to modify working conditions in the cotton mills, the debate undoubtedly focused on the life prospects of very young children laboring twelve to sixteen hours per day. The millowners could certainly be counted on to raise economic arguments against a change in the rules. If current debates serve as a guide, it would be asserted that the new institution prohibiting child labor would make their product more expensive (that is, the institutional change would be inflationary). We might also suppose that the millowners would complain that the change would render them less able to compete against foreign firms in nations whose institutional structure was more "business friendly." Finally, millowners might well have expressed concern that the new institution would lower the income of families whose children could no longer be in the labor force. By casting a social choice of this nature in purely economic terms, we see immediately that the debate gets framed in economic-efficiency terms. The reformers could only fall back on the argument that it was uncivilized at this time in history to have children in the mills rather than in school. The opponents of institutional change would likely cast the debate so that static calculations of an economic kind were advanced as arguments against a new institutional arrangement that has little to do with economics, yet a great deal to do with alternative visions of the future—children who are in school rather than in the mills. We are reminded that institutional change concerns whose interests will be advanced or impeded by some particular institutional arrangement. These choices are inherently of a rationing nature. And this is why I refer to them here as *rationing transactions*.

Notice that the mere presence of economic implications from institutional change is not sufficient for institutional change to be seen as, and to be evaluated as, solely an economic issue. Some economists are too easily captivated by the notion that because economics as we have come to define it is the science of choice, it is therefore the only science of choice. From this idea comes the quite obvious non sequitur that there can be no rational choice without the blessing of an economist or two. Given that much of contemporary economics employs the circular logic of revealed preference to "explain" choices consistent with preferences, it should be obvious that we are unable to say anything meaningful about the substantive reality of so-called rational choice. Despite this problem in the realm of the individual actor, many welfare economists have too eagerly insisted on a standard notion of rationality in collective action—that the net present value of all benefits and costs must be positive (or at least nonnegative) in order that an action might be considered socially preferred (Arrow et al. 1996). When the political process results in institutional change in the absence of this finding, Paretian economists are quite sure that once again the special pleaders have maneuvered politicians into yet another inefficient giveaway that reduces social welfare. This peculiar conclusion is simply the necessary entailment of positivism and consequentialist welfarism, and yet such dubious provenance seems not to preclude frequent criticism of much public policy being advanced with great certitude (Palmer, Oates, and Portney 1995).

Of course, institutional change is not always as some of us would wish it to be. Some institutional change appears inexplicable, and all of it produces gainers and losers. It is no mystery why the gainers tend to like particular institutional changes. Nor is it hard to see why the losers cannot be expected to rejoice. But the key questions concern how to understand the reasons for particular policies, and how to regard the gains and losses that attend institutional change. Farmers denied access to DDT must find another means to control crop pests. But of what long-run economic significance is this? Those who care about public health and bald eagles will obtain relief from the new rule. Are the economic interests of farmers logically commensurate with the destruction of important parts of the ecosystem? Is the momentary disruption of a particular industrial technology of the same significance as the quite irreversible elimination of bald eagles? While it is clear that the pest-control strategies of farmers will inevitably be more expensive at the outset—we deduce this from knowledge that farmers, given a choice, and being clever managers, would use the most cost-effective *legal* means of pest control—this fact is not sufficient (or even pertinent) to the social choice of whether to ban DDT. This conclusion follows necessarily from the realization that there exists a number of pest-control options open to farmers, all them arrayed in some manner based on their cost-effectiveness. The elimination of one strategy simply renders other strategies economically feasible—and now "efficient" to pursue.

If Paretian economists are to be consistent in their commitment to general equilibrium analysis, then the ban of DDT in the political arena is not different from some market-driven outcome that suddenly renders DDT no longer to be the cheapest pest-control strategy. What if some essential ingredient was no longer available in the market? Why is it that a market-driven elimination of DDT as a feasible technology—a price increase driven by a new scarcity of some pertinent raw material—is regarded as legitimate, while a ban on a deadly product is somehow regarded as untoward "interference" in the market? Why is it thought necessary to determine the willingness to pay for bald eagles and weigh this amount against the alleged "costs" to farmers of switching to a new pest-control strategy? The demise of bald eagles has a single plausible cause—DDT. Of course, scientific findings may someday emerge to exonerate DDT, at which point we might easily predict that the ban on DDT would then be lifted. The options for killing plant pests in agriculture are numerous, with only one of those options (DDT) being, at the moment, the cheapest (most efficacious). But being the "best" among the panoply of choices is not sufficient reason for selecting this option when it entails the social costs of eliminating the population of eagles (and perhaps other creatures).

We see that the preference for market-based outcomes rather than collective action (public policy) springs from the notion that market-driven change is the result of the wondrous invisible hand, while collective action to ban DDT is the result of willful intent to harm one group (farmers) while helping another group (those who care about bald eagles). Notice the appeal to magic. The market, through its alleged abilities to divine social values, gives the optimal technology trajectory that then generates the optimal pest-control strategy. Notice that the word optimal is simply another term for cheapest in terms of what the farmer has to pay to control pests. But, of course, by using the cheapest means on one set of accounts, the farmer manages to shift costs to others in the form of harm to bald eagles. Because there is no market for bald eagles, this situation is immediately labeled a market failure. Enter the Paretian economist to declare whether or not it is optimal to make farmers stop killing bald eagles while they go about their business of also killing crop pests. If it is not deemed efficient to bring about this new state of affairs (banning DDT), then it seems that there is no market failure and the eagles deserve to die—on economic grounds at least. Some welfare economists are inclined to say that if politicians should decide to ban DDT, then it must be for political reasons and not for rational economic reasons. We see here that "the market" is used as a basis to malign collective action when that political action differs from what is thought optimal in the light of prescriptive calculations predicated on market circumstances.

This strained case for freedom and markets was made by Hayek when he pointed out that coercion should be regarded as a restraint on what an individual may do when that restraint is the result of the will of other individuals and that "we should not regard as coercion the restraint on what an individual can do imposed upon him by 'physical circumstances' " (Viner 1961, p. 231). Because one's "physical circumstances" can quite easily be regarded as one's situation in the market, it is natural for those who prefer markets to point out that any change from the status quo by collective action, unless it has unanimous assent, constitutes coercion. Jacob Viner, in commenting on Hayek, noticed a rather serious flaw in Hayek's logic:

> Freedom is thus defined as freedom *from* subjection to the will of others, and not as freedom *to do* anything in particular, or for that matter to do anything at all, in the sense of power or ability or opportunity to do it. . . . It is to enable him [Hayek] to maintain a sharp distinction between "coercion" as meaning willed restraints on others and the restraints from "physical circumstances" that Hayek puts so much stress on what A "wills" with respect to B as distinguished from what impact A's behavior has on B regardless of whether A had B in mind or not. (Viner 1961, p. 231)

Notice that if individual A successfully "wills" some restraint on individual B, then that would constitute coercion of B by A. However, if the status quo institutional arrangements are such that A can behave in a manner that is seriously detrimental to the interests of B—but A remains oblivious or indifferent to B's suffering—this would not qualify as coercion in Hayek's eyes. This allows those who defend markets and the institutional status quo to suggest that when individual B decides to seek relief from this unpleasant situation, this manifestation of will on the part of B, coupled with B's necessity to seek some official sanction to be relieved (usually in the form of government action), comprises the essence of coercion upon poor A who is simply doing what she has always done. Notice that if B had the will to alter A's behavior but, instead of relying upon the state, had attempted to bargain with A over the interference and had failed, then the status quo would be reaffirmed by the welfare economist as efficient, and B would simply be out of luck. The so-called freedom of the market would be affirmed over the tyranny of collective action. It is not logical, but it is the received wisdom.

As a defense of minimal government and laissez-faire, Hayek's selective conception of coercion serves his normative purposes. In fact, this view of will and intent is common in the standard account of externalities.

Here we are told that externalities are unintended side effects of some other direct action; the steel mill makes steel, but as an unintentional by-product, it also fouls the air. Collective action to reduce that pollution is often seen as coercion of the polluting firm. Many welfare economists advocate an approach that allows bargaining between polluter and victim. If the victim cannot pay enough to induce the polluter to stop, then it is, according to the standard view, socially optimal that the pollution continue and that the victim either move away or suffer in silence. But is it credible to assume that externalities are unintentional visitations of costs on others? When the steel mill is planned, the owners or manager certainly know the recipe for making steel, and they know that it will entail a certain quantity of coal being burned and that the smoke from that combustion must go somewhere. How this part of the production process can be dismissed as "unintended" is curious indeed (Schmid 1978, p. 41). And it seems odd to suggest that the efforts of those (individual B) suddenly harmed by A's actions are engaged in coercive behavior if they decide to seek relief from the legislature rather than offering payments to A so as to be relieved of the harms. Why, exactly, is it compelling to insist that B must offer payments to A in order to be liberated from the visitation of unwanted costs from A?

We see that institutional change is often regarded, prima facie, as interference in the allegedly natural processes of the market. But this judgment rests on the false premise that the current price structure that guides rational calculation is logical and socially ratified. In actuality, what exists at any particular moment in an economic system is nothing but the mechanical and thus accidental coalescing of thousands of prior collective and individual actions that together create a set of ordered relations from within which today's prices will emerge, and today's atomistic choices will take place. If one believes that prices actually come from markets, then they reveal themselves quite capable of believing that milk actually comes from plastic bottles. Why this prevailing and quite arbitrary constellation of prices and costs carries any normative significance for public policy remains unjustified. Its only plausible claim to credibility is that we are thought to live in a "market economy," and thus by implication the outcomes of market processes are thought to be presumptively beneficent. But this is not a reason for the automatic sanctification of market outcomes—it is mere validationism. The status quo ante institutional setup merely exists. To imagine that the status quo ante is natural is to commit the naturalistic fallacy. To imagine that the status quo ante serves some useful and transcendent purpose—say, to enhance social welfare—is to commit the teleological fallacy. The status quo ante has but one redeeming feature: it protects those well served by it, and it harms those who are thereby disadvantaged. Indeed, advocacy of laissez-faire is simply a rallying cry for those now made comfortable by the status quo ante institutional setup. It is rather like those with an agreeable portfolio of economic assets insisting that the primary purpose of government is—but, of course, they mean ought to be—the protection of property rights. One looks in vain for the poor and miserable advancing this assertion.

FINAL CAUSE

We see that the conventional approach to the consideration of institutional change invokes the concept of consequentialist welfarism in an effort to pass judgment on the efficiency properties of proposed changes that are concerned with, indeed motivated by, rationing—that is, altering or reallocating—the gains and losses of future economic agendas. The Paretian economist errs by imagining that this process is correctly informed by the circular concept of economic efficiency. The Paretian economist also errs by grounding the evaluation of institutional change on the doctrine of mechanical cause. That is, mechanical cause is the process of evaluating future outcomes in terms of the present. But, of course, this is not how individual choice and action are formulated, and it is certainly at odds with how democratic societies undertake public policy. Public policy is correctly modeled as choice that considers present actions and their entailments in terms of the future. For public policy the pertinent question becomes, Will a commitment to the present institutional structure get us where we wish to be in the future? If the answer to that question is not promising, then a new institutional setup is called for. This process is informed by the concept of final cause—the purpose to be served by a new institutional setup. Notice that the desired outcome in the future constitutes the reason for the action whose resultant will be a modified institutional setup. The probable (and desired) outcome explains (is the reason for) the collective action that is the cause of the institutional change that will plausibly result in the desired outcome. We can say, therefore, that the plausible outcome provides evidence of sufficient reason for the new institutional arrangement.

Final cause permits us to understand that DDT was banned not because it was suddenly economically efficient to do so (a mechanical cause), and not because environmentalists suddenly acquired more "power" vis-à-vis agricultural interests (an ex post rationalization). DDT was banned because there gradually evolved a new collective commitment to the idea that bald eagles, and perhaps other animals, were worth the disruptions to pest control in agriculture—not "worth it" in welfare economics terms, but simply worth it in terms of creating a future that, on balance, seemed the better one to embrace. Pragmatists would suggest that we were able, collectively, to mobilize better reasons for a future with bald eagles than without them. The same can be said for alterations in British work rules in the nineteenth century, for the ban on fox hunting with hounds, for a change in the side of the road on which one drives a car in Sweden, and for the establishment of the national park system in America. Final cause reveals to us that children living in poverty are fed breakfasts (and possibly lunches) in schools not because they may not get them at home, and not because it is the socially optimal thing to do. They are fed for the reason that there is robust evidence that they will be happier, healthier, and more attuned to learning if they are not hungry. If we really believed that the future is understood in terms of the present, then it would be easy to allow schoolchildren to remain hungry and distracted. After all, it is costly to feed them from the public purse, and the present value of the comparative benefit streams is quite uncertain. But because public policy forces us to think of the present in terms of the future, feeding school-children comes to be seen as quite the obvious thing to do. We do this not on utilitarian grounds but on the grounds of more compelling outcomes in the future—in this case, their enhanced educational prospects.

Final cause would allow us to see that rules putting children in schools rather than in the workplace is not logically advocated or denounced on the basis of whether economic efficiency will be thereby advanced or harmed. The banning of deadly chemicals cannot be evaluated on efficiency grounds. There is no meaningful way to evaluate on efficiency grounds an institutional change that puts Sweden's drivers on a different side of the road. Indeed, the 1994 referenda in Finland, Norway, and Sweden whether to join the European Union—an institutional change of dramatic proportions—certainly did not lend themselves to analysis on welfare economics terms in which there emerged a single "rational" truth rule. Of course, the protagonists raised a number of issues, and much of the discussion was carried out in what we might regard as a general benefit-cost framework. But the idea of computing a net present value of a yes or no decision on such questions is absurd. The citizens of those three countries cast their votes, after long months of debate, in terms of their own individual sense of which future they found most compelling. Each person, in the course of contemplating the decision, searched for the best reasons by which it might be possible to fix his or her belief about the future either in or out of the European Union. It could not possibly be otherwise.

With the idea of final cause in hand, it is helpful to think of public policy—the process that entails institutional change in democratic states—as an exercise in practical inference (von Wright 1983). A syllogism of practical inference brings together two kinds of premises. The first I shall call the volitional premise. A *volitional premise* is a want statement, or a proposition concerning an end of action. The volitional premise can be thought of, in the language of final cause, as a desired outcome in the future for the sake of which a particular policy action *must* be undertaken now. If the emerging desire is to address problems of atmospheric ozone, then certain actions are required. If the emerging desire is to address the pollution of the Baltic Sea, then particular actions are required now. If the emerging desire is to make sure that a nation's youth are prepared to assume the responsibilities of citizenship, then particular actions are required now. We see here the application of *prospective volition*—the human will in action, looking to the future, contemplating ways in which the future might and should unfold. If nothing is done in each of these instances, then it is possible to contemplate the future and the probable outcomes to be realized under existing institutional arrangements. If those probable outcomes are regarded as undesirable, then the existing institutional arrangements that parameterize individual domains of choice—fields of action—will be seen as instruments whereby different possible futures are possible and, with some care, plausible. This brings us to the epistemic premise.

The *epistemic premise* draws on scientific and traditional belief (some prefer to call it scientific and traditional knowledge) to offer a plausible guide for necessary action if the volitional premise is to be realized. If it is intended that atmospheric ozone be protected then the epistemic premise represents the proposition that chlorofluorocarbons must be eliminated from everyday use. If it is intended that the Baltic must be protected, from further nutrient enrichment, then the epistemic premise reveals that nitrogen and phosphorous loadings must be reduced by some specific amount. If it is intended that children will grow up to be responsible citizens, then they must be required to stay in school until they reach a certain age and have acquired particular life skills. Notice that estimates of the monetary benefits arising from these future states are not a necessary or even a credible part of the decision process. Which is not to say that the costs of various means to reach these desired outcomes are irrelevant. But welfaristic estimates of the benefits in order to justify these outcomes are neither necessary nor sufficient for rational choice.

It is worth emphasizing again that new public policy starts with a consideration of particular desired outcomes in the future (the volitional premise). The epistemic premise—of the form, "if Y then X"—connects the desired outcome (Y) with the necessary action (X) to achieve that outcome. Notice that the epistemic premise is both a prediction and a prescription. The epistemic premise prescribes what must be done (X) in order that the desired outcome (Y) might be achieved. And the epistemic premise predicts that the desired outcome (Y) will be realized if a particular action (X) is undertaken.

The conclusion of a syllogism of practical inference is referred to as a practical necessity. That is, the conclusion points to the practical necessity of deploying the means (X) implicated in the epistemic premise in order to attain the end (Y) implicated in the volitional premise. The necessity of the conclusion of practical inference follows from the nature of the syllogism. Notice that the volitional premise is clearly not of the form:

Y is desired if the benefits of Y exceed the benefits of ~ Y ("not Y").

The welfare economist might be expected to put this as: iff $\Sigma\$V_Y > \Sigma\$V_{-Y}$. Nor is the volitional premise of the form:

Y is desired if the benefits of Y exceed the costs of X.

Rather, the volitional premise states what *must* be done. In democratic states, these declarations of what must (or ought to) be done emanate from the judicial and parliamentary branches of government. That is, after all, the reason why these branches of government exist. It is in the discourses of parliaments—and the considerations of the courts—that debates about the relative merits of Y and ~Y take place. Although Paretian economists may feel uncomfortable at the prospect of making choices without prices (and thus without monetary estimates of $\Sigma\$V_Y$), this is a misplaced concern (Vatn and Bromley 1994). Democratic structures and processes exist for precisely those purposes.

It is common in such discussions to consider future outcomes in terms of the discounted monetary benefits and costs. Doing so entails discounting the interests—the life prospects—of future persons. This happens in standard welfare economics analysis because the future is considered in terms of the internal rate of time preference. The internal rate of time preference is the one relevant to currently living agents as they contemplate deferring consumption into the future—perhaps next year, perhaps longer into the future. However, the external rate of time preference, the rate at which those now living discount the utility of future persons, is the pertinent rate for intertemporal choice, and this rate is not reflected in any prices faced by living agents, and it is therefore unavailable to us. For this reason, the external rate of time preference is not a choice variable that can be used to inform public policy about the future (Bazelon and Smetters 1999). Notice that it is not our consumption that is being deferred, because it is not our consumption in the future that matters (because we will not be here to consume). Intertemporal choice, in which those of us presently living compare our present consumption (and investment) decisions against the consumption decisions of future persons, entail interpersonal comparisons of well-being. Long-run intertemporal choice is interpersonal choice. The idea that the gainers could compensate the losers is incoherent. The standard story, that we can compensate future persons by not correcting serious environmental problems and generating yet more wealth to pass on to them—in their increasingly degraded environment—simply compounds the fallacy of standard approaches to public policy.

Interestingly, and paradoxically in light of standard thinking among some welfare economists, the political process brings the future into view. Individuals may contemplate their future in terms of the institutional structure within which they are embedded, and which defines for them acceptable domains of choice. But individuals cannot change that institutional structure; only collective action can alter the choice domains of individuals. And in contemplating that structure and its possible alteration, the future is all that matters.

We see that a welfare analysis of environmental policies in which the costs are borne today—say, in the form of higher carbon abatement costs—while the discounted benefits accrue in the future to persons not yet born constitutes choice in which the future is considered in terms of the present. Those of us now living stand as dictators over the environmental assets to be inherited by future persons, and in the standard economic approach to that problem we act in our interest, not in the interest of future persons. It remains to be explained how this approach can possibly be said to maximize social welfare over time. The standard approach simply assures that the time stream of all possible future discounted net benefits is as large as possible to those of us now living and choosing. This is acting according to how the future serves the present. When the future is discounted, the future serves those of us living in the present very well indeed, because discounting will discourage environmental policies in which we bear many of the adjustment costs, while the benefits accrue to future persons.

This issue has usually been framed in terms of the quest for the appropriate rate of discount, but that is only part of the matter. Under all collective choice settings the question inevitably arises, What is right with respect to the future? Welfarism cannot answer that question. Instead, the ethical choice can be thought of in terms of the Rawlsian veil of ignorance—what decision would be taken about global climate change (or any policy) by risk-neutral agents who were ignorant of whether they would live today or a hundred years from now? In the language of a superfair game, intertemporal policy would be framed in terms of "no envy." That is, no agent, upon learning when she would live, would wish to trade places with any other time-identified agent. Notice that the pertinent question is not what climate endowment those of us living now prefer to leave for future persons. Rather, the problem concerns how can the tyranny of time's arrow be solved in the interest of all present and future persons. The no-envy constitution addresses that problem.

This brings us back to the notion of prospective volition—the human will in action, considering the present in terms of the future. That is, what actions must be taken now in order that the future shall be better than the past and the present? This vision sees reasons for action running from the future back to the present. This vision of the policy problem requires the concept of final cause, which allows us to understand that new policies to reduce pollution emerge not because it is suddenly economically efficient to reduce pollution, but because of a collective commitment to how the future ought to be constituted. Chlorofluorocarbons were not eliminated because lawmakers discovered that the net present value of the ban was positive. Chlorofluorocarbons were banned because of a collective commitment to restore atmospheric ozone. Finland and Sweden did not join the European Union because the citizenry was presented with a welfare analysis revealing that the net present value of doing so was claimed to be positive. These countries joined because the citizenry contemplated a future in and out of the EU and concluded that being in was plausibly better than being out. The citizens of Norway made the opposite choice.

IMPLICATIONS

The idea that the market—or a marketlike welfaristic calculation—is the proper analytical approach for social choice has a durable grip on many economists. Those of conservative persuasion use helpful economic concepts to advance their preferred political dogma. Because the status quo ante is invariably defined as the logical and inevitable result of "the market at work," conservative economists can sanctify this mystical process and thereby resist proposals to rectify "market failures"—discrimination in the workplace, environmental pollution, high rates of unemployment, flaws in the health care system, to name just a few. "The market" is a useful metaphor for conservative economists to continue to keep government "interference" in that market at bay. Those economists of a liberal persuasion admit a role for government, but insist that its actions must be held in check by strict adherence to what they imagine to be objective efficiency criteria. This double standard among liberal economists provides—or so they want to believe—rigorous and objective cover for their liberalism. Conservative economists are, in a sense, more honest. However, even these economists manage to conjure their self-serving requisite truths by selectively picking which part of the large corpus of economics they shall deploy at particular moments. But regardless of political persuasion, many economists are eager to invoke—to hide behind—what they have come to believe is the wondrous scientific rigor of received economic doctrine. This behavior denies public policy of many valuable insights that a more honest economics—an economics committed to the working out of the reasons for particular public policies—could offer.

Although the syllogism of practical inference is suggestive, notice that it begs the question of how volitional premises and epistemic premises are formulated. How, exactly, do we know what we want? How can we be sure that we know how to get what it is we think we want? The problem now is to turn our attention to the different ways by which individuals come to believe what it is they hold to be true. Following Pierce, we must now come to grips with the idea that the sole function of thought is the production of belief. We must explore how humans undertake structured thought for the explicit purpose of producing belief. And this task shall occupy us throughout all that follows.

CHAPTER TWO

The Task at Hand

> There is an uneasiness that has spread throughout intellectual
> and cultural life. It affects almost every discipline and every
> aspect of our lives. This uneasiness is expressed by the opposi-
> tion between objectivism and relativism, but there are a vari-
> ety of other contrasts that indicate the same underlying anxi-
> ety: rationality versus irrationality, objectivity versus
> subjectivity, realism versus antirealism.
>
> —Richard J. Bernstein, *Beyond Objectivism*
> *and Relativism* (1983).

CHALLENGING PRESCRIPTIVE CONSEQUENTIALISM

My main purpose here is to offer an epistemological vision and approach—a theory of action—that stands in stark contrast to the ubiquitous prescriptive urge that necessarily flows from commitments to what
Richard Bernstein refers to as objectivism, rationality, and realism. Standing opposed to these modernist certitudes we find the derogatory ideas of
relativism, irrationality, and antirealism. There can be little doubt that the
first trilogy (objectivism, rationality, realism) is privileged in the modern
mind, whereas the latter (relativism, irrationality, antirealism) is regarded
as encompassing all that is distasteful and ambiguous about postmodern
thought and practice. Indeed, the terms themselves cannot but be understood as conveying odious qualities. Who can possibly aspire to be a relativist, to be irrational, or to be antirealist? Modernism celebrates firm
prescriptive convictions. Prescriptive economics of the consequentialist
variety—assertions about efficiency, optimality, socially preferred policies, and potential Pareto improvements—is a necessary part of the modernist project imbued with notions of objectivism, rationality, and realism. I here challenge the core catechisms of the modernist trilogy. What
follows is a pragmatist's challenge to a priori consequentialism and its
manifold presumptuous assertions and prescriptions.

In addressing the universal prescriptive urge, Richard J. Bernstein has
written:

> By "objectivism" I mean the basic conviction that there is or must be
> some permanent, ahistorical matrix or framework to which we can
> ultimately appeal in determining the nature of rationality, knowledge,

truth, reality, goodness, or rightness. An objectivist claims that there is (or must be) such a matrix and that the primary task of the philosopher is to discover what it is and to support his or her claims to have discovered such a matrix with the strongest possible reasons. Objectivism is closely related to foundationalism and the search for an Archimedean point. The objectivist maintains that unless we can ground philosophy, knowledge, or language in a rigorous manner, we cannot avoid radical skepticism.

The "relativist" not only denies the positive claims of the objectivist but goes further. In its strongest form, relativism is the basic conviction that when we turn to the examination of those concepts that philosophers have taken to be the most fundamental—whether it is the concept of rationality, truth, reality, right, the good, or norms—we are forced to recognize that in the final analysis all such concepts must be understood as relative to a specific conceptual scheme, theoretical framework, paradigm, form of life, society, or culture. Since the relativist believes that there is (or can be) a nonreducible plurality of such conceptual schemes, he or she challenges the claim that these concepts can have a determinate and univocal significance. (Bernstein 1983, p. 8)

We see here in quite clear terms the nature of the challenge that lies ahead. Objectivism is the guiding light of reductionist reason, whereas relativism is the denial of the existence of a universal (reductionist) Archimedean point. In the West, religion once held a firm grip on the Archimedean point, and then Platonic philosophers gladly took control of its safekeeping. Philosophers became happy and eager foster parents who sought with much dedication (and some cleverness) to raise it to adulthood where it could, finally, begin to do the really difficult work. Pragmatists deny the existence of an Archimedean point.

The challenge therefore, is to spell out a pragmatic theory of human action, of economic institutions, and of institutional change, while avoiding the crippling flaws in standard modernist epistemology of such prominence in the social sciences.

CONSIDERING THE PRAGMATIC ALTERNATIVE

Imagine a rope. Imagine the entwinement of multiple strands. Imagine the augmented strength of the rope by this collation of various strands, each of which brings its own capacity for hard and valuable work. The very act of entwinement produces strength quite beyond the capacity of the individual and separate strands.

The rope I construct here is intended to do demanding work. That work entails an understanding of human action, and an understanding of the implicated economic institutions that define domains of human choice—individual and collective fields of action. In particular, the central purpose of the necessary work is to help us understand why and how economic institutions change and evolve. A few economists have, for some time now, been intent on developing a theory of institutional change. This quest has centered on making institutional change endogenous to economic processes and to economic models. This effort is misguided precisely because endogeneity is just another word for nothing left to choose. And if someday there is a "theory" of institutional change in which economic institutions are no longer objects of choice but follow necessarily and mechanistically from relative prices (and from circular notions of efficiency), this dubious accomplishment will have necessarily stripped the concept of economic institution of any coherence and pertinence to economic theory and economic practice. Endogeneity will have reduced institutional change to nothing but a machine process.

What is needed here is not mechanism. What is urgently needed is, instead, a theory of institutions and institutional change built on the concept of prospective volition—the human will in action, looking to the future, and deciding how that future ought to unfold. The prospect of attaining particular outcomes in the future constitutes the reasons for humans to undertake specific events today—whether acting as individuals, or acting collectively in those democratic entities (legislatures, parliaments, administrative agencies, courts) created precisely for the purpose of considering and implementing institutional change. When we get a grip on those reasons, we will get a grip on why institutions change.

This particular rope entails five strands.

Economic Institutions

The first strand of our rope concerns the idea of economic institutions. Clarity here starts with the recognition that economic institutions constitute and define the legal foundations of any economic system. The preeminent American institutional economist John R. Commons thought of institutions as indicating what "individuals *must* or *must not* do, . . . what they *may* do without interference from other individuals, . . . what they *can* do with the aid of collective power, . . . and what they *cannot* expect the collective power to do in their behalf" (Commons 1924, p. 6). Notice the legal content and entailments here *must, must not, may, can* (with the aid of the collective power), and *cannot* (expect the collective power to help us do). This quotation from Commons captures the full essence of economic institutions as I use that concept here. Notice also, that those institutions falling at the "informal" end of the spectrum—the norms, habits, standard practices, customs, traditions, and conventions that provide important boundaries to, and parameters for, much individual and collective action—receive much less attention here than do the legal variety.

Public Policy

Having stipulated what economic institutions are, let me now address the second strand of the rope. Institutional change is the raison d'être of public policy in any economic system. I submit that public policy is collective action in restraint, liberation, and expansion of individual action. On this stipulation, we see that the purpose of all public policy is precisely to change economic institutions. The result of public policy is therefore new (different) economic institutions. More particularly, new economic institutions redefine who must or must not undertake some specific action, who may undertake certain actions without interference from other individuals, who can undertake certain actions with the explicit aid of the collective power, and who cannot expect the collective power to undertake certain actions in their behalf.

Abduction

The third strand of our rope concerns an old but neglected way of fixing belief. Aristotle and later philosophers called it diagnosis. I follow Charles Sanders Peirce and call it the method of hypothesis, or abduction. Many scientists imagine that induction and deduction constitute (and exhaust) our ways of fixing belief. But abduction offers valuable insights and prospects to those who are seriously interested in discovering the reasons for particular events. An abductive argument is of the form:

> The surprising fact, C, is observed:
> But if A were true, C would be a matter of course,
> Hence, there is reason to suspect A is true.

That is, abduction starts when particular circumstances and events are encountered and we find ourselves in need of an explanation (Hands 2001, p. 223; Hoover 1994, p. 301). That is, human action is animated, ab initio, by doubt or surprise. Peirce talked of the "irritation of doubt." Why is that tree in my garden dying? Why am I feeling dizzy? Why did that airplane crash? Why is my car sputtering? Why did that spacecraft disintegrate on reentering the Earth's atmosphere? Abduction allows us to deploy specific known relations and particular assumptions to formulate propositions (testable hypotheses) with the intent of explaining those particular events. If your car will not start on a cold morning, abduction is the process your mechanic will deploy in quest of a reason. If you have a fever, abduction is the process your doctor will deploy as she ponders the reason for your fever. If you are a forensic pathologist, you ponder the cadaver in quest of the reason for death. If you are an engineer struggling to explain the destruction of a spacecraft, abduction is your avenue to explanation. The essential purpose of abduction is the production of belief about specific events. To quote from Charles Sanders Peirce, "the action of thought is excited by the irritation of doubt, and ceases when belief is attained; so that the production of belief is the sole function of thought" (Peirce 1957, p. 36).

Human Action

The fourth strand of our rope concerns a theory of human action. Here again Peirce offers an important insight: a belief is that upon which we are prepared to act. I combine this notion with the volitional economics of John R. Commons, and the idea of created imaginings from the work of G.L.S. Shackle, to challenge—and to go beyond—the standard economic approach that regards the ends of action as fixed and insists that the individual need only address alternative means to those predetermined ends. I am certainly not alone here. Many writers suggest that it is precisely here that rational choice theory goes off the rails, for the simple reason that the concept of choice as it is used in economics becomes incoherent. Or, as Amartya Sen has observed, it turns the idea of choice into a mere play on words (Sen 1977). Notice that if ends are given, and all that remains is for the individual to compute the most efficacious means to achieve those ends, this is not choice but mere calculation. Individuals who can only calculate are not choosing among alternative actions but are calculating to find the "best" means. Notice that this route leaves the individual, once the calculations have been made, with no choices to make. As long as the individual could not "rationally" have done other than what the calculations revealed to be the rational choice, the agent did not exercise choice (Lawson 1997). It is here that Shackle enters the picture.

> Conventional economics is not about choice, but about acting according to necessity. . . . Choice in such a theory is empty, and conventional economics should abandon the word. . . . The escape from necessity . . . lies in the *creation of ends*, and this is possible because ends, so long as they remain available and liable to rejection or adoption, must inevitably be experiences by imagination or anticipation and not by external occurrence. Choice, inescapably, is choice amongst thoughts, and thoughts. . . . are not given. (Shackle 1961, pp. 272–73)

I argue that the concept of prospective volition offers promise to the subject of individual choice and action. And if individuals, in the process of arriving at choice, must contend with ends as well as means, then it necessarily follows that groups of individuals engaged in collective action must do so as well. Indeed, recent work suggests an ironic aspect of rational choice theory, and one that holds important implications for the subsequent development of a pragmatic theory of action. That is, rational choice theory works best when there is little choice to make. Specifically:

> [We] believe that rational-choice explanations are most plausible in settings in which individual action is severely constrained. . . . In the absence of strong environmental constraints, we believe that rational choice is a weak theory, with limited predictive power. . . . rational-choice explanations are more powerful when their object is the behavior of political parties as opposed to voters. The primary reason for the asymmetry of explanatory success is that consumers and voters face less competitive environments than firms and parties. We fully realize the irony of our contention: the theory of rational choice is most powerful in contexts where choice is limited. (Satz and Ferejohn 1994, p. 72)

Commons connects the individual to the working rules of going concerns—firms, villages, households, and nation-states. For within any going concern, some individuals are in a position to play an important role in the construction of new working rules (institutions). These individuals are known as directors, owners, managers, bosses, supervisors, headmen, husbands (in some societies), wives (in other societies), and both husbands and wives jointly in many societies, leaders, judges, legislators, and administrative rule makers. The choices that individuals make today are embedded in—and, to a certain extent, products of—the actions of yesterday's volitional agents. These extant working rules provide the scaffolding for today's choices and, in so doing, transmit yesterday's "economic values" to individuals who must make choices today. To Veblen, this idea captures the essence of cumulative causation. Commons called this a process of "artificial selection" because it allowed for the evolution of going concerns without the contrived deus ex machina of "natural selection"—the magic mechanism of spontaneous order. To Commons, evolution in human systems is "artificially" created by human volition, what I call prospective volition. How many days of paid holiday are associated with this particular job? What is the going wage for this type of work? What proportion of income is subject to taxation? What structures may I build on this land that I own?

We see that individual choice is already set in motion and parameterized according to prior collective decisions by those to whom the society under study (the going concern) has granted the authority to determine "economic values." John Dewey maintained that we are "always arriving in the middle" of life, as when one walks in during a movie rather than at its beginning. And we may be absolutely certain that the answer to questions about paid holiday, going wage, taxation, and allowable structures on a parcel of land have evolved over time in response to new perceptions of what seems better, at the time, to do about paid holiday, going wage, taxation, and allowable structures on particular parcels of land.

> A key element of Commons's theory is his reinterpretation of the etiology of economic values. No longer are those values perceived to emerge spontaneously from natural forces, as in the mechanical equilibrium theories of mainstream economics. Commons instead discerned that the general pattern of economic values observed to obtain in a given "going concern" (economy) are in a fundamental sense the cumulative volitional creation of those who have consecutively possessed the power or delegated authority to decide upon the content of the concern's working rules. (Ramstad 1990, p. 87)

The "content of the concern's working rules" is precisely the scaffolding within which individual action is first animated, and within which "reasonable" (workable and consensual) solutions to new problems are created by those who must act. The same holds, quite obviously, for collective action (because collective action is but the collation of individual action within designated entities, such as boards of directors, the courts, or the legislature). If we keep in mind that economic institutions are human constructs, and if we understand why institutions are thought to be in need of change, we might then understand how individuals and groups (including formal law-giving bodies) follow abductive inference in the fixing of a new belief and connect that new belief to the existing institutional setup. This connection is necessary if the existing institutional arrangements are suddenly to be judged unsuitable for bringing about desirable futures. How is it that in a short period of time many nations have prohibited smoking in public buildings? How is it that within a few years of establishing a plausible link between aerosol sprays and the ozone "hole" over Antarctica, aerosols have been practically eliminated in consumer goods? How is it that child labor, once thought to be normal, is now seen as appalling? How is it that the industrial workweek, once in the range of sixty hours, is now approximately forty hours throughout the industrial world, and on its way to being thirty-four to thirty-five hours? How is it that slavery, once quite prevalent came to be seen as a moral outrage? How is it that automobile seatbelts are now required in practically all developed nations? These institutional changes came about because individuals came to hold new beliefs. That is, they began to imagine that the world—*their* world—would be a better place under a new institutional setup.

I develop the general outlines of a theory of action that offers clarity concerning the process whereby existing outcomes come to be seen as unacceptable, and how new outcomes that seem to offer a more promising future are formulated. When we understand the nature and purpose of institutions, and when we understand that differing institutions are the reasons for differing outcomes, we will be close to the formulation of a theory of economic institutions and of institutional change.

Settled Belief

The final strand in our rope concerns individual and collective determinations of settled belief. By settled belief I mean the arrival at a point in the consideration of possible action that individuals or groups can finally and honestly declare, "this seems the better thing to do at this time." When we can say to ourselves (or to our colleagues in the parliaments, the legislature, administrative agencies, or the court chambers) that we have reached a decision, it means that our settled deliberations have given us a new coherent belief. And, again, a belief is that upon which we are prepared to act. In effect, we have now found sufficient reason(s) to alter specific institutional arrangements in the interest of—for the purpose of— modifying particular economic outcomes in the future.

Pragmatism offers conceptual guidance here through the ideas of warranted belief (or warranted assertion) and valuable belief (or valuable assertion). *Warranted assertions* arise from settled belief emanating from a community of individuals thought to have special epistemic sanction to study, ponder, undertake research about, and then pronounce on particular matters. Our term for this community of individuals is *a scientific discipline*. The purpose of these epistemic communities—whether comprising astronomers, sociologists, economists, historians, geneticists, or ichthyologists—is to tell the rest of us what we ought to believe about specific issues. Their purpose is to produce warranted belief. Individual and collective action will often be informed by consulting the assertions of a particular discipline. The usual term for this consultation with the "experts" is to see what the science says about this matter. Is genetic engineering a threat to naturally occurring plants and animals? Will my outdoor wedding be rained out? Why am I feeling lethargic? What was the cause of World War I? Can I expect inflation to increase over the next year? For the most part, epistemic communities offer warranted assertions predicated on warranted belief.

But not all assertions from an epistemic community (a scientific discipline) are warranted assertions. Specifically, only those assertions that enjoy widespread assent within a discipline earn the right to be regarded as warranted assertions. The purpose of warranted belief is to help the rest of us figure out what we ought to believe. But we are not mere passive vessels into which warranted belief is poured and immediately acted upon. As discerning agents (*Homo sapiens*) we have the obligation to consider pronouncements from scientific "experts" and decide for ourselves whether we will now hold to our prior belief or change it. *Valuable belief* (or assertion) is a warranted assertion that can be justified to an audience of attentive sapient agents intent on a particular action. A valuable belief is one upon which I am now prepared to act. Do I believe what the meteorologists tell me about the chances of rain on August 27? Do I believe what the geneticists tell us about genetically modified corn? Is this particular explanation of World War I compelling and plausible?

It should not surprise us that there will be times when the warranted belief (or warranted assertion) of the experts will be found interesting but not necessarily compelling. Some warranted belief may well be quite impertinent to the rest of us. Not all warranted belief is valuable belief. In practical terms, as sapient agents we are under no special obligation, upon hearing the warranted belief of a particular disciplinary community, to stop what we are doing and immediately adopt that particular belief. We have the right to demand justification for discarding what we now believe. If the proffered justification by the experts is regarded as deficient, we have not yet been presented with valuable belief. Pragmatism insists that the choice of what to believe is ours, not theirs.

Volitional Pragmatism

In epistemological terms, I seek here to move economic prescriptions about what is best to do away from the flawed doctrine of logical positivism to which it fell serious victim in the 1930s under the forceful influence of Lionel Robbins. Ironically, philosophers had abandoned positivism about the time that most economists succumbed to its dubious appeal. In a larger sense, I seek here to make economic prescriptions about what is best to do in a particular policy setting more consistent with democracy. In that sense, this work is a project of hope. Specifically, I develop the broad outlines of a reconstituted economics on the expectation that if prescriptive economics can be rescued from the defective state into which it has fallen under the false promises of positivism and consequentialist welfarism, economists might once again have something valuable and useful to say about public policy. I call my approach volitional pragmatism.

PART ONE

On Economic Institutions

CHAPTER THREE

Understanding Institutions

> [T]he renewed interest in institutions on the part of many economists can be recognized as a growing conviction that satisfactory understanding of economic performance requires going beyond the lean logic of at least stripped down neo-classical theory.
>
> —Richard R. Nelson and Bhaven N. Sampat,
> *Making Sense of Institutions as a Factor Shaping Economic Performance* (2001).

LIBERATION AND RESTRAINT

Institutions are the rules whereby going concerns—families, clans, villages, firms, nation-states—regularize and channel individual action and interaction. Institutions define and specify opportunity sets, or fields of action, for the members of a going concern. Put somewhat differently, institutions are the means whereby the collective control of individual action is given effect. The study of institutions brings us into direct contact with the socially constructed norms, working rules, and entitlements that shape and influence individual fields of action. The tradition in economics has been to explain behavior in terms of prices, preferences, and the maximization of utility. However, utility is merely an index, not a reason for action. Desires can function as explanations for action only if there are reasons for those desires. Understanding human action requires understanding not desires (or preferences) but reasons. The human will in action, looking to the future, constitutes plausible reasons for choice and action. When applied to the realm of public policy, again the human will in action, looking to the future, offers clarity of thought about the reasons for particular institutions—which then provides modified fields of action for individuals and groups of individuals. Understanding reasons for particular institutions entails gaining clarity regarding the essence of institutions. That is, we are here concerned with rules and with the reasons for rules.

Understanding the institutional foundations of a market economy poses a somewhat novel conceptual challenge. Contemporary economics has come to be defined as the study of self-interested individuals choosing among alternatives so as to maximize utility (or "welfare"). In such choice-theoretic terms, institutions are regarded as constraints on individual maximization algorithms. One common definition insists that "Institutions are the rules of the game in a society or, more formally, are the humanly devised *constraints* that shape human interaction" (North 1990, p. 3; emphasis added). In what follows I offer a challenge to this notion of institutions as constraints. To reveal the general lines of this challenge, notice that if institutions are seen as constraints, then the economist is obligated to explain why these constraints exist in a market economy. Are we to suppose that institutions are nothing but the inevitable product of pernicious "rent seeking" and the perverse redistributive tendencies among odious political entrepreneurs? On this view, it is easy to gain the impression that unfettered markets and autonomous individual behavior are natural human phenomena against which these "humanly devised constraints" impose conditions that impede the beneficent properties of presumptively "free" markets.

Clarity is found by regarding institutions as both liberation and restraint of individual and group action. Does it not seem odd to regard the prohibition of child labor as nothing but a constraint on business firms? Are not children liberated by such a rule? How is it possible to regard a ban on DDT as only a constraint? Are not those who care for bald eagles (and other animals) plausibly devastated by that chemical compound liberated by the prohibition of its use? How is it possible to regard urban growth boundaries only as a constraint on the relentless march of houses and strip malls into green space at the urban fringe? Are not those who treasure rural amenities liberated by such restrictions? We see that in each case new institutions simply modify choice sets—fields of action—for atomistic maximizing individuals. To regard institutions as simply constraints is to reveal an unsubstantiated affinity for the status quo ante and then to reify the current situation by referring to it as "the market." If one lives in a market economy, then the status quo ante—by being called "the market"—is privileged in any discussion of desired or necessary policy change. We see that laissez-faire easily becomes just another term for protecting the status quo ante institutional setup in the interest of safeguarding those well served by that particular status quo.

A clear understanding of institutions requires that we see them as both liberating and restraining individuals. In fact, the proper way to regard institutions is that they define choice sets—fields of action—for members of a going concern (family, clan, village, firm, nation-state). With a proper focus on institutions as constitutive of social and economic relations rather than as simply constraints on those relations, we can begin to bring useful analytical attention to bear on these essential aspects of an economic system. This new perspective places emphasis on institutions as structural parameters in an economy rather than as mere constraints on some prior and allegedly natural entity called "the market." There is, after all, no such thing as the market. There are, instead, arenas of exchange that are the product of prior human creation. Any market is a social construct, and changes in the parameters of that construct—new institutional arrangements—are also human creations.

If we start by recognizing that institutions define fields of action for individuals (and groups) in society, then there is hope that we might explain their existence at any particular time and build explanatory models to understand the forces that cause institutions to change. But more is required. We must expand the scope of economics beyond the narrow definition, dominant since Lionel Robbins (1932), that economics concerns the allocation of scarce means to meet conflicting ends—the consideration of which is not admissible to economic analysis or professional comment by economists. But of course there are good and bad ends, just as there are good and bad reasons. Is a nation-state where children collect garbage from the streets on a par with an equally poor nation-state where they are in school? Is there no difference between institutional arrangements that allow, perhaps even encourage, child pornography and those that encourage young musicians? When economists insist that we have nothing to say of a "scientific" nature about the merits of alternative ends, two mistakes are made.

First, this reluctance implies that we have no professional competence or obligation to point out the serious economic and social implications of children picking garbage rather than being in school. And those implications must not be reduced to the trivial absurdity that it may just be more "efficient" for children to work in carpet factories (or to collect roadside litter) instead of being in school. The second mistake is that assertions about our need to restrict ourselves to matters of objective "science" deceive the listener (and the speaker) into believing that when economists do pronounce not on ends but on means, such pronouncements are indeed objective and value free. This deceit is a fiction. The standard obligatory silence on ends leaves the impression that many economists imagine employment as prostitutes is not economically and socially different from employment as teachers. How is it that economics has come to see silence on such matters as the essence of "scientific" rigor? The answer is to be found in the false promises of logical positivism and its adherents who imagined that—with sufficient hard work—objective "truths" would be revealed through models of possessive individualism.

In contrast to this stunted economic vision, the study of institutions reinforces the point that economics must come to be seen as the study of how individuals and groups organize themselves for their provisioning. Only on this broader definition will economists be able to undertake careful study of the institutions that define the domains of choice for individual and group action and to engage in structured and meaningful conversations about good and bad ends and good and bad reasons for particular actions. Doing so will require a new theory of human action. Before I develop that theory, let us return to the subject of institutions.

On the Collective Control of Individual Action

The study of economic institutions concerns three fundamental realms of human thought and action:

1. *Ethics* deals with the rules of conduct arising from the inevitable conflict of interests, necessitated by scarcity, and enforced by the moral sanctions of collective opinion.
2. *Economizing* deals with the rules of conduct arising from the inevitable conflict of interests, necessitated by scarcity, and enforced by the collective accounting sanctions of profit or loss.
3. *Jurisprudence* deals with the rules of conduct arising from the inevitable conflict of interests, necessitated by scarcity, and enforced by the organized sanctions of collective (and state-sponsored) violence. (Commons 1931)

By "violence" we should understand that Commons meant that the modern state holds the monopoly on coercive action in the sense of arrest, imprisonment, and even—in rare circumstance—capital punishment. In other words, retribution and revenge have gradually shifted from being a matter for individuals and families to arrange to one of the collective authority. In the phrasing of Oliver Williamson, transactions are less and less the province of "private ordering" but are, instead, enforced by the collective power of the state carried out by government agents.

Because our interest in economic institutions is, for the most part, concerned with working rules and property relations (I largely ignore the realm of custom and tradition), it is easy to understand the emphasis on ethics, economizing, and jurisprudence. That is, economic institutions represent the application of ethics and jurisprudence to the ubiquitous economizing behavior that defines our daily life. More specifically, existing economic institutions represent the ethical judgments of those who, in our past, were in a position to determine which institutional arrangements were adopted. We see that current institutions are a mirror on—a reflection of—prior scarcities, prior purposes, prior values, prior economic agendas, and prior political processes. Once those institutions are in place, individuals and groups engage in economizing behaviors that hold economic (and noneconomic) implications for themselves and for others. The study of institutional economics insists that the economist incorporate all three types of sanctions—ethics, jurisprudence, economizing—into efforts to explain institutions.

Any economic system is defined by—parameterized by—collectively ascertained and articulated rules and entitlement regimes that indicate what individuals must or must not do (duty), what individuals may do without interference from others (privilege), what individuals can do with the aid of the collective power (right), and what individuals cannot expect the collective power to do in their behalf (no right). The ethical realm constitutes the epistemic grounds (the reasons) for these institutions, the jurisprudential realm provides the articulation and ultimate enforcement of these institutions, and the economizing realm provides the arena in which individuals act in a domain parameterized by these institutions (the rule structure), yet subject to the prospect of financial gain or loss.

But whence does this apparatus arise, and how (and why) does it persist? The quick answer is that economic institutions arise from the prior choices and actions of the authority system in the nation-state. In this political domain, there is a continual reassessment of existing institutional arrangements, which is motivated by an emerging sense that current institutional arrangements are not well suited to new settings and circumstances. That is, current behaviors, parameterized by prevailing institutional arrangements, no longer seem to conduce to agreeable outcomes. Institutional change now seems necessary. We see the end result of these prior deliberations when we ponder the institutional arrangements in place in various countries at the same time in history. Some nations are rather indifferent to new fathers, whereas in Norway new fathers are required to take one month of paid paternity leave early in the life of their new child. New mothers receive more-generous leaves and are guaranteed their former job when the leave period comes to an end. Similar rules are the norm in other parts of northern Europe, though quite unheard of in America. In most of Europe, workers receive four to five weeks of annual leave, plus normal national holidays. In some other countries, workers receive only two to three weeks of annual leave. Why—for what reasons—do these institutional differences exist? They exist precisely because democratic processes in nation-states rest on, and act upon, different priorities. In this case, citizens and leaders of different nations hold different visions about the role of family and work in national life.

These visions and priorities drive the law-making process, and it should be no surprise that when new visions and priorities begin to emerge, new institutions will likely emerge as well. We say that economic institutions are manifestations of collective action in restraint, liberation, and expansion of individual action. When I say *collective* action here I mean that new economic institutions (not norms and conventions, but new working rules and new entitlement regimes) are products of the processes and structures of governments. That is, economic institutions are given form and content (and enforcement) by the agents of the state we call government. The term *government* is here used to include the hierarchical structure of a village, a clan, or some other going concern. That is, the idea of government need not imply only those authority structures (and authoritative agents) found in industrialized societies. Each of these authority systems denoted by government represents collective authority residing in a leader, a parliament, a judicial system of some sort, or some combination of these.

We must pause and recall that the tradition in economics is to regard "collective action" as something that individuals jointly do for themselves as an alternative to individual action in market transactions. The large literature on clubs and other collective action focuses on levels of contributions, on free riding, and on incentives to contribute to the collective purposes of such groups. Indeed the popularity of game theory in economics finds its explanation in efforts to model action when individuals are involved in joint (mutually dependent) activities that hold differential benefits and costs depending on the actions undertaken by others.

The concept of collective action used here differs in important ways from this tradition. If we are to understand the meaning of economic institutions in democratic market societies, it requires that we give primacy to the governance structures that parameterize (define and redefine) individual realms of choice. Paramount here would be the legislative-parliamentary function. We know that such entities are the law-giving bodies in democratic societies, and we also know that laws represent the fundamental institutions (working rules, property relations) of any society. What is less well understood is that the legislative-parliamentary activity of democratic societies is the essence of collective action. This law making is collective precisely because democratic societies create legislative-parliamentary bodies for no other reason than to craft (and recraft) the institutional foundations of the going concern we call the nation-state. We can consider these institutional arrangements as collective consumption goods, because their use by one or more individuals does not diminish their capacity to do work for others. Some economists call them public goods, although the adjective *public* is often confusing. It is better to refer to them as collective consumption goods; they are nonrivalous in consumption, and once they are made available for one person, they are available for all persons (they are nonexcludable). The interest in the former Soviet Union to get "institutions right" is precisely pertinent here. A market economy works better if there is a collectively determined legal regime to define individual fields of action. When that collectively designed and enforced institutional structure is absent, as it still is to some extent in the former Soviet Union, economic transactions must be "privately ordered (enforced)."

Members of nation-states agree, explicitly or tacitly, to abide by the rules promulgated by their law-giving entities. This does not imply unanimous agreement in principle with all of the undertakings of law-giving bodies, but it does imply general acquiescence in behavior of members of the entity governed by the relevant law giving body. We may say that law-giving is the essence of collective action in redefinition of individual action. In constitutional democracies, the judicial branch will have a role to play in assuring that the results of law giving are consistent with guiding constitutional principles. And, of course, the judicial branch is essential to arbitration between individuals (or groups) in a society. Even the actions of the judicial branch, including the decrees of a single judge, are the essence of collective action. Such judicial decrees are collective because, in virtue of her sanctified role (official position) in that society, a judge speaks both *to* and *for* all members of the polity.

Given this definition of collective action in democratic societies, we see that the state, through its organizations and processes, is necessarily a party to every transaction. I say necessarily because the state must agree which transactions shall be allowed. Hallucinogenic drugs, slavery, and extortion are classes of transactions that are not allowed in most societies. That is, members of the nation-state assert, through their law-giving entities, that these particular transactions shall not be permitted. Once particular transactions have been deemed by the collective to be acceptable, there remains the problem of state ratification of contracts and other aspects of transactions. After all, if contract disputes arise, where do the aggrieved parties go but to the nation's courts? Nation-states cannot avoid being a party to every transaction. By agreeing to be a party to every transaction, the state agrees that it always stands ready to consider the interests of all citizens. By agreeing to be the enforcement agent for private transactions, the state is declaring that it cares about the well-being of individuals who choose to enter into contracts. And the state is signaling that it recognizes the high social and economic costs to arise from contracts broken on a whim.

By being a party to all transactions, the state defines important aspects of the individual, and the state liberates and expands the powers of the individual. Official categories define who we are and what we may do. The terms *husband* and *wife* are legal concepts, and so the state sets the minimum age (even the gender) for which individuals may acquire those appellations. The age of majority must be collectively determined, and this is often contentious. During the Vietnam War, America's youngsters—old enough (eighteen years of age) to be drafted and to "die for their country" (as they were inclined to put the matter)—were denied the opportunity to purchase alcoholic beverages (twenty-one years of age in most states). In virtually all modern societies an individual must be above a specific age to be licensed to drive an automobile. The terms *worker* and *supervisor* carry legal entailments and open up varying ranges of command and obedience between the parties. The idea of *owner* carries with it a wide range of opportunities in the firm, for owners are central to all contracts over the necessary factors of production. And the owner is the residual claimant on all profits—and the residual risk bearer in the case of negative profits. We see that an individual's legal personality is determined by collective action in the parliaments and in the courts.

In addition to restraining and liberating individual action, institutions expand the realm of individual action. To have a right in something—a civil right, a contractual right, a property right—is to have the capacity to compel the state to come to the defense of your particular interest. Again, we see that the state defines the individual in important social and economic ways (owner, worker), but it also empowers individuals bearing that definition with inordinate powers over the machinery of state—government agents. To have a right is to have the ability to command the agents of government to come to your aid. If I notice a prowler in my backyard late at night, I have the right to command that the sheriff arrive as quickly as possible. Should my pleas for help be met with an insistence that the sheriff would be happy to drop by following coffee break, I would have plausible grounds for disciplinary grievance. I cannot be made to wait while the sheriff enjoys coffee. We see that rights expand the power of the individual over agents of the state.

We should also come to understand the state as a domain of redistribution of advantage, opportunity, and therefore of income and wealth. Within the boundary of the nation-state, struggles over particular institutional arrangements occur. What shall be the new minimum wage? Should the social security system be changed, and if so, how? How shall health insurance be organized and financed? Shall there be paid maternity leave, and if so, how many days with full pay shall be allowed? Shall there be paternity leave? If so, how will it differ from maternity leave? These conversations serve to define the realm of activity we recognize as the nation-state. After all, the citizens of Sweden would be unlikely to have a serious and legally binding conversation about these topics with the citizens of Australia.

With this understanding of how institutions enable and control transactions in democratic societies, what I call rationing transactions and to which I shall return shortly, it now seems useful to introduce a second kind of transaction in a market economy. A *bargaining transaction* is one that occurs between legal equals—a willing buyer and a willing seller. Bargaining transactions concern the legally sanctioned transfer of ownership over future net benefit streams between the participants to such transactions. The buyer acquires ownership (not just possession) of a new benefit (income) stream, with the state standing as the only entity that can bestow the concept of "ownership" over objects, settings, or circumstances. The seller receives (usually) money that can then be invested to produce a new income stream, or spent on some other item that will produce a new benefit stream. Commons reminded us that there are always four parties to a bargaining transaction: the successful buyer, the successful seller, the disappointed buyer, and the disappointed seller. The two dominant ideas in bargaining transactions are *persuasion* and *coercion*. When bargaining "power" is approximately equal, persuasion will dominate. On the other hand, when one party enjoys an economic or political advantage over the other—despite the fact that they are equal before the law—we may expect to find coercion rather than persuasion being the pertinent climate of a bargaining transaction. In a market economy, where most individuals must sell their labor power if they wish to eat, those engaged in bargaining transactions cannot really be said to be entirely free participants in such negotiations. Despite what some market apologists wish for us to believe, freedom does not come from the ability to choose among alternative market (bargaining) transactions—all of which may be inferior (Sen 1993). Rather, freedom comes from not having to participate in any bargaining transaction (Macpherson 1973). If you cannot eat unless you enter into some bargaining transaction (in the labor market), you are not really free from coercion.

Despite the popular conception of a market economy as an arena of ubiquitous bargaining transactions, in reality a market economy is an arena of pervasive command and obedience (Simon 1991). This brings us to the third class of transactions in a market economy, the *managerial transaction*. Managerial transactions concern not the transfer of wealth, as in bargaining transactions, but rather the creation of wealth. Unlike bargaining transactions, in which both participants are nominally equal before the law, the realm of managerial transactions entails superior and inferior participants. Another contrast is that, unlike the bargaining transaction, in which there are four participants, the managerial transaction concerns but two parties. The master (boss, foreman) gives orders, and the servant (workman or other subordinate) must obey on pain of sanction. We see that the dominant idea in managerial transactions is that of command and obedience. There will, of course, be struggles over reasonable and unreasonable demands and willing and unwilling obedience. Notice that the definitions of "reasonable" demand and "unwilling" obedience must be ascertained by the law-giving entities in a democratic market economy. We also should notice that what once was regarded as a reasonable demand in a managerial transaction in the late nineteenth century will likely differ considerably from what is considered a reasonable demand at the dawn of the twenty-first century. We see that what is consid-

ered "reasonable" is itself a product of collective action in liberation, restraint, and expansion of individual action. These deliberations define the
socially acceptable domains of both bargaining and managerial transactions. That is, the very definition of "reasonable" will be (and is) continually renegotiated and thus redefined by the law-giving and law-judging
entities in a democratic society. As noted, institutional economics recognizes the essential roles of ethics and jurisprudence in defining the continual evolution in our ideas about acceptable realms of economizing behavior. We would say that the economy is always in the process of becoming.

We may now return to a more explicit treatment of the previously mentioned rationing transaction. *Rationing transactions* are regarded as
transactions precisely because the various affected parties in a democratic
nation-state engage in conversations and negotiations over the very concept of reasonable working rules (institutions) that shall define the acceptable and unacceptable parameters of bargaining and managerial transactions. These negotiations, occurring in the legislatures or parliaments and
in the courts, entail argument and pleading. Only when a decision has
been rendered by the law-giving or law-judging bodies, or both, do we
encounter command and obedience. These transactions are considered to
be rationing because it is in their very nature to ration—to redirect—
streams of benefits and costs across various individuals and groups into
the future. In rationing transactions, the "superior" is not an individual
(boss, supervisor) but a "collective" (legislatures-parliaments, courts).
Notice also that the "inferiors" are not employees but all of us in our
various roles and capacities. The dominant idea in rationing transactions
is again one of argument and pleading. When I say that new public policy
is a new collective action in liberation, restraint, and expansion of individual action, it is the rationing transaction that embodies (captures) this
idea. The legislature and the courts, in their actions, reconstitute economic advantage and disadvantage. Any law, and any legal decree, advantages some and disadvantages others. They are advantaged and disadvantaged because the new economic institutions ration—redirect—the flows
of beneficial and harmful settings and circumstances. Some of those beneficial and harmful effects may well be monetary. But they need not be.

In grasping the theory of action that is to come later in the book, it is
essential at this juncture to understand that all three classes of transactions—bargaining, managerial, rationing—entail thought and negotiations directed toward the future. That is, institutional change is motivated
and acted upon with the future clearly in mind. Existing institutions are
not explained by the choices and actions of those living at this moment.
Instead, by shaping individual perceptions of current settings and circumstances, existing institutions—crafted in the distant or recent past—affect
(define) the acceptable (legally permissible) choices of individuals living

today. In other words, the institutions of one period are the result of collective action in the past, sometimes as recently as last year's legislative session, or yesterday's judicial decree, but also the quite distant past. We must see that the values and priorities and commitments of the past are projected into the present in the form of the prevailing institutions under which we live. Similarly, as those of us now living struggle with the problems of what seems better to do, we will project the answers to those challenges, in the form of new institutions, on to those who will follow us.

One of the most compelling challenges to Adam Smith's utopian economic philosophy has been advanced by Commons in his criticism of that wondrous deus ex machina—the "invisible hand." Commons insisted that Smith was conjuring divine providence, not the human will in action, as the fairylike mechanism whereby the butcher, the brewer, and the baker in their alleged self-interest could quite inadvertently benefit others. Notice that to assume this is to assume accidental providence, a rare occurrence in our world. Hayek reified this particular version of magic by calling it "spontaneous order." This seductive metaphor continues to buttress utopian claims about the manifold wonders available—as some like to put it, "free of charge"—from thoroughgoing market processes. Unfortunately for the utopians and their happy stories, we live in a world not of spontaneous—or providential—order but a world of constructed order. Institutions constitute that constructed order.

IMPLICATIONS

We can begin to understand economic institutions when we see them as the essential ordering—the architecture—of our existence. Institutions represent collective restraint, liberation, and expansion of individual action. A proper understanding of the meaning of economic institutions and of institutional change requires an acceptance of three realms of sentient action: the realm of ethics, the realm of economizing, and the realm of jurisprudence. In any society, ethics and jurisprudence combine to parameterize the realm within which the calculation of profit and loss (economizing) shall, may, and may not be undertaken. Institutions determine which benefits and costs in the grand scheme of individual and group economizing shall, may, and may not fall on which parties. The evolutionary—and mutually reflexive—properties of ethical beliefs and jurisprudential reasoning continually redefine the acceptable domains over which costs may be shifted and benefits retained. We see, therefore, that the concept of income (and of profit) is itself a social construct. If this is doubted, engage an accountant with good knowledge of American and European accounting protocols in a conversation. You will quickly learn how the concepts of profit and loss differ under two distinct social, economic, and political settings. The concept of profit, an idea of some interest to most economists, is itself constructed.

The collective political entity we call the state must, of necessity, be a party to every transaction. It could not be otherwise. The manner in which the state is involved in every transaction varies according to the issues in play. For some issues, simple working rules are sufficient. For others, where claims over future income streams are at stake, property relations are necessary. The exact structure of these different kinds of institutions needs to be explored and clarified.

CHAPTER FOUR

The Content of Institutions

> The law, in its majestic equality, forbids the rich as well as
> the poor to sleep under bridges, to beg in the streets, and to
> steal bread.
>
> —Anatole France, *Le Lys Rouge* (1894)

CONSTRUCTED ORDER

In the previous chapter I developed the idea that economic institutions
are the product of law-giving and law-judging entities—legislatures or
parliaments and the courts. With this idea in mind we can see that, at any
moment, one must regard an economy as a set of structured relations.
That is, when considering any economy we must immediately bring
into view the institutions that define, structure, and give meaning to
that economy. These institutions include, but are not limited to, the structure of property rights, contract and bankruptcy law, the law of credit,
general business law, the law of marriage and divorce, and the law of torts
and accidents. These institutions serve to order—give structure to—our
daily lives.

Political philosophers have long recognized that out of scarcity comes
conflict, but out of scarcity and conflict also comes mutual dependence.
From the conjunction of conflict and dependence arises the universal
imperative of order. Adam Smith finessed the essential problem by suggesting that order was the logical and providential outcome of the age-
old problem of provisioning. Smith suggested that it is not from the
beneficence of the butcher, the brewer, and the baker that we are fed but
from the full play of their self-interest. On this telling, the division of
labor, animated by self-interest, would bring forth both material wealth
and individual liberty. This idea is very comforting. How wonderful to
avoid the difficult business of having to agree upon mechanisms for
achieving—and the rules for evaluating—that constructed order. How
very lucky we are that this order will simply emerge unorchestrated and
uncoordinated from that which comes most easily to all of us—the full
expression of possessive individualism.

Indeed, it is such a happy prospect that the idea of magic comes to
mind. Hayek was so inspired by this notion that he called it "spontaneous
order" (Hayek 1960). And, in a direct challenge to the durable economic

maxim that there is no "free lunch," Hayek managed to find one. Ironically, those most inclined to insist that there is no free lunch are usually the most energetic in suggesting that Adam Smith's invisible hand is just that. Spontaneous order is the economic equivalent of the physicist's perpetual motion machine. And, as with perpetual motion, the concept of spontaneous order is a grand and splendid fantasy. The reality of the human condition is that it falls to various forms of human associations—families, villages, clans, nation-states—to construct the order that will parameterize and define individual domains of choice (fields of action).

When we come to see institutions as the working rules of going concerns, we can begin to grasp the fundamental distinction between the everyday use of the term institution—as being synonymous with an organization such as the Federal Reserve System or a university—and the use that is the core subject of inquiry here. Notice that organizations such as the Catholic Church or a corporation acquire their meaning from the working rules (institutions) that define them. We see this by supposing that one is attempting to explain to a child the concept of Catholicism—or any religion. That "explanation" necessarily comprises a description of the working rules of the organization, as well as the beliefs (also working rules) of Catholics. Notice that "beliefs" must be understood as a commitment to the working rules of the Catholic Church and therefore constitutive of what it means to be a Catholic. One cannot be a Catholic by holding to the rules (and correlated beliefs) of Buddhism.

If we shift our gaze to the idea of a university, the explanation of this organizational form would, as well, entail a list of what it does and does not do, how it does and does not function, and the roles that individuals play within it. Notice that each of these descriptions (or explanations) of organizations reduces to a description of the working rules of the going concern. In one sense, the working rules are the organization. Likewise, if one wishes to explain the concept of a corporation, one necessarily defines it in terms of the rules that differentiate it from a sole proprietorship or from a limited partnership. These working rules (institutions) are constitutive of the organizations they describe.

By being constitutive I have in mind the idea that it is the working rules of an organization that both give that organization its identity and meaning to the outside observer, and those same working rules determine how its members or employees actually carry out their activities. We "know" the Federal Reserve by what it does, and how it does those things it has been empowered to do. We "know" a university by what it does (educate students, produce research), and by how it goes about doing those acknowledged activities (organized lectures of a certain frequency and duration, research laboratories). And it should be obvious that it is the working rules of the Federal Reserve—or of a university—that indicate what it does, and how its employees shall carry out their respective tasks. By your rules you shall be known. Once the working rules and their emanations are apprehended, few sapient beings can plausibly suppose that the Federal Reserve educates young people in classrooms and that universities control the money supply. Charles Sanders Peirce had a more elaborate version of this idea. "Consider what effects, that might conceivably have practical bearings, we conceive the object of our conception to have. Then, our conception of these effects is the whole of our conception of the object" (Peirce 1934, p. 1).

Understanding going concerns—whether firms, government agencies, universities, or nation-states—requires that we make a connection between the working rules of those going concerns and the apprehended effects to which those rules give rise. To Peirce our conception of those effects constitutes our conception of the going concern. We see that the working rules (the institutions) comprise a set of conditions indicating what individuals can and cannot do (if they wish to remain a member of the organization), and what they can and cannot expect the organization to help them do (if they remain members). The working rules (the institutions) define the organization. In that sense, organizations are not institutions (working rules), they (organizations) compose institutions (working rules). These institutions: (1) define an organization with respect to the rest of the world; and (2) spell out the internal nature of the organization. These two types of institutions are found in the enabling legislation, the constitution, the bylaws, the charter, or the administrative rules of organizations. With respect to a corporation the first type of institution articulates the necessary steps that must be followed to become a corporation, and to remain one. The second type of institution articulates how officers are appointed, how the financial records shall be kept, and how administrative decisions are to be made.

Because institutions are collectively determined rules that define acceptable individual and group behavior, they are sets of dual expectations. The concept of an institution is one of mutualities—of correlates and of dualities. This correlative nature was recognized by the legal scholar W. N. Hohfeld (1913, 1917), who postulated four sets of dualities as the essence of legal relations among individuals in a society. These legal correlates (right-duty, privilege–no right, power-liability, and immunity–no power) were incorporated into the institutional economics developed by John R. Commons, who used slightly different terminology to form the basis of his analysis of collective, economic, and social relations.

All human activity requires regularizing rules that facilitate social processes; the calendar and the clock are such rules. Time is a social institution that provides regularity and structure to our daily lives. In any social setting behavioral norms (institutions) define acceptable actions for the members of the polity. These institutions may be secular or they may be religious. Individuals of the Jewish and Muslim faiths do not eat pork and usually prefer that food be prepared in certain ways. Catholics, at one time, were under some compunction not to eat meat on Fridays. Some religions discourage dancing, the playing of cards, smoking, and the consumption of alcohol. Other religions are silent on alcohol, and some permit having multiple wives.

Our daily life is replete with rules—customary and formal—that are both positive and negative signals concerning individual behavior. Notice that an institution that restrains Alpha (who may be an individual or a group or class of individuals) simultaneously liberates Beta (who may be an individual or a group or class of individuals). The idea that institutions are only constraints apparently emanates from the idea that markets are natural mechanisms that operate best without "interference." But institutions cannot logically be seen as constraints on markets for the simple reason that markets cannot possibly exist without an institutional structure in place that indicates ownership, what is a cost, and who must pay whom in particular situations. And, as we know, markets not only constrain but also liberate.

We recognize the reciprocal nature of institutions when we see that I can no longer burn the leaves raked from my yard in the autumn, nor can I allow my dog to roam the neighborhood unrestrained. At the same time, my asthmatic neighbor no longer need suffer from the smoke I once generated by burning my leaves, I no longer must repair the damage to my shrubs from roaming dogs, nor need I reclaim my yard from the unwelcome depositions of a time when all dogs ran free. Speed limits indicate how fast I may drive, and how fast I can expect other motorists to drive. Food and drug standards assure me that my cheese is indeed cheese, my meat is indeed meat (and reasonably safe), and that the malaria pills I take are—within certain probabilities—safe.

The distinctive architecture of Paris, with its mansard roofs, is a reminder that institutions can give rise to behaviors and particular outcomes that, over time, become not only the norm but also symbols of great beauty and admiration. The mansard roof is a clever response by the architect François Mansart (1598–1666) to a rule on taxation of building height. Owners of buildings, always in need of more space in an increasingly crowded urban landscape, proved amenable to innovative architecture, borrowed by Mansart from Italy, that managed to hide an additional story under the roof, thus rendering it exempt from taxation. An alternative account is that the hidden floor under the sloping roof arose because of a restriction rather than a tax on building height. Either way, the mansard roof provided more space for the owner and has come to define a particular class and era (Beaux-Arts) of architecture.

Other institutions are more subtle but no less important. In Great Britain, and most of its former colonies, one drives an automobile on the left-hand side of the road. Until September 3, 1967, motorists in Sweden did the same. In the majority of other nations one drives on the right. It really does not matter on which side of the road people drive as long as they all do it on the same side. The choice of a side of the road for driving holds no important economic consequences, but it does regularize behavior. Other forms of regularizing institutions are called habits or norms. Elderly people are usually treated with some deference, very young children warrant special attention when near roads, and in most countries individuals will respect the sanctity of queues.

Our interest in institutions arises because new public policy is simply a new constellation of institutions formulated in the legislative, executive, or judicial realms. Because new institutions at the national, regional, or local level represent collective action in restraint, liberation, and expansion of individual action, a new law or a new rule from the legislative branch (or from the courts) is simply an alteration in prior collective action (or mere custom) that now modifies extant choice domains of individuals. Some will be aided by those new working rules, and some will be harmed. Those so harmed by the new institutional setup will likely lament government "interference" in what they imagine to be some historically sanctified and therefore justified reality. Those previously harmed under the status quo ante institutional setup will relish their newfound relief.

If it is considered the norm that people be allowed to smoke in public places, then collective action (by, for instance, a city council) to alter that behavior will be viewed by those who wish to smoke as an invasion of their existing presumptive "right" to smoke in such places. Indeed, that is precisely how smokers will regard (and lament) the new institution. Notice that preexisting behavior, whether or not it is officially (legally) sanctioned, over time takes on the aura and the presumption of a right, but especially in the mind of those well served by the status quo ante. Of course, there was never a law stating that it was legal to smoke in public places, any more than there was a law declaring that chemical factories may dump whatever poisons they wish into a nation's rivers. These existing behaviors are simply an artifact from an earlier time when there was "no law." Indeed, it is often the case that there is still no law against such things. We may recall that expectorating was once regarded as quite acceptable behavior, and that loud belching constituted the ultimate compliment to a cook. Few today would choose to exercise their presumed "right" to expectorate or to belch in public, but neither would they be likely to complain about their loss of freedom for this new situation. As Commons insisted, the individual mind is formed by accommodating itself to prevailing customs and practices (Ramstad, 2001). In this we become, to a certain extent, who we are in virtue of what the prevailing institutional arrangements predispose—indeed, often force—us to become. And how could it not be this way? Children of today fail to see anything interesting about telephones that do not require landlines, nor are they much puzzled by the emerging custom in many countries that marriage no longer seems a necessary precondition for their existence. And adults will very soon believe it quite "normal" that public places, including cramped airplanes, are no longer characterized by revolting clouds of cigarette, cigar, and pipe smoke. Children, never having lived through the alternative institutional regime (with its smoky outcomes), may be excused for not appreciating the difference. They are socialized into, and therefore become habituated to, very different settings and circumstances from that of their elders. And by being so habituated, they are different from the rest of us.

Various forms of regularized behavior become codified in a variety of ways. In early landlord-tenant relations, it gradually became the norm that the renter would need to pay a deposit as security against possible future damage to the dwelling—a performance bond, as it were. Soon this practice appeared in most rental contracts, and it became the legal duty of the tenant to make the deposit. Conversely, it was the right of the landlord to receive it (Schmid 1986). As this practice was transformed from one of custom to the "law," the landlord had a duty to return the deposit if the dwelling were vacated in satisfactory condition and the tenant had the right to expect that proper behavior would result in the return of the deposit. It is also often the case that the deposit must be placed in a segregated interest-bearing account so that it cannot be used for other purposes. If there is no damage, the deposit plus accrued interest must be returned to the tenant. Customs evolve into laws when there continues to be good reasons for that evolution. And other customs either remain so or eventually disappear. Indeed one may think of the legal domain as simply the codification of earlier customs that were found to have enduring pertinence (value).

Our daily existence is therefore defined and structured by institutions that are the product of prior collective action. Institutions are necessarily the manifestations of collective action for the simple reason that individuals cannot formulate collective arrangements of acceptable and unacceptable activity; only collectives can do this. That is the essential purpose of collective action in the political realm—to do to us (and for us) what we cannot do to (and for) ourselves. This realm of collective action structures fields of individual action, or choice sets. The institutions that emanate from the legislatures and the courts define new arenas of choice, and of forbidden action, from within which individuals may or may not go about the business of their daily life. But, when institutions change, those whose actions are newly constrained will invariably complain about government "intervention" or their "loss of freedom." Notice the incoherence of this claim.

According to Commons, the volition of the authoritative agents (the legislature and the courts) produces, with a purpose in mind, the institutional structure to which all of us become habituated in our daily lives. That is, the "volition of the authoritative figure(s) . . . is the 'cause' of the behavior its hoped-for attainment elicits from citizens of the going concern" (Ramstad 1990, p. 81). By becoming habituated to these institutions, each of us must then be understood to be acting not of free will but predicated on what Commons would call the "institutionalized mind." Once a problem in the ongoing process of economic life is encountered—that is, once the prevailing institutional arrangements are thought to give rise to unwanted outcomes, the usefulness—the social legitimacy—of those institutions is thrown into doubt. The institutions become suspect precisely because the behaviors they plausibly induce are now found wanting.

Paradoxically, the formulation of a "workable solution" to the emergent problematic situation is inseparable from these customary practices to which all individuals have become accustomed. That is, the habituated mind comes to see current practices, choices, and actions as normal, right, and correct. Commons called this the "instituted personality." And this brings us to the idea that the purposes and expectations toward which problem-solving thought will be directed are instances of what Commons called institutional causation. In different words, prevailing institutions are the plausible cause of the emergent problem, and therefore new institutions will become the plausible cause of the solution to those emergent problems.

Precisely because individual choice is shaped by current working rules (by the extant institutional setup), and because current market forces and processes are themselves reflections of (predicated upon) these volitionally created working rules, it becomes incoherent for individuals thus shaped (thus instituted) to object to institutional change by the courts or the legislature on the grounds that such change would be coercive, or that it would interfere with their exercise of "free will," or that it would somehow inhibit their "freedom." Such claims are bogus precisely because their customary action against which change is now to be gauged was itself not an exercise of free will or freedom. The human mind, by habituating itself to the evolving institutional setup, had already been shaped by the processes of socialization—by "naturalizing" that which it had gradually come to regard as normal (Ramstad 1990, p. 81).

For precisely the same reason, complaints about the subversion of allocative efficiency by virtue of new institutional arrangements—a tax, a zoning restriction, a mandate to provide health benefits to all employees—

cannot be taken seriously. Such complaints, and the studies seeking to document the extent of the new "distortion" in the economy, are counterfeit because those conducting the studies ought to know that allocative efficiency calculations must always be understood in light of the institutional setup that indicates which instances of costs and benefits—whether or not they happen to be monetized at the moment—must be recorded. The issue therefore cannot be cast as one of allocative efficiency. The only intellectually honest (and theoretically correct) way to consider these new institutional arrangements is to inquire as to whose will—whose interests—are to govern the creation of these new institutional arrangements. And what purposes are to be served by these new working rules? All other questions are bogus and merely diversionary.

The central point here is that the concept of the habituated mind leads to the interesting fact that institutions are barely noticed until they are about to undergo change. Suddenly we are reminded of the connection between the working rule and our habituated action in light of that rule. It is not that we so much mind changing the rule. Rather, it is our rule-based and quite habituated action that is suddenly precious to us. Rules are hardly worth fighting over. Habituated actions, what we imagine to be the "normal" state of affairs, are most certainly worth a good fight. And especially is the habituated action of others worth a good fight if that action—smoking in public places, the destruction of some charming piece of nature—has now become loathsome to us.

The contentious nature of institutions is to be found less in their existence than in their modification. This characteristic necessarily follows, as we have seen, from the fact that individuals raised and socialized in a particular institutional environment are without a reference point for judging and evaluating that particular institutional structure. Their point of reference is never what once was; their only reference point is whether the existing structure of working rules serves useful purposes (to them) now and into the foreseeable future. Wittgenstein showed us that our language (and hence our sapience) ends where our world ends, and vice versa. Only when there is a necessity for institutional change do people tend to become defensive about the status quo ante that is suddenly threatened. We may notice here an analogue to the "olfactory gradient" in which humans are able to smell only differences in odors, not the normal (background) odors, in our lives. Enter a kitchen in which some glorious dish is being prepared and one is assaulted by the magnificent smells. After a moment the marvelous odors do not go away; only our ability to smell (detect) them disappears. Our sense of smell quickly adjusts to a new "norm," and we no longer notice the charming odors. We are soon habituated.

THREE CLASSES OF INSTITUTIONS

Norms and Conventions

Norms and conventions are the noncodified though generally accepted
regularities in behavior that bring order, civility, and predictability to
human relationships. Norms do not arise from the rulings and declarations of authoritative agents with the coercive power of the state behind
them. Norms are best thought of as the things our mother taught us.
Norms are the inherited practices of everyday life that constitute much of
what it means to be socialized into a particular culture. There have never
been any discussions and collective decisive rulings that people from East
Asia shall eat with chopsticks, while those from European origins shall
eat with metal knives, forks, and spoons.

The enforcement of norms and conventions tends to reside close to the
individual. That is, young people are socialized into a pattern of living
that, for the most part, entails the apprehension and adoption of family
and community habits of mind. The inculcation of such behavioral expectations, and their enforcement, resides in the family and its logical exten-
sions. This is not to deny the importance of norms that work at the larger
level of social interaction throughout our adult lives. But the norms we
learn when young are largely enforced by our own codes of conduct as
we mature. Indeed, social misfits, while not necessarily criminals, are
those who have rejected some of the norms and conventions that the rest
of us regard as our social (and possibly personal) obligations.

We see, therefore, that norms and conventions must be distinguished
from the class of institutions for which there exist formal (codified) enforcement mechanisms. Drivers in the United Kingdom were never asked
to reach agreement regarding on which side of the road they shall drive.
So while specific driving patterns emerged as a custom (or as a norm), the
social costs of nonconforming behavior in this realm (as opposed to the
realm of the choice of eating utensil) means that compliance processes
must be set up by the state to enforce conformance with an evolved norm.

Working Rules

Emerging from conscious social action and entailing a formal structure
of authoritative rules and sanctions is a second class of institutions in
which we find rules that carry the expectation of legal sanction. These
rules must now be understood in their more formal—that is, legal—cloth-
ing. Because institutions are collective rules that define socially acceptable
individual and group behavior, they are sets of dual expectations. The
concept of an institution is always one of correlates (of dualities). To Com-

mons, institutions are the working rules that indicate what "individuals *must* or *must not* do (compulsion or duty), what they *may* do without interference from other individuals (privilege or liberty), what they *can* do with the aid of collective power (capacity or right), and what they *cannot* expect the collective power to do in their behalf (incapacity or liability)" (Commons 1924, p. 6).

Before turning to an elaboration of these Hohfeldian correlates, it is necessary to draw a distinction between legal relations and a legal system. Obviously, no society can function in the absence of social order. The institutional arrangements of that going concern—that society—create the social order that allows it to function and to survive. The ways in which those institutions are promulgated and enforced constitute the legal system of that society. It is not necessary that the legal system have courts, lawyers, and jails. It is sufficient that the society have a structured set of rules and sanctions that result in social order. We might think of this as the society's authority system. These institutions need not be codified rules, nor do they need to be secular rather than religious. What matters is their recognition on the part of the members of the collectivity. When this happens, there is a legal system. It is a legal system in the broadest interpretation of the term. The societal recognition of a specific set of ordered relations among individuals is a legal relation.

Turning now to Hohfeld's fundamental legal relations, imagine two individuals, Alpha and Beta. Recalling that legal relations are also group specific, imagine Alpha to be a person (an individual) and Beta to be all other persons; one social entity (Alpha) may be an individual or a group against another social entity (Beta), which may be an individual or a group. The four fundamental legal relations are shown in Table 4.1, with slight modification from the Hohfeld terminology.

In the Hohfeld scheme, a *right* means that Alpha has a state-sanctioned and enforced expectation and assurance that Beta will behave in a certain way toward Alpha. As an example, Alpha has an expectation that Beta will not act against Alpha's interests. A *duty* means that Beta must behave in a specific way with respect to Alpha. This means that Beta must not act contrary to Alpha's interests. Notice that the dual of Alpha's legal position is Beta's legal position; Alpha has the right, Beta has the duty.

The second correlate is that of privilege and no right. If Alpha has *privilege* with respect to Beta, then she (Alpha) is free to act without regard for the implications that may befall Beta from that action. For instance, Alpha is free to discharge toxic pollutants into a river in which Beta seeks to catch fish. Beta, by standing in a position of *no right* to Alpha's privilege, is unable to gain relief from this instance of cost shifting. If Beta should seek relief, he would be told that there is "no law" against Alpha's actions. Beta has no rights. In May 2000 the so-called Love Bug virus,

TABLE 4.1
The Legal Correlates

	ALPHA	← →	*BETA*
Static Correlates	Right	← →	Duty
	Privilege	← →	No right
Dynamic Correlates	Power	← →	Liability
	Immunity	← →	No power

released in the Philippines, overwhelmed e-mail systems worldwide and caused tens of millions of dollars in damage. Prosecutors in the Philippines dismissed all charges against a man accused of releasing the virus because of a lack of applicable laws. Again, privilege is a situation of "no law," and so one person is free to visit harm on others without regard for the consequences.

The difference between the right-duty correlate and the privilege–no right correlate can be further clarified. Consider the issue of solar collectors. If my neighbor is free to allow her shade trees to grow to a height such that my solar collector would become useless, she has legal privilege and I have no right with respect to solar rays. On the contrary, if a new local land-use law should protect me against the incursion of shade, then I would suddenly have a right to the sun's rays and she would have a duty not to interfere with my access to that source of energy. In this instance, it is my right to expect that sunlight will not be interrupted, and it is her duty to see that such does not occur. Notice that these are static correlates that define legal relations at a particular time.

From a dynamic aspect, to have *power* is to have the ability to force other individuals into a new legal situation against their will. If Alpha has power, then she may put Beta in a new legal situation not of Beta's choosing. And whence does this ability come? This ability springs from the capacity of Alpha to enlist the coercive power of some authority (the state) to impose her will on Beta's choice domain (field of action). The state (or the pertinent authority system) becomes an essential participant in the exercise of Alpha's power with respect to Beta. When Alpha has power, Beta suffers from a *liability* to the capacity of Alpha to force Beta into a new and unwanted legal situation. If Beta is not exposed to Alpha's attempt to create a new legal relation inimical to Beta's interests, then we say that Beta enjoys *immunity* in the face of Alpha's efforts to put Beta in an unwanted legal position. In the face of Beta's immunity, we would say that Alpha has no power. To have *no power* means that Alpha is unable to put Beta in a new legal situation that is not to Beta's liking.

The Hohfeldian scheme is symmetrical with respect to the position of Alpha and Beta. That is, the legal relation is identical regardless of the position from which the relation is viewed (Alpha or Beta). The difference lies "not in the relation which is always two sided, but in the positions and outlook of [Alpha and Beta] . . . which together make up the two converses entering into the relation" (Hoebel 1942, p. 955).

We can regard these four legal relations as being either active or passive. The right-duty and the power-liability relations are active in that they represent imperative relations subject to the authority of the state (or the appropriate authority system). On the other hand, the privilege–no right and immunity–no power relations are passive in that they are not subject to direct legal enforcement. Instead, these latter correlates define the limit of the state's legal activities. That is, they indicate types of behavior in which the state has no interest. As we see in the case of privilege, the state declares that it is none of its direct concern if Alpha pollutes a river (and kills the fish) of interest to Beta.

In modern legal systems, every right that Alpha has upon Beta is given effect by the obligation held by the state to compel Beta to abide by the duty incumbent on Beta. That is, to have a right is to know and to expect that the coercive power of the state will be continually brought to bear on those who bear a duty against your right. Indeed, there is more to the story. To have a right is to be able to compel the state to protect your interests. Notice that if Alpha has a right, this is more than being a mere passive recipient of the state's direct support. Rather, the state agrees, when it grants a right to Alpha, to stand ready to defend Alpha's interests against the claims and incursions of others. That agreement is manifest in the state's coercion against those with a duty against Alpha's right. We see, once again, that the state is a party to every transaction.

Property Relations

Finally we come to the third level of institutional arrangements, which concern income (or benefit) streams arising from the ownership of particular valuable objects or circumstances. We call these particular institutional arrangements property relations. Property relations, along with what have come to be called civil rights, are the most fundamental social constructs among members of a political community. Whereas civil rights laws are entitlements concerning the expected behaviors of all members of a polity toward each other, property relations concern collective assurance among members of the polity with respect to particular income (or benefit) streams—usually (but not only) associated with the ownership of land. Small wonder property relations are contentious.

With a clear understanding of the fundamental working rules—rights, duties, privilege, no rights—it is straightforward to extend these legal correlates to situations that represent the prospect for monetary gain or loss. To have a right with respect to a particular activity (say, the right to free assembly or to free speech) is to have the capacity to compel the state to protect your ability to assemble or to speak. To have a right with respect to a stream of future economic benefits is to have the capacity to compel the state to protect—and perhaps to indemnify if necessary—your control over that income stream. The first of these we call a civil right. The second of these we call a property right.

Property rights obtain their empirical content from the imposition by the state—or a comparable authority system—of a duty on all others to forbear from interference with the income stream accruing to the owner of the object or circumstances so protected. As we consider the analysis of property relations, it is important to resist the temptation to cast these relations in dyadic terms—the owner against an all-powerful and meddling government. Clarity is possible only if we understand that property relations are not dyadic—a person (usually called an "owner") against government. Rather, property relations must be seen as triadic. That is, property relations must be understood as social arrangements that define the relations among: (1) one person (or several persons) whom we will call the "owner(s)"; (2) an object or circumstance of value to the owners as well as to others; and (3) all other persons in the polity. When we consider property relations in this manner, it allows us to comprehend the essence of property relations as foundational social institutions.

The empirical reality of property relations is that they situate all members of a polity in a particular position with respect to valuable assets and circumstances. The essence—the empirical content—of ownership is the socially sanctioned ability to exclude others. A copyright prevents others from benefiting at the expense of the creator. A patent gives temporary protection to the inventor. Private property in land and other related assets sanctions exclusion of others. When I am precluded from infringing the patent of one who has labored many years on some invention, it seems that little harm can result. But exclusion can, in certain settings, impose real costs. Herein resides the contentious nature of property rights in land and other valuable objects. If the gold fields of South Africa are owned by a single large corporation, then economic relations throughout the economy cannot help but be affected in a particular way. If the vast majority of the best agricultural land in a particular nation-state is owned by a few large and aggressively dynastic families, then the social costs of landlessness and related social pathologies cannot be so easily dismissed. As Henry George put the matter, "Place one hundred men on an island from which there is no escape, and whether you make one of those men the absolute owner of the other ninety-nine or the absolute owner of the soil of the island, will make no difference either to him or to them" (George 1955 [1905], p. 347).

Property relations are inevitably contentious economic and social relations. To be the owner of something of great economic value is to find oneself in a rather comfortable situation on two counts. First, as indicated, to have a right (in this case a property right) is to have that wonderful capacity to compel the coercive power of the state to come to your aid in protecting your economic interests. I have characterized this situation as institutional change that expands individual action. When the state grants a property right, it is, of necessity, also acknowledging a durable obligation on its part to defend the interests of those to whom the property right has been granted. As if this assurance were not a sufficiently advantageous position to occupy, one other material advantage must be noted. To own something of economic value in a market economy is to put one in a position of a seller. In a market economy one always wants to be a seller rather than a buyer. Moreover, as a seller, one wants to be in a position as a seller of more than just one's labor power. If one has only labor power to sell in a market economy, one is at the mercy of those in need of buying labor power. If one owns not only labor power but other assets of significant economic value—land and other forms of capital—then one is twice a seller. Economic advantage in a market economy accrues to those with a diversified and providential asset portfolio who stand in a position of seller rather than buyer.

To most observers the word ownership is clear: the full rights left to an individual after certain governmental restrictions and reservations are taken into account. We can agree that individuals (and groups) own land and related assets, and we know that the market price of such assets is a function of the covenants placed on it by previous owners, as well as the working rules set down by the community in which it is situated. Ownership implies a degree of limited and constrained sovereignty of the owner. But, as noted, that limited sovereignty for the owner represents liberty for the neighbors. The owner's duty to refrain from undertaking the extraction of sand and gravel is the neighbors' right to a dust-free future. The owner's duty not to build a tavern on an urban parcel is the neighbors' right to quiet evenings.

It is essential to consider the essence of property to be an income or benefit stream (Bromley 1991; Macpherson 1973). That is, we must consider property to be a benefit stream that individuals (or a group of individuals) hope to be able to capture and control into the future. On this understanding, property relations entail the constellation of entitlements that give that benefit stream its empirical content. When I acquire a property right (a legally sanctioned property interest in something), it means that I can rely on the authority system of the polity in which I live to protect my claim to that benefit stream—to my property. Indeed, as we have seen, I can demand that protection from the authority system. Property rights concern expectations that are sanctioned by the collectivity and enforced by the collectivity at the will and command of the holder of the right.

The social content of property originates in the fact that the state must agree to stand ready to defend an owner's interest in the income stream. Why should the state agree to this arrangement? Because those who define the purpose of the state, the authoritative agents, agree that it is in their interests to do so. There is no mystery, after all, why those who own economic assets will insist that it is the purpose of the state (and of its government) to "protect property rights." One rarely hears this insistence from those without assets protected by property rights. Contention over property relations arises because historical access to some income stream—say, the ability to avoid costly processing of industrial wastes by discharging them directly into a nearby river—will invariably be regarded by the current beneficiary of this favorable situation as a right to that income stream (the avoided costs). This ability, a legal privilege, to discharge industrial wastes into a river represents no secure claim at all. In terms of the legal correlates, the industrial polluter is simply enjoying privilege and in so doing is free to act without regard for the interests of others. This is a regime of no law with respect to waste disposal practices.

Property relations are more than codified institutional arrangements specifying who may use an object of value, who controls the use of that object, and who may receive the benefits from that object. Property relations, along with the other state-defined working rules and entitlements, are also the legally sanctioned capacity to impose costs on others. That is, the correlates of privilege for Alpha and no right for Beta define a situation in which Alpha is free to disregard costs imposed on Beta, and the latter has no avenue for registering objections to this situation. The absence of clear property relations with respect to solar rays means that my neighbor can impose costs on me in terms of allowing her shade trees to invade my access to the sun. Notice that this situation of privilege and no right was not important or contentious, except for avid gardeners and sunbathers, until new technology permitted me to generate electricity from the rays of the sun. Once I had the technical capacity—and the interest—to generate my own electricity, then the legal arrangements permitting shade on my roof were suddenly quite unsatisfactory to me. In fact, prior to my interest in solar power, I may well have benefited from my neighbor's shade in the summertime. But suddenly, I am surprised.

That is, when a new technical opportunity and my new interests in solar energy coalesced, the extant property relations became central to my idea of what seems better to do about shade and solar collectors. At that moment, the structure of actual (not presumptive) rights became important because those property relations indicated who must pay to have their interest protected against the costs imposed by other parties. Under the existing property relations I am suddenly bearing unwanted costs in the form of shade in an area in which I would like to place a solar collector. My neighbor's trees impose costs on me. I could, of course, as the hyper-Coaseans would have it, simply offer to pay my neighbor to cut down her tall trees. If I am unable to outbid her love of those trees, then she keeps the trees and I must forgo my interest in a solar collector. The hyper-Coaseans would quickly announce that efficiency had been served by this failure to negotiate a bargain. But what if I am able to buy out her interest in tall shade trees and thus place my new solar collector in a nice sunny spot where it will work to good effect? The hyper-Coaseans would then declare that particular outcome—a very different one by the way—to be efficient. And energy conservation would be enhanced. Notice that the hyper-Coaseans would be able to declare both outcomes—very different in economic futures—to be "efficient." We see that efficiency can be used to explain and to justify either economic outcome. Some decision rule.

But we must cast these property relations in a broader context. At some point it is not difficult to imagine that a number of my neighbors will wish to install solar collectors on their roofs. The question then becomes, at what point is the larger social interest well served by a change in the property relations concerning shade and solar collectors? We need not, at this point, occupy ourselves with all of the larger economic and political niceties of this gradual shift in relative scarcities between shade and access to solar rays. The example is strictly heuristic. But it is not in doubt that, as in so many situations, the balance of interests in favor of solar collectors and against unwanted shade will shift. When some point is reached, those who seek solar access will manage to change the local rules (property relations) so that shade trees may no longer block access to solar collectors. These new property relations will bestow a new income stream—in the form of cost savings—on those who wish to install solar collectors, and this new legal opportunity will become capitalized in the value of dwellings in this particular jurisdiction. There is now a property right in the sun's rays. We see once again that these interdependencies among economic actors affect settings and circumstances that eventually bestow differential economic advantage and disadvantage on different parties.

Let us consider these interdependencies in more detail. Imagine two individuals characterized by the right-duty and privilege–no right correlates. Assume that Alpha has a right and Beta has a correlated duty. How do these correlates manifest themselves in everyday life? Consider first the right-duty correlate. The right that Alpha has can be of several possible types. The most valuable type of a right is one in which Beta may not interfere with Alpha without the latter's prior consent. For example, Beta may not pick flowers from Alpha's garden without the latter's permission.

Alpha's right is protected by a property rule, and Beta has a duty that is proscribed by a property rule protecting Alpha (Bromley 1991).

A right protected by a property rule means that the party wishing to contravene that right must approach the right holder and initiate the bargaining process. Here Beta must approach Alpha. This is the essence of protection for Alpha by a property rule, and it conforms to what most of us have in mind when we are told that an individual has a property right in some object or circumstances. But there is a second way in which Alpha's property right might be protected. Assume that Beta may interfere with Alpha's interests—contravene Alpha's right—but this interference is accompanied by Beta's knowledge that compensation will be required ex post. In this instance, Alpha has a right that is protected by a liability rule. We see this form of protection of Alpha's right when there is difficulty in anticipating certain outcomes that may adversely affect Alpha.

Oil spills from tankers provide one example of this property relation. A coastal nation has a right to be free of unwanted oil spills, and this right is protected by a liability rule that requires compensation from shipowners after the fact (after a spill occurs). Notice that this form of protection is useful because, in the case of accidents, it does not make sense to assume that the two parties would agree to a price before the fact. But they do agree to a form of protection of the right of coastal nations to be free of unwanted oil by an arrangement—a liability rule—whose exact financial extent can only be determined after an accident. The shipowner (Beta) has a duty to pay some damages to the coastal nation (Alpha) whose interests are protected by a right given effect through a liability rule. Of course, some accidents—say, the explosion of a nuclear reactor at an electricity-generating facility—cannot be foreseen or protected against, and though "inalienable" in the strict sense of the word, courts of law may still become the venue wherein compensatory damages are assessed. The difference between this situation and protection by a liability rule is that with the latter it is understood that certain outcomes are more frequent—perhaps even "expected"—but the victim has a regularized expectation to be made whole.

Finally, Alpha's right might be given protection through an inalienability rule. Under this rule, Beta may not interfere with Alpha under any circumstances; there is no price at which Alpha would agree to the interference, and expost compensation is not an option. We tend to find inalienability rules in those areas where it is important to protect individuals from serious damages—say, toxic chemicals in food or in domestic water supplies. The outright prohibition of certain chemicals means that Alpha is protected by an inalienability rule, and Beta has a duty to make sure that Alpha remains free of such compounds. Notice that compensation may still be demanded by the right holder, but this recourse would arise through judicial proceedings in the case of malfeasance.

We see that within the rights-duties correlate there are three different ways in which Alpha's *right* may be given protection, and thus there are three ways in which Beta's duty might be effectuated. When Alpha has a right protected by a property rule, Beta must approach Alpha to see if there is scope for a bargaining transaction. When Alpha has a right protected by a liability rule, Beta may proceed to act with due prudence but with the understanding that, if there are costs visited on Alpha, then Beta must be prepared to pay compensation—such necessary compensation being set by a third party. Finally, when Alpha has a right protected by an inalienability rule, there is no price that would permit Beta to interfere with Alpha, nor may Beta proceed to interfere with Alpha comfortable in the knowledge that, should something go wrong, some level of automatic compensation will rectify the situation.

Let us now consider the second set of correlates, those pertaining to privilege and no right. Recall that privilege is a situation in which Alpha may undertake actions that may be detrimental to Beta, but Alpha need hold no particular concern for the interests of Beta about such interference. Here, Alpha may interfere with Beta and can only be stopped if Beta agrees to buy off Alpha. In this instance Alpha is the interfering party, while Beta is the receiving party; it is Beta upon whom costs are being imposed by Alpha's actions, yet it is Beta who must initiate action to prevent the harm being imposed. Mitigation would consist of Beta buying out Alpha. In this case Alpha's privilege is protected by a property rule against Beta's no right. To return to the example of solar collectors, in the absence of a right to solar rays the only way I can influence my neighbor's management of her trees is to buy her off. Because I have no right, it will cost me money to have my interests represented. When I do not have the law on my side, and when the extant property relations are not to my liking, my interests can only be given effect if I spend money.

The second property relation under the privilege–no right correlate is that where Beta may stop interference from Alpha but in doing so must be prepared to compensate Alpha. Again, the exact compensation would be determined by a neutral third party. In this situation Alpha still has privilege with respect to Beta—that is, Alpha may still impose costs on Beta. If Beta wants those costs to stop, then it will be necessary to pay some compensation to Alpha. As in the right-duty correlate, this second form of protection for Alpha is one of a liability rule. Also, as previously, the compensation is to be determined by a third party rather than as a process in which Alpha and Beta engage in bargaining. Protection of a right by a property rule implies the force of injunction and prior bargaining; both parties must agree to a price, or there will be no change in

TABLE 4.2
Rights Protected by Property Rules, Liability Rules, and Inalienability Rules

Alpha	Beta
Right	Duty
Alpha has a right protected by a property rule.	Beta has duty against Alpha's protection by a property rule.
Alpha has a right protected by a liability rule.	Beta has duty against Alpha's protection by a liability rule.
Alpha has a right protected by an inalienability.	Beta has duty against Alpha's protection by an inalienability rule.
Privilege	No Right
Alpha has privilege protected by a property rule.	Beta has no right against Alpha's protection by a property rule.
Alpha has privilege protected by a liability rule.	Beta has no right against Alpha's protection by a liability rule.
Alpha has privilege protected by an inalienability rule.	Beta has no right against Alpha's protection by an inalienability rule.

the status quo. Protection of a right by a liability rule entails efforts to rectify grievances after the fact with the necessary settlement (the compensation) not being subject to the relative strength and wealth of the antagonists but rather to be set by the neutral eye of a third party (usually the state). These static legal correlates are depicted in table 4.2.

The relations in table 4.2 are static in that they describe, at any moment, the extant entitlement structure. In a dynamic setting, the particular forms of entitlements found within the two separate correlates are a function of the way in which power is exercised by Alpha as against the liability of Beta. Notice that liability here is in reference to a position of being legally vulnerable to the desires of Alpha to create a new legal relationship. The liability rule just discussed represents a form of legal compulsion to be held financially liable for one's actions. There is an important distinction between Beta having financial liability toward Alpha because Alpha is protected by a liability rule, and Beta being legally vulnerable (having liability) to the whims of Alpha in her exercise of power. Duty in the face of Alpha's right is not the same as liability to Alpha's power.

When Alpha exercises power, there are several ways in which that might affect Beta. The three kinds of entitlements found under the right-duty correlate and the three types of entitlements found under the privilege–no right correlates represent six possibilities. The final set of legal correlates—immunity and no power—is covered by the inalienability rule. That is, Alpha is immune to the actions of Beta to create a new legal relationship that will bind Alpha. Alpha enjoys inalienable protection against the inability of Beta. The relation between rights, property, and property rights is depicted in table 4.3. The dominant forms of property relations are depicted in table 4.4.

The Economic Effects of Institutions

We now see how prevailing institutional arrangements, especially those concerning property relations, legitimize the realization of particular benefit streams for certain individuals in an economy, and how those same institutional arrangements therefore legitimize the imposition of costs in that economy. In other words, institutions indicate which costs must be considered by various decision-making units. Until recently, workers had a very limited property right in their labor power, and so it was inexpensive for early industrialists to ignore the costs to those workers suffering injury in the workplace. From the conceptual framework presented in the preceding section, we would say that workers had no right, and industrialists had privilege. One can understand the history of the modern labor movement as being primarily concerned to redefine these legal relations. As noted previously, we would say that these redefinitions occurred through rationing transactions that redefined the realms of reasonable and unreasonable demands and of willing and unwilling obedience embedded in managerial transactions.

Once it became more expensive for the owners of factories to ignore the interests of workers—that is, once workers had a property right in their future income stream—it became more costly for owners of factories to be so cavalier about safety. Suddenly it was in the interest of owners to invest in improved working conditions. Concerted political action by workers, and the corresponding activities of their unions, facilitated the legal conversion of their situation of no right into one of right. Owners of factories were moved from a position of privilege to one of duty. In this respecification of legal relations, not only did the pertinent institutional arrangements undergo change, but workers soon enjoyed a new realm of economic opportunity compared with their former condition. The new property relations liberated workers and restrained the owners of factories. In altering their legal relations, we would say that workers exercised power as against the liability of factory owners. Of course, workers could not do this alone. A fuller account would indicate that, over time, workers were gradually able to enlist the aid of a sufficient number of others who could help persuade the larger political community to begin to see—to come to regard—the existing institutional arrangements as "unreasonable." Gradually, minds were changed about what seemed better, at the time, to do. Peirce would tell us that new belief emerged from the focused

TABLE 4.3
Rights, Property, and Property Rights

RIGHTS

Rights allow an individual to compel the coercive power of the state to come to her assistance. Rights do not entail passive support by the state but rather active assistance for those with rights. That is, the state stands ready to be enlisted in the cause of those to whom it has granted rights. We say that rights *expand the capacities* of the individual by indicating what one can do with the aid of the collective power (Bromley 1989; Macpherson 1973; Commons 1924).

PROPERTY

Property is not an object but is instead, a value. When one buys a piece of land (in the vernacular, a "piece of property"), one acquires not merely some physical object but rather control over a benefit stream arising from that setting and circumstance that runs into the future. That is why one spends money (one benefit stream) in order to acquire a different benefit stream ("ownership" of a new benefit stream arising from the fact of ownership). Notice that the magnitude of that new benefit stream is a function of the legal parameters associated with it. The price paid to acquire that new benefit stream is none other than the expected discounted present value of all future net income appropriable from "owning" the thing. This is why property is the value, not the object (Bromley 1991; Macpherson 1973, 1978).

PROPERTY RIGHTS

Property rights bring together legal concepts of rights and duties with settings and circumstances (including objects) capable of producing income (Becker 1977; Bromley 1989, 1991; Christman 1994; Hallowell 1943; Hohfeld 1913, 1917). Property rights parameterize the nature and extent of income appropriable from control of income-producing settings and circumstances. Trademarks, copyrights, and patents are forms of property rights. All are forms of rights in property (the future value), and duties for nonowners.

consideration of the unwanted effects arising from existing institutional arrangements. William James would tell us that it now became better to believe that workers should not be treated as they had been previously.

We see that a labor contract is an arena of correlated rights and duties. The existing institutions define which costs may legally be ignored, and thus which costs may be legally visited on others. This struggle between those causing such costs—and those on whom they fall—is at the heart of

TABLE 4.4
Assets and Property Regimes

We might usefully think of three general property regimes, and one regime that is not defined in terms of property rights at all.

STATE PROPERTY

The political community is the recognized owner of the asset. Individuals in the political community may benefit from the asset but must observe rules of the government agency responsible to the political community.
Examples: national forests and parks, military bases, government office buildings.

PRIVATE PROPERTY

Individual members of the political community have a recognized right to benefit from the asset, subject to legislative mediation and judicial review. Nonowners have a duty to allow owners to behave as above.
Examples: Fee-simple land and buildings, automobiles, personal objects.

COMMON PROPERTY

A group of owners holds rights in common, including the right to exclude nonowners. Individual owners have specific rights and duties with respect to their ability to benefit from the asset, subject to legislative mediation and judicial review within the larger political community. Nonowners have a legal duty to respect boundaries of the regime.
Examples: Irrigation districts, condominiums, the Swiss alps (pastures).

RES NULLIUS

There is no legally recognized group of users or owners. The asset is available to anyone; it is an open-access resource.
Examples: The high-seas fishery (outside of national 200-mile limits), the atmosphere (in the absence of pollution laws).

Source: Bromley 1991

conflicts over the legal foundations of a market economy. When someone complains about government "interference," we may immediately understand this lament to be motivated by the new unwelcome realization that costs that are currently being shifted elsewhere may no longer be visited on others. The party now bearing those unwanted costs cannot be expected to complain about government interference. One person's government interference is another's government protection. Constraint for Alpha is liberation for Beta.

This new inability to continue to ignore certain costs by shifting them to others is obviously unpleasant to those who have grown comfortable with the status quo. Small wonder they complain. When regulations of the workplace were first introduced, including the prohibition of child labor, factory owners no doubt complained about government "interference" in their freedom to run their business as they (the owners) saw fit. Notice here that if government had failed to act on behalf of the interests of the children, it is quite improbable that this inaction would be seen as government "interference" in the lives of the children. When governments sanction—perhaps through inaction—those currently able to shift certain costs on others, few consider this protection of the status quo an example of government "interference" with those now bearing such costs. Yet, when governments decide to protect those currently being visited with unwanted costs—those with duty, no right, liability, or no power—that action is invariably referred to as government "interference" with the party enjoying a right, privilege, power, or immunity. Put another way, when the right, privilege, power, or immunity of certain economic agents is jeopardized by citizen complaints and political action, government quickly becomes the enemy. And the talk inevitably turns to a claimed loss of "freedom."

Factory owners at one time had the legal sanction (they had privilege) to treat workers (including children) as they wished. When workers began to mobilize to seek relief from working twelve to sixteen hours a day, six days per week, factory owners were able to call on the coercive authority of the state—and its police—to crush these early workers' movements. Those killed in such protests were demonized as troublemakers, and the police were usually absolved of any wrongdoing. In our terminology, workers had no right.

With respect to pollution, factories and farmers have, until quite recently, been able to discharge effluent into the nearest river while those who objected to this practice were invariably denounced as meddlesome troublemakers. Those adversely affected by this pollution were in a legal position of no right. Factories and farms were in a legal position of privilege to treat waterways and the atmosphere as their private waste-disposal facility. Farmers behaved as if they had a presumptive right to allow their cows' manure to wash into streams. At one time, meatpackers had the presumptive right to sell any product on which they might make a profit, regardless of the health implications for those who might eat that product.

All of these presumptive rights—legal privilege—have been challenged and found not to have been a right at all but merely a historic practice. But this critical assessment of traditional practices, and its subsequent reversal through collective action in the legislatures and in the courts, did not occur without struggle by those who would be inconvenienced by the need to absorb those costs that were formerly imposed on others. These redefinitions of socially acceptable realms of opportunity—fields of individual action—constitute the essence of public policy. They are examples of rationing transactions that redefine the legal foundations of the economy.

IMPLICATIONS

Human action is parameterized by institutions—norms and conventions, working rules, and property relations. It is incoherent to use choice-theoretic techniques of standard welfare economics to advocate the adoption of "efficient" institutions precisely because institutions determine which costs must be accounted for by which economic entities. Cost shifting occurs when some individuals are able, because of the status quo institutional setup, to disregard those costs that they now impose on others. Indeed, that is the essence of economic institutions: they indicate who must pay for which costs, and who is able to shift particular costs to others. Pareto irrelevant externalities is a term much in favor by those who believe in the ability of atomistic bargaining to solve all "relevant" externalities—by which they mean those which impinge on "efficiency." But this escape clause simply rationalizes (justifies) those settings and circumstances in which efficiency calculations fail to find evidence that cost shifting should be stopped on efficiency grounds. The circularity in this approach is evident and complete.

Rationing transactions are those in which collective action redefines the institutional setup within which individuals are free to choose. Those well served by the status quo ante will be the first to complain of government interference and will, quite possibly, lament their alleged loss of "freedom." Others, newly liberated from unsatisfactory settings and circumstances, will be inclined to celebrate their new liberation.

A complete understanding of institutions now requires that we turn our attention to the problem of understanding why institutions change (or do not change), and how prevailing institutional arrangements can be seen as explanations for particular behaviors and social outcomes.

CHAPTER FIVE

Institutional Change

> Outcomes of *available* actions are not ascertained but
> created. We are not speaking . . . of the objective recorded
> outcomes of actions which have been performed. Those ac-
> tions are not "available." An action which can still be chosen
> or rejected *has no objective outcome*. The only kind of out-
> come which it can have exists in the imagination of the
> decision-maker.
>
> —G.L.S. Shackle, *Decision, Order and Time*
> *in Human Affairs* (1961)

RECEIVED TRUTHS

Prevailing accounts of institutions and institutional change are predicated
on an epistemology of positivism and consequentialist welfarism. Indeed,
the "new" institutional economics differentiates itself from the classical
institutional economics of Commons and Veblen in the belief that it now
brings to the task a level of theoretical exactitude and empirical truth that
eluded the classical institutionalists. The new institutional economists
start from the presumption that economics is *the* science of choice. They
are committed to the doctrine of methodological individualism. They
tend to see institutions as constraints on the otherwise efficient working
of free exchange among atomistic utility-maximizing individuals. And
they seek to make this same choice-theoretic structure the mechanism
whereby institutional change can be understood and explained. More seriously, they seek to make institutional change endogenous to models of
economizing behavior.

For example, Douglass North suggests that, by pressing ahead with
this theoretical project, the new institutionalists can, with sufficient hard
work, produce that ever-elusive grand synthesis whereby all the social
sciences can at last be unified under the reigning doctrine of neoclassical
economics. This glorious future would reassure the place of economics as
the linchpin of the social sciences—psychology, law, history, sociology,
and economics—all predicated on, and carefully elaborating, the grand
axioms, assumptions, and models of neoclassical economics. In advocating this utopian agenda, North was moved to write:

Defining institutions as the constraints that individuals impose on themselves makes the definition complementary to the choice theoretic approach of neoclassical economic theory. Building a theory of institutions on the foundation of individual choice is a step toward reconciling differences between economics and the other social sciences. The choice theoretic approach is essential because a logically consistent, potentially testable set of hypotheses must be built on a theory of human behavior. The strength of microeconomic theory is that it is constructed on the basis of assumptions about individual human behavior (even though I shall argue for a change in those assumptions . . .). Institutions are a creation of human beings. They evolve and are altered by human beings; hence our theory must begin with the individual. At the same time, the constraints that institutions impose on individual choices are pervasive. Integrating individual choices with the constraints institutions impose on choice sets is a major step toward unifying social science research. (North 1990, p. 5)

North seems to have rather more confidence in the ability of contemporary economics to explain choice than we find among those who have devoted their professional careers to this difficult challenge—and therefore might be presumed to know something about it (Bowles 1998; Hodgson 1988, 1998; Lawson 1997; Little 1949; Rabin 1998; Sen 1977, 1982; Shackle 1961, 1992). Indeed Lawson reminds us of the substantive idea of "choice" in economics:

So prevalent is the rhetoric of choice, indeed, that Duesenberry famously concludes that what distinguishes the subject (from sociology) is that "economics is all about how people make choices." . . . Yet it isn't. In the formal "models" found in mainstream journals and books, human choice is ultimately denied. For if real choice means anything it is that any individual could always have acted otherwise. And this is precisely what contemporary "theorists" are unable to allow in their formalistic modeling. . . . although the reality of choice appears to be widely acknowledged by economists in their more informal discussions and public pronouncements, the exercise of choice is a phenomenon that is always absent from the formal substantive analyses. . . . Instead, individuals are represented in such a way that, relative to their situations, there is almost always but one preferred or rational course of action and this is always followed. Despite some suggestive rhetoric, human doings, as modeled, could not have been otherwise. (Lawson 1997, pp. 8–9)

Notice that choice, as modeled in economics, leaves individuals with no choices to make. In such models, humans are but passive automata—

"homogeneous globules" in Veblen's caustic phrase—responding without thinking to external stimuli. If this is choice, then the word has lost any plausible meaning. In the standard account, individuals have but one choice to make—the one that maximizes utility at that moment. This is not choice for the same reason that if you cannot move, then you are not *choosing* to stand still. G.L.S. Shackle offers this observation:

> Conventional economics is not about choice, but about acting according to necessity. Economic man obeys the *dictates* of reason, follows the *logic of choice*. To call his conduct choice is surely a misuse of words, when we suppose that to him the ends amongst which he can select, and the criteria of selection are given, and the means to each end are known. . . . Choice in such a theory is empty, and conventional economics should abandon the word. (Shackle 1961, pp. 272–73)

Those who imagine that the standard theory of choice offers auspicious ground on which to build a grand synthesis of institutional change stand alone against a large number of the very best theorists who understand the comprehensive barrenness of "choice theory" in economics. And this brings us to the second problem with North's grand strategy—his wish to make institutional change endogenous in economic models of maximizing behavior. Throughout North's work on institutions and institutional change, one sees repeated reference to the desire—indeed, the necessity—to incorporate institutional change into the formal models of economic theory (North 1990). This quest for endogeneity springs from the fact that one cannot explain events in economic terms if they are exogenous to standard economic models of choice. So the theories of the new institutional economists are built in strict accord with the reigning epistemology: positivism, methodological individualism, rational agents, unexamined (yet socially constructed) scarcities, and endogenous institutions whose transformations and refinements are asserted to be explicable by the same price-theoretic algorithms that animate individual consumers and producers.

If these price-theoretic algorithms offered plausible explanations of individual choices, especially of collective choices, then such models might stand a chance to offer possible grounds for a theory of institutional change. But they do not and thus they cannot. If we suppose that we have explained (as opposed to justified) behavior when we find that it is consistent with a particular piece of theory, then we have acquired belief of a very meager kind. More important, we have terminated our inquiries precisely where they will soon start to pay large explanatory dividends. Premature claims of victory are only part of the problem. The flaw of confirmationism is compounded by the belief that economic phenomena can be fully understood by reference to independent variables that are themselves strictly economic in character. Any effort to explain economic phenomena by reference only to economic phenomena introduces a fatal circularity into economic work. To quote Joseph Schumpeter:

> [W]hen we succeed in finding a definite causal relation between two phenomena, our problem is solved if the one which plays the "causal" role is non-economic. We have then accomplished what we, as economists, are capable of in the case in question and we must give place to other disciplines. If, on the other hand, the causal factor is itself economic in nature, we must continue our explanatory efforts until we ground upon a non-economic bottom. (Schumpeter 1961, pp. 4–5)

The point here is simple: one has not explained economic phenomena—and institutional arrangements are the essence of economic phenomena—until one encounters one or more *noneconomic* independent variables. This is an unwelcome proposition for those who wish to make institutional change endogenous in economic models. Despite this, the press for endogeneity is unlikely to be abandoned for the simple reason that, if only institutional change can be thought of as endogenous in economic models, then the triumph of economics will be complete. That is, all of human action, not only individual maximizing but also the choices about the institutional foundations of all human association and interaction, will be explicable in terms of relative prices and utility maximization. This would be some grand synthesis.

However, the project is doomed on logical grounds. Once something is made endogenous, it is no longer capable of being explained by the structure within which it is embedded. By virtue of its embeddedness, it is now indistinguishable from the system of which it is a part—the "two" things are, in fact, one thing. The rear sprocket of a bicycle is mechanically linked (by a chain) to the front sprocket. One does not explain the turning of the rear sprocket by appeal to the empirical claim that the front sprocket is turning. The turning of one is the required turning of the other; they are a single entity within the structure of which they are a part. One would only seek an explanation if the rear sprocket failed to turn when the front one did. Notice that the link between the two sprockets is pertinent to explanation in the latter case but not in the former. We will devote considerable attention to the problem of explanation in subsequent chapters.

For now, notice that one can explain the turning of the rear sprocket only if one is prepared to look beyond the structure that ties the two events together—that embeds the one in the other. That is, an explanation that allows one to escape the trap of mechanical entailment can only be found if one looks for an exogenous source (the application of force to the front sprocket) of the turning of the rear sprocket. This is precisely the same reason why conventional economics does not—and cannot—

have an explanation for individual choice. Individual choice is endogenous in economic models, and by being endogenous it no longer qualifies as choice. Its endogeneity strips it of any capacity to differ from that which its very structural dependence preordains for it. This is not choice but mere mechanism. The rear sprocket has no choice but to turn as the front sprocket dictates. The endogenization project of the new institutional economists is correctly understood as an effort to reduce institutional change to nothing but mechanical determinism. Melvin Reder has something to say of this doomed endeavor.

> Associated with the assumption of stable preferences, but logically distinct, is the "thrust for endogenization." A leading manifestation of this tendency is Stigler's attempt to explain—and constrain—the behaviour of political decision makers, but this is not the only one. . . . Successfully to endogenize a new variable is to enhance the explanatory power of economics. . . . However, it must be noted that where variables are made "endogenous," they can no longer serve as objects of social choice. . . . To the extent that variables are endogenized—choice is explained—"society's" freedom of choice is seen as illusory. Freedom appears to consist not in power of choice, but (*pace* Hegel) in recognition of necessity. This is not a likely conclusion for followers of Adam Smith, and surely not one they desire, but one from which they can be saved only by failure of this direction of research. (Reder 1982, pp. 34–35)

We see that the gain in "explanatory power" for economics comes at the cost of producing plausible explanations of institutional change. Such explanations should, I suggest, be an abiding goal of the social sciences. But such explanatory coherence can only be secured if the quest for endogenization fails—as it must.

Beyond Endogenization

While the fuller development of a theory of institutional change must await the development of volitional pragmatism in subsequent chapters, I here offer a synoptic overview of the general outlines of that theory. The essential task here is to find a way to think about institutional change without getting beguiled by the quest for endogeneity and its necessarily deterministic mechanisms. We need, in other words, a theory of institutional change grounded on reasons rather than on mechanism. To Schumpeter, the answer was to be found in locating that noneconomic "bottom" on which actual human choice gains solid footing. To suppose that this essential human enterprise can be reduced to the mechanism of economizing models—models in which choice is, by definition, not choice at all but rather the reality of acting out of necessity—is to reveal a flawed understanding of the essence of economic institutions.

I therefore start with the proposition that institutional change must be seen as an example of what John R. Commons called "rationing transactions." The idea of a rationing transaction is appropriate because institutional change entails the restructuring—the redefinition—of plausible futures for members of a nation-state. Parliaments and courts ration (realign) new income and cost streams for members of society. To Commons, it was the authority system in a nation—its parliament, its courts, and its administrative agencies—that effectuates this rationing under pressure from members of the citizenry at large. We see here an example of the human will in action, looking to the future, and forming plausible images of how that future might—indeed, how it ought to—unfold. Parliaments and courts qualify as the essential locus where this process occurs. Institutional change is best understood as the essence of public policy. That is, policy is nothing but thinking about, weighing, and ultimately choosing among alternative institutional setups that will give rise to alternative imagined and plausible futures. Rationing transactions—institutional changes—redefine realms of individual action and thereby redirect income flows. But the futures of central concern to citizens, members of parliaments, and the courts are only imagined futures (Shackle 1961).

To Shackle, actions that can still be chosen or rejected on the basis of their plausible implications for the future have no objective outcomes associated with those available actions. The only outcomes that such actions can have merely exist in the mind—the imagination—of the decision maker(s). This means, quite simply, that outcomes of available actions are not ascertained (or discovered) but created. This is a central aspect of volitional pragmatism. Specifically:

> Outcomes of available actions are only imaginable, and in the process of imagining them we do not *ascertain* those outcomes—rather we *create* those outcomes.

This distinction between discovering (ascertaining) and making (creating) lies at the heart of the current struggle in philosophy between adherents to the classic dyads—facts versus values, mind versus body—and those who reject the demarcationist program so central to Plato, Kant, and Descartes (Rorty 1979, 1982, 1999). I return to this matter in subsequent chapters. For now, we need to stay focused on the very real issue of how institutions evolve under the influence of the human will in action, looking to the future.

Again, I follow Shackle in suggesting that institutional change entails the formulation and implementation of created imaginings. This approach may be easier to apprehend if we start with the idea that all institutional change entails three steps. The first step is recognition on the part of affected individuals that the status quo institutional setup induces particular individual behaviors, the aggregate of which gives rise to realized outcomes that are no longer regarded as acceptable or as reasonable.

Perhaps the health care system is creaking under excessive demands for service, a shortage of health professionals, and antiquated facilities. Perhaps air pollution is bad and getting worse. Perhaps a nation's schools are failing to meet the expectations that parents and politicians have for them. Perhaps the food supply has come under suspicion for harboring contagious diseases. Perhaps there are concerns about genetically modified organisms making their way into natural habitats and destroying particular ecological settings. These unsettling circumstances do not just materialize out of thin air nor do they exist without a reason. Rather, they are the products (results) of individual behaviors that are themselves the inevitable and "rational" economizing entailments of the existing institutional arrangements. That is, the health care system is a going concern whose operational parameters—its working rules—give rise to those traits that render its performance either agreeable or a source of widespread individual and collective disgust and agitation. Air pollution exists because factories and automobiles are at liberty to disgorge air pollutants at will.

Some schools are bad because of flawed incentives surrounding the operation of those schools, because some teachers are uninspired (and uninspiring), because some students are distracted and unruly, and because buildings are often wretched (Bromley 1998). Animal diseases that would normally be spotted by government veterinarians slip through because of some functional problems in staffing levels, morale, testing procedures, or training. One cannot plausibly attribute these failings to flawed prices. Rather, the explanation is to be found in the institutional arrangements embedded within—and indeed defining—the respective going concerns.

We see that the existing constellation of institutions gives rise to individual behaviors, the aggregate of which generates acceptable outcomes, or else such behaviors generate unacceptable outcomes. The emerging awareness of defective outcomes is at the root of a growing dissatisfaction with the status quo ante, and it is precisely these dissatisfactions that become the essential catalyst of nascent demands for institutional change. One may think of this catalyst from two different perspectives. One possibility is to suppose that institutional change is motivated by the shared desire to generate potential gains from creating new ways of doing things. I prefer an alternative hypothesis. That is, I suggest that institutional change is motivated, ab initio, by an inchoate yet emerging recognition that something must be done about existing institutional settings and their associated outcomes to mitigate probable harms that would otherwise emanate from a continuation of the status quo ante institutional setup. On this view, institutional change is provoked and motivated by a shared apprehension concerning unwanted created imaginings in the future. This perspective accords explicit recognition to the work in prospect theory indicating that humans have a greater distaste for losses from a status quo position than for the gains that may arise from changes in that status quo (Kahneman and Tversky 1979; Tversky and Kahneman 1987).

Once this galvanizing condition has been met, institutional change still requires two more conditions. The first of these concerns new created imaginings. We may usefully regard these imaginings as families of hypothetical propositions of the sort, "if X_i, then Y_i," where the subscript i relates to the proposition held by the ith member of the community, whether citizen or politician. The essence of created imaginings is that they allow members of a democratic society to create mappings of plausible outcomes (imaginings) from the enactment of new institutional arrangements. Just imagine what the health care system might become if only we could increase the number of doctors by 20 percent over the next five years. Imagine how the wait for elective surgery might be reduced if only we could increase the number of spaces in hospitals by 10 percent over the next decade. Imagine the improved health status of 40 million Americans now unprotected by health insurance if they could suddenly receive some level of health insurance coverage and thereby have the means to devote greater attention to their overall health status.

Of course, individuals will create different imaginings about possible outcomes. This should not surprise us. As Shackle says, we have different imaginings because the available actions are novel events in our lives. We have not done that before, so why should it be supposed that each of us could have definitive data and similar imaginings concerning precisely what will transpire? As Shackle says, "An action which can still be chosen or rejected has no objective outcome" (Shackle 1961, p. 143). This is precisely why there are consultants, parliamentary (legislative) committees, elaborate hearings, independent research organizations ("think tanks"), advisers, experts, and indeed entire sectors engaged in the task of creating plausible imaginings. If the task were easy and straightforward, many people would need to find other lines of work.

Once there is an emergence of plausible created imaginings, we begin to approach the final stage of institutional change—policy formulation. Democratic market economies are in continual need of new created imaginings as new problems and new opportunities arise almost on a daily basis. Those who celebrate the dynamic properties of markets are telling us only half of the story. The real dynamism of democratic capitalism is that the existing institutional arrangements are regarded as the indispensable malleable architecture for adaptation. With this idea at hand, it is easy to see that this cacophony of created imaginings will evolve from just that—an inchoate cacophony—into a slowly coalescing and emerging consensus that begins to narrow the range of institutional alternatives and plausible imaginings.

If only these X might somehow be altered in the following ways, then we could, within ten years, reasonably expect to have Y doctors entering practice each year. Think what that would do for current backlogs in the health care system!

When the process of sifting and winnowing through the various created imaginings reaches the point that several of them have come to dominate the others, the third essential component of institutional change comes in to play. This final stage is the actual process whereby the working rules (or entitlements) are modified for the explicit purpose of implementing one of these dominating created imaginings. We may properly consider this emergent and now reigning imagining as the reason for the new institutional arrangements. That is, the emergent created imagining is the outcome in the future for the sake of which the new institutional arrangements must be implemented now. This dominant imagining comprises the sufficient reason for the new institutions. It explains the institutional change.

The process is repeated ad infinitum in a democratic market economy. That is, such economies are engaged in a continual process of: (1) assessing existing settings and circumstances; (2) searching for plausibly causal (epistemic) connections between those outcomes and the institutional arrangements on which they are plausibly predicated; (3) formulating new created imaginings; (4) working out the political arrangements to discard the most implausible imaginings; (5) searching for and articulating the plausible mappings between surviving created imaginings and the institutional arrangements that are their plausible explanations; and (6) undertaking collective action in the parliaments, the executive branch, and the courts to modify the implicated institutional arrangements from their status quo configuration to a new and plausible configuration that will—on the newly accepted emergent imagining—plausibly lead to the desired outcomes in the future.

I have suggested that public policy can be understood as collective action in restraint, liberation, and expansion of individual action. And I have argued that the essence of public policy is that of rationing (redefining) economic settings and circumstances. Public policy is the essence of a rationing transaction because the actions of the legislatures or parliaments and the courts redirect or reallocate economic opportunities for differentially situated individuals. Public policy necessarily advances the economic and social agenda of some individuals and impedes the economic and social agenda of others. Individuals will struggle to have their interests represented in that process, but there can be no doubt that public policy is precisely concerned with such reallocations of relative advantage in the economy.

Institutional change is a central aspect of the modern nation-state precisely because the essence of our existence is the continual adaptation to new settings and circumstances, new opportunities, and new unwanted outcomes. The puzzle is not that institutions undergo reconsideration and alteration. The analytical challenge for social scientists is to understand why these processes look as they do in democratic market economies. There are instances, of course, in which two or more individuals undertake conversations and negotiations over the working rules that define and parameterize their relationship to each other, or to third parties not included in these conversations. Labor negotiations are precisely of this sort. But a necessary component of any such discussion and negotiation is the status quo ante in which some institutional structure is already in place.

Of course, some institutional change does not necessarily entail parliaments or the courts, though, as noted, the extant institutional structure—the product of prior parliamentary actions and judicial decrees—provides a framework within which these other institutional transactions occur. Consider an institutional transaction involving a prospective employee and her supervisor. The conversation may pertain, for example, to the employee's desire for nonstandard work hours in order to be able to take care of a very sick mother. This is an example of a managerial transaction, and we know that the essence of managerial transactions is command and obedience. But talk of command and obedience tends to make things seem more rigid than they in fact are. In reality there will be scope for negotiation over reasonable and unreasonable demands and willing and unwilling obedience. If the worker's demands are too extreme, the supervisor may well withdraw the offer of employment. But recall that there are higher-level institutional arrangements that constrain the actions of the supervisor. If the supervisor's demands are too extreme, the prospective worker may look elsewhere. But the worker is not without an ally in this transaction. That is, the worker can fall back on existing institutions that define fair labor standards. The worker will bring labor power to the firm, and the firm will pay that worker for her contributions to the firm's objectives. But if the demands of the supervisor are "unreasonable," then the potential employee has legal recourse. And just where is it determined that the demands of the supervisor are or are not "reasonable"? This idea is worked out in the parliaments, in the courts, and in the administrative agencies whose writ includes "fair" labor practices. And what exactly are "fair" labor practices? They are the accepted practices of the day in the particular economy (the nation-state) under consideration. Is there an oracle to which we may turn for edification on what is "fair"? One has not yet been found. What is deemed to be "fair" will emerge from the settled deliberations of legislative, legal, and administrative entities charged with considering precisely that issue. What was "fair" in 1890 in America will, not surprisingly, look rather different from what is considered "fair" in 2005. What was fair in India in 1920 will have differed from what was fair in France that same year.

The two parties engaged in this particular institutional transaction will reach some agreement—a set of working rules—that will henceforth define acceptable realms of behavior on the part of both the worker and the supervisor. Such negotiated working rules will rest on top of (that is, supplement) existing norms, customs, and working rules about "fair" and "reasonable" practices in this particular line of work. As these negotiations begin, both parties will construct (and then reconstruct) what they imagine they prefer as they gain more information about what they come to believe they might be able to have. As Shackle would put the matter, in the process of imagining plausible outcomes we do not discover those outcomes, we create them. It is quite possible that when the negotiations started, both parties held quite different ideas about what they wanted in the way of acceptable outcomes. And, as in all transactions, the parties soon realized that divergent expectations and desires induced them to reconstruct their imaginings about the preferred (best?) outcome. The transaction is completed when the two agree or decide to stop the conversation. Their deliberations have been settled when they arrive at some compatible belief or when they agree to stop talking.

We see that institutional transactions of this sort, if repeated often enough between workers and bosses at this particular firm, will, over time, evolve into a set of standard practices—we may think of them as shop rules—that will parameterize future conversations and negotiations. The idea here is simple: "At company X, this is how we do business." These working rules become the accepted standard, and until something unforeseen arises, these particular rules will serve to define realms of behavior for workers and this particular firm in all future dealings. We have here an example of managerial transactions that result in working rules by which this firm becomes known. If those evolved working rules are generally agreeable to both parties, if we have workable mutuality, this may well be the end of the matter. If, on the other hand, the firm refuses to accommodate what are generally seen as reasonable and legitimate concerns on the part of its workers, then a very different outcome will emerge. Efforts may arise to organize workers into a union. Some workers may file grievances with a government agency whose writ entails fair labor practices. Notice again that all of these institutional transactions occur within an existing structure of economic institutions previously determined by legislative action and decrees in the courts. For instance, do workers have the legal ability to meet to discuss their conditions of employment? In England, the Combination Acts of 1800 were intended to suppress strikes and the formation of trade unions. Other countries had similar institutional arrangements dedicated to preventing workers attaining better working conditions. We see that managerial transactions are necessarily embedded in the larger institutional structure of a nation-state. In essence, a boss (and the police) could simply say to workers, "sorry, you have no right to strike or to meet for the purpose of organizing a union." And if workers took it upon themselves to meet for such purposes, they could be, and often were, arrested and confronted with an unpleasant justice system. Such were prevailing attitudes at the time in many nation-states.

Is it legal for a worker to seek time off to care for a sick mother? In some countries the answer is yes, in others the answer is no. Is it "reasonable"? Again, that will depend upon the country. Recall that a managerial transaction is one in which a legal superior (boss) negotiates with a legal inferior (employee). The essence of this type of transaction is one of command and obedience, with the realm of acceptable commands always being under the collective control of parliaments and courts. By way of contrast, the bargaining transaction entails legal equals.

The standard bargaining transaction is the stuff of everyday life: I enter a shop, acquire an object whose change in ownership is the reason for my visit, dispense the requisite currency to the clerk, and depart the owner of less liquidity (money) but now the owner of some new item that gives me more pleasure than the money I just surrendered. Such bargaining transactions entail precious little "bargaining" these days, although if one is in the souks or bazaars of some far-off place, there might be a great deal of bargaining going on. The point here is that such transactions epitomize what is usually meant by "the market." The key idea is that ownership has changed hands. We may usefully consider these bargaining transactions as being, in reality, commodity transactions. That is, all commodity transactions belong to the class of bargaining transactions, whereas bargaining transactions can occur over commodities or over the informal rules that affect how legally equal individuals shall interact in the future.

Imagine two neighbors whose property boundary passes quite near the base of a very large tree. In most settings, the person on whose land the (majority of the) tree is rooted is the legitimate owner and should be able to do as she wishes with the tree. In most settings, the accepted norm is that the two neighbors talk and seek to reach an amicable agreement about the maintenance of this shared asset-burden. After all, the tree provides shade to both, but also drops large quantities of leaves in the autumn, the clearing of which may well burden both owner and nonowner in rather equal shares. Indeed, it is possible that the large tree shades an area in which the neighbor wishes to plant a vegetable garden, in which case the shade becomes a nuisance instead of an asset. In this setting, the bargaining transaction may become much less amicable than the rather standard bargaining transaction of everyday life. The pruning of branches may similarly fall to both parties, although the owner of the tree is legally responsible for this activity. A number of agreements must be reached between these two parties, agreements that will constitute the standards of behavior vis-à-vis this shared tree. Notice that if one of the neighbors should move away, a new conversation (agreement) will be required. Unlike the managerial transaction discussed previously, the two parties here are legal equals, though of course the owner of the tree must carry both the benefits and costs of ownership. But similarly situated neighbors have reached a wide variety of creative arrangements down through the ages—such norms of behavior constituting the essence of economic institutions.

These examples illustrate two distinct forms of institutions and of institutional change. The workplace (managerial) transaction concerned the evolution of enforceable rules that will bind worker and supervisor. The two neighbors reaching agreement on tree maintenance concerned the evolution of norms. We see that both norms and rules comport with the earlier definition of institutions as indicating what individuals must or must not do (duty), what they may do without interference from other individuals (privilege), what they can do with the aid of the collective power (right), and what they cannot expect the collective power to do in their behalf (no right).

In the case of rules between supervisor and employee, these rules are embedded in a larger institutional matrix that specifies domains of choice available to both the employee and the supervisor. What can the employee ask for, and what can she demand? Likewise, what can the supervisor ask for, and what can she demand? The realms of acceptable asking and demanding have been worked out previously through rationing transactions. In the case of evolved norms defining the realms of behavior of neighbors with a shared tree, these norms are also embedded in a larger institutional structure—one party legally owns the tree, and the neighbor has legally specified rights to be free of unwanted nuisance from that tree. In each case—workplace and tree management—the two parties are able to reach some agreement over the norms and rules that will govern their future interaction. In these negotiations, the respective parties bring to the conversations their particular imaginings concerning plausible desired outcomes, and they most certainly have some preconceptions about which of those imagined outcomes seem "best" to them. But in each case we cannot doubt that the conversations and the compromises lead not to the discovery of what is "best" (optimal) in the grand sense of that term. Rather, the creation of new imaginings concerning plausible outcomes forms the envelope within which eventual agreement is reached. Once there is agreement, both parties may well regard the resolution as the "best that could be obtained under the circumstances." With that said, it is difficult to suggest that the settled deliberations are somehow deficient because they do not comport with how choice is modeled in economics. To that issue we now turn.

FINDING REASONS FOR ACTION

Since the early 1950s, economists have developed a particular way of talking about, and thinking about, human action (Cooter and Rappoport 1984). The presumption of utility maximization leads us to postulate human action as if choice were predicated on clear notions of outcomes and clear notions about the requisite pathways to achieve those outcomes. Of course, we admit uncertainty and address this by attaching probabilities to both outcomes and pathways. Notice that the essence of this branch of economics is purposeful (and rational) welfare maximization on the part of individuals. Few economists would disagree with the proposition that our subject concerns the making of optimal choice in situations of scarcity. Individuals are said to consider their options and choose the one that is best for them. This much is both axiomatic and circular. It is axiomatic because it follows from general covering laws governing individual choice as we treat that subject in economics. It is circular because we assume rationality before decisions are taken, and once they are taken, we assert that they must have been optimal (and rational) or the individual would have done otherwise. Notice that rationality pertains to choices that are consistent with preferences—whatever those preferences may be. And it is precisely here that economics confronts but fails to address the tension—indeed, incongruity—between preferences and welfare. For there are many preferences held by individuals that cannot possibly be said to conduce to their welfare, unless one chooses to define enhancing "welfare" as simply that which individuals choose to do after they have consulted their "preferences." The circularity here is apparent and debilitating.

But institutional change—collective action in restraint, liberation, and expansion of individual action—is not about choosing among competing brands of toothpaste or cheese. Institutional change redefines realms of choice (fields of action) for individuals, including the chemical content, labeling, and safety of both toothpaste and cheese. Institutional change reallocates income and wealth streams. Institutional change forces some people to change the ways they have been doing certain things. Institutional change liberates some of us from the offensive—or merely annoying—behavior of our neighbors. Institutional change rearranges the signposts in our life that reveal what we can and cannot do, what we may and may not do, what we must and must not do, what we can expect the collective power (the authority system) to help us do, and what we are powerless to do in the face of particular behaviors of others that do not please us.

Institutional change is not about otherwise satisfied people coming together to enter into welfare-enhancing commodity transactions—buying and selling ownership of future benefit streams in the service of improving utility (or "welfare"). Institutional change often modifies what it is that we are able to buy and sell. Institutional change modifies how fast we may drive, what we may eat, what we may do with land we own, perhaps what we must wear when we drive motorcycles, what the safety features must be of the cars we buy, how we must treat those who work for us, and how we must act with respect to those for whom we work. Institutional change indicates how much of our income must be paid in taxes to pay for collective goods and services, how often our garbage will be collected, what we must and must not put in that garbage, and how that garbage must be presented at the curb for the benefit of those whose job it is to collect garbage.

The purpose of collective action—and the business of the political entities in nation-states—is to confront the manifold ways in which we get in each other's way, and to craft remedies for these emerging problematic settings and circumstances. Whether village councils, county boards, provincial committees, national parliaments, supranational bodies such as the European Parliament, or the United Nations, the task of institutional innovation is an ongoing exercise in searching for plausible and acceptable solutions to new awkward and unwanted realities in the human condition.

Much of the literature in introductory economics leads one to believe that atomistic bargaining is the dominant (and preferred) form of institutional change. This approach makes institutional change seem analogous to Pareto-safe moves inside the trading lens of an Edgeworth box. On this telling, both parties have something to gain, and the extent of the gain to each is a function of their ability ("power") as bargaining or negotiating agents. And economists are satisfied when those negotiations result in an inevitable movement to the "efficiency locus" (the contract curve). Many economists seem to imagine that institutional transactions are precisely of this form—the unrestrained seeking of mutual advantage through bargaining transactions. By this means, institutions mutually evolve as new scarcities and new relative prices render past institutional arrangements suddenly "inefficient," and thus the economy is once again in need of being restored to the contract curve along which efficiency reigns. A more appropriate term for the contract curve, however, is a conflict curve. For along this curve individuals are able to impose their will on others; perhaps Alpha can push Beta to a lower indifference curve. And it is here that some individuals will be able to enlist the collective authority of the state to move them along that conflict curve. More profoundly, it is also here that these same individuals may be able—with the indispensable assistance of the collective power—to alter the very nature of the conflict curve in a way that further enhances their relative advantage vis-à-vis others in the economy.

Some accounts of this process seem to imply just how unnecessary government really is in the matter of institutional change (Ellickson 1991). Not only are governments alleged to be unnecessary in matters of institutional change; governments are often imagined to be unnecessary in the establishment of institutions in the first place. Those who find these accounts compelling apparently fail to understand that the idea of property rights in the absence of the state is a logical contradiction. Such stories are presented as harmonious bargaining episodes in which both (or all) participants get precisely what they want. On reading these accounts, one is put in mind of pastoral stories about cattle ranchers and corn farmers calmly reaching an optimal Coasean agreement over the poaching of corn by errant cattle insufficiently attentive to property lines. Left out of these utopian allegories is any mention of the existence—at the time of the felt need for serious bargaining between farmers and ranchers—of extant property regimes that already define the parameters within which ranchers and farmers are said to engage in their mutually beneficial bargaining.

Because there can be no doubt that the corn farmer is the owner of the land on which his corn is growing, and someone else's cattle are munching, one must ask why is there a need for bargaining in the first instance? Do we seriously imagine farmers settled at the kitchen table eagerly calculating their reservation price for corn still on the stalk rather than delivered to the local grain elevator? While one solution seems missing in these standard stories, it has certainly crossed the mind of more than a few farmers. That solution, if neighborly conversation is insufficient, is to threaten the rancher with some unpleasant event, or to shoot the cattle that are enjoying the corn. This act would certainly get the attention of the rancher. The cattle are, after all, trespassing. As the attentive farmer might put the matter, "Why should I have to pay ranchers to keep their cattle out of my fields?" And to allude to the role of purpose in human affairs, the farmer may well insist that he is in the business of farming for the purpose of raising corn so that he might then sell it to the highest bidder. He might add that he did not become a farmer in order to be compensated by ranchers for unwanted livestock lounging about in his fields.

But, of course, this reminds us again that all of the wistful bargaining tales of such endearment to the hyper-Coaseans are necessary artifacts of the larger institutional structure within which bargaining takes place. That is, which party to the transaction is protected by the status quo ante institutional setup? For example, in the eastern part of the United States, where crop farming is the normal land use, those who own cattle and sheep are legally liable to keep their animals out of farmers' fields. If an animal should get into a field and create damage, then financial liability falls on the owner of the animal. I have earlier defined this as a property right protected by a liability rule. In this legal regime, animals must be fenced in. By contrast, in the western part of the United States, where arid conditions preclude farming except in isolated patches of irrigated plots, liability runs the other way. Here, those who wish to undertake crop farming must bear the financial obligation of keeping cattle and sheep fenced out. The difference is reflected in whether a region is governed by herd laws or by fence laws (Sanchez and Nugent 2000).

The point is that the celebration of atomistic bargaining as the proper pathway to efficiency in matters of economic institutions fails to tell us much about how the existing institutional setup bestows differential advantage on the bargaining parties. More seriously, this literature leaves the impression that the preferred institutional change emerges from consensual individual bargaining, whereas government "interference" with market processes is the inevitable and undesirable consequence of political meddling by parliaments or legislatures and the courts. Such accounts of institutions and institutional change are not useful to the clear understanding of economic processes.

IMPLICATIONS

Institutional change is simply the working out of new legal parameters that will define possible realms of individual action. Public policy is collective action in restraint, liberation, and expansion of individual action. Of course, two neighbors can evolve institutional arrangements—norms of behavior—for the stewardship of a shared tree. And, of course, a potential worker and her supervisor can bring about mutually agreeable schedules of work. Many economists have an affinity for these stories precisely because such accounts allow for the full play of what it is we do in economics—build models of rational choice wherein individuals may seek optimal outcomes. But this realm of institutional change is of trifling importance in comparison with collective action in parliaments or legislatures and courts of democratic market economies. Here we must seek to understand the reasons for collective action that restrains, liberates, and expands individual action. If we are to understand reasons for such collective action, we must abandon deterministic mechanical formulations that see public officials as perverse utility maximizers. We must also formulate a more honest heuristic of the process whereby individuals create, as they engage in collective action, plausible imaginings of future outcomes, and plausible imaginings of pathways whereby those outcomes might be brought to fruition. This formulation of collective action requires that we now develop the concept of volitional pragmatism.

PART TWO

Volitional Pragmatism

CHAPTER SIX

Fixing Belief

> The object of reasoning is to find out, from the consideration of what we already know, something else which we do not know.
>
> —Charles Sanders Peirce, *The Fixation of Belief* (1877)

FROM THOUGHT TO BELIEF

The standard approach to economics is embedded in the hypothetico-deductive method. On this approach, primitive axioms (covering laws) inform the search for particular assumptions and applicability postulates that will then suggest hypotheses to be tested against data from the "real" world. The axioms entail postulates of rationality, self-interest, stable preferences, and the alleged desire to maximize utility. In such exercises, the truth content of the axioms is not in dispute. Indeed, the core axioms of economic theory are rarely subjected to tests of their veracity. This is the essence of foundationalism. Although received theory may be tested on occasion, it is more common to find that our work ends when we find results that are alleged to be validated by theory, or to be consistent with theory. Indeed, the keen confidence with which some Paretians will pronounce on the allegedly "optimal" policy arises, in no small measure, from the conviction that most social problems can be properly regarded as but part of this standard deductive model.

This commitment to deduction arises, in part, because many of us imagine that there is but one way of knowing (McCloskey 1983). Indeed, one of the unfortunate legacies of logical positivism is that several generations of economists have been taught that there is only one way to truth—relentless adherence to what has come to be called *the* scientific method (as if there were but one). The essence of the accepted method is its reliance on specific covering laws (axioms). These covering laws provide the conceptual grounding for the scientist, and they receive their importance from a basic conviction of modernism that there can be no rigorous scientific belief unless the pursuit of that belief is firmly embedded in a set of a priori received truths. This is what we mean by the nomological aspect of modern science.

Indeed, as suggested earlier, a serious impediment to scientific progress arises because most practitioners, having been socialized to believe the truth content of these covering laws, find it difficult to question them. To do so is to seem disloyal to the discipline into which one has been socialized. The enterprise of "normal science" is essentially concerned with working in a way that is supportive of these general axioms and truth claims (Kuhn 1989). We may think of a paradigm as an organizing framework for a community of practitioners (a discipline) bound by their tacit agreement regarding which questions are worth asking—and therefore which questions are idle. Stanley Fish (1989) would call a discipline an "interpretive community." I use the term *epistemic community.*

An essential prerequisite to gaining an understanding of economic institutions is to start with the recognition that most nomological commitments impede open-mindedness. More seriously, such commitments lead aspiring scientists—and here I have economists particularly in mind—to imagine that there is only one way to acquire knowledge that constitutes the necessary precursor of belief. Therefore, if we are to make necessary headway in our quest to understand economic institutions and institutional change, we must first enhance our understanding of how scientists come to know what they claim—at the moment—to know. What is the process by which scientists acquire the knowledge that allows them to fix their belief in a certain matter? Despite what most economists assert about *the* scientific method, there are in fact three methods by which scientists fix belief: deduction, abduction, and induction. We now consider these three ways of fixing belief, beginning with deduction, the most common approach.

Deductive Belief

> *Rule:* All the beans from this bag are white.
> *Case:* These beans are from this bag.
> ∴ *Result:* These beans are white.

Deductive belief derives from systems of propositions whose purpose is to explicate the relationships among axioms (*rule*), particular assumptions and applicability postulates (*case*), and particular outcomes (*result*). Deduction is a class of inference in which a conclusion follows necessarily from one or more given premises—axioms (often called major premises, here called the *rule*) and assumptions and applicability postulates (often called minor premises, here called the *case*). This necessity of the conclusions following from the premises arises from a central property of deduction—that the conclusions are necessarily involved in the premises. In its purest form, deduction requires that the conclusion (these beans are white) be of lesser generality than one of the premises (all the beans from this bag are white). The outcomes—the findings—of deduction are necessarily prefigured by the structure of the analytical engine constructed to produce that particular belief. Notice that in the preceding syllogism, the result (these beans are white) is deduced from the rule and the case without explicit reference to the beans themselves—that is, without the need of actually looking at the beans to see what their color might, in fact, be. The deductivist puts more faith in the rule and the case than in the actual subject of interest (these beans, from this bag, which, it is claimed, contains only white beans). On these grounds, the beans could not be any color except white. Notice that the lack of a need to consult the beans regarding their color is central to an economist's ability to declare that some particular choice enhanced "welfare" or was "rational." Utility, welfare, and preferences are unobservable and thus not measurable. No need to worry. We don't need to observe or measure them—we are deductivists.

It may help to see deduction in its pure form if we consider a problem somewhat removed from economics. Consider an airplane lost at sea, and all that is known is its point of origin and intermittent radar sightings that end while the airplane is still in the air. The quest for fixing belief here concerns the urgent need to reduce the size of the area over which a search must be conducted so that there is the greatest possible chance of finding the crew and passengers alive. The relevant axioms (rule) here include the law of gravity and various laws of aerodynamics. The case includes assumptions concerning the behavior of this particular kind of aircraft under various conditions, such as engine failure, mechanical problems that compromise particular steering mechanisms, instrument failure, fuel level, and resiliency in the face of pilot error. Finally, the case also includes applicability postulates consisting of the known observable data in this particular search and rescue mission, including weather in the immediate area, ocean currents in the probable crash zone so that adjustments might be made for drift of the lifeboats (if there are any), the experience of the pilot, weight of the plane at takeoff, duration of the flight when it disappeared from radar, last known speed, elevation and heading, and probable visibility. At this point there might be speculation as to the probable cause of the crash, such as engine failure, sudden incapacitation or disorientation of the pilot, or sabotage. But diagnosis of the cause (why did this plane crash?) is, at this moment, less important than determining the best place in which to search. That is, where did this plane crash?

We see that the search-and-rescue mission uses an analytical engine (deduction) to produce (deduce) the most probable area in which the wreckage might be found. That is, hypotheses are formulated to suggest the most probable area in which to begin the search. Notice that the rule (gravity, aerodynamics) is less crucial to the "fineness" (accuracy) of the

hypotheses than is the case (the assumptions and the applicability postulates). Notice, as well, that the more realistic are the assumptions, and the
better is the empirical content (the applicability postulates) of the analytical engine, the smaller (the more accurate) will be the optimal search area.
And the smaller the search area, the greater the probability that survivors,
if any, might be quickly rescued. We would judge the model (analytical
engine) by the accuracy—not the precision—of its prediction. An accurate
model may not be precise, and conversely. A precise model might say,
"search in this particular area of 12.65 square kilometers," yet miss the
real location of the wreckage (be inaccurate).

Notice that the predictive accuracy of the model depends on its ability
to describe—by way of the case (the invoked assumptions and applicability postulates)—all of the circumstances prior to the crash of the aircraft
into the ocean (as well as the circumstances of possible drift after the
crash). Notice also that the fundamental problem here is to determine
where and *how* the plane crashed, not *why*. That is, how it crashed will
help to facilitate the immediate location of possible survivors. This is deduction in its pure form.

In economics we find a classic application of deduction in the theory
of international trade. We know that free trade between two countries
can benefit both if each country exports the goods in which it has a comparative advantage. From this we also know that free trade conduces to
efficiency and is therefore desirable. How do we know this? We know it
because we can build a deductive analytical engine to "prove" it. The
story usually starts with a Ricardian world in which each country has
only one factor of production, labor, that produces two goods—say, wine
and cheese. We then suggest that unit-labor requirements indicate how
much labor time it will take to produce a unit of wine or a unit of cheese.
This is the technology set. We then derive a production possibilities frontier showing the maximal quantities of each product that can be produced
with the available supply of labor. With one factor of production, the
opportunity cost of producing wine is a linear function of how much
cheese is produced. To find the optimal level of production, we must know
the prices that wine and cheese will fetch in the market. The resulting
supply of wine and cheese will depend on the wages paid in each sector.
Labor will allocate itself according to which sector pays the higher wages.
Comparative advantage tells us that this economy will specialize in that
good (cheese) for which the relative price exceeds its opportunity cost
(forgone wine). In the absence of trade, the economy under study would
be forced to produce both goods (if we assume a demand for both), but
this would require that the relative price of cheese equal (not exceed) its
opportunity cost. In the absence of trade, the relative price of goods must
equal their relative unit-labor requirements; technology is deterministic.

Now we introduce trade and, in doing so, augment the simple model with a new assumption.

To make the story interesting, we require that the technology in each of the two countries differs—otherwise they are still "one country" separated only by transport costs. Now let technology reveal that the ratio of labor necessary to produce a pound of cheese compared with that needed to produce a gallon of wine is lower at home than it is abroad—yet another assumption. The domestic economy's relative productivity in making cheese is higher than it is in making wine. In other words, the domestic economy has a comparative advantage in making cheese. Once trade is permitted, the relative prices of cheese and wine in each country are no longer determined by technology in each country. This constitutes a "finding" of our analytical engine. General equilibrium across both countries requires that relative demand must equal relative supply. Each country specializes in the production of the good for which it has the relatively lower unit-labor requirement (technology again). We learn that countries whose relative labor productivities differ across industries will specialize in the production of different goods and that this specialization will allow individual countries to enjoy positive gains from trade with others. The simple world of only one factor of production can be expanded to include multiple factors of production—yet another assumption.

As we recount this familiar story, we see (as with the airplane search) the essential components to any analytical engine. First, we have a few central axioms drawn from the canon of orthodox economics. These would include the proposition that factors of production are freely mobile between wine making and cheese making, that consumers are self-interested and rational and they therefore choose wine or cheese in a manner that is consistent with their preferences, that producers and consumers have full and costless information about their options, and that prices and wages are determined by the free interplay of supply and demand in each market. We call these axioms rather than assumptions because they constitute the core premises or "basic laws" of economics. The axioms represent the received wisdom of the discipline. One might regard them as the unchallenged rules of economic behavior.

The second component of an analytical engine—the case—augments the axioms and gives the analytical engine a closer conceptual connection to the particular problem at hand. These assumptions flesh out the axioms and render the analytical engine pertinent to a discussion of trade. What are these assumptions? Again, we have the assumption that there is only one factor of production, though we might also consider more than one factor. We have the assumption that technology is fixed. We have the assumption that only two goods, wine and cheese, are produced. We have the assumption that transportation costs are zero. We have the assumption of a linear transformation of cheese into wine (along a linear production possibilities frontier). And we have the assumption that a second country has a different technology set than does the domestic economy.

From the conjunction of the axioms and the assumptions, the economist constructs an analytical engine permitting the derivation of certain conclusions (hypotheses) with respect to the issue of international trade. The findings suggest, for example, that the supply of wine and cheese will depend on the wages paid in each market. In the absence of trade, we show that the domestic economy would be forced to produce both goods (if we assume a demand for both). In the absence of trade, the relative price of goods must equal their relative unit-labor requirements. When trade is introduced, relative demand must equal relative supply, and the exploitation of each nation's comparative advantage allows both of them to be better off than would be possible in the absence of trade. Or, rather, we should say that each country will end up producing those commodities for which it has a comparative advantage and that consumers will thereby gain because the resulting prices will be lower than if there were no trade. The components of an analytical engine are therefore:

AXIOMS + ASSUMPTIONS

The axioms entail the essential neoclassical canon that allows us to look at the problem as an economist, through "an economic lens" as it were, while the assumptions provide subject matter, content, and specificity. Together the two components constitute an analytical engine permitting the generation of insights and hypotheses concerning a particular economic issue. One derived proposition is that there can be gains from trade. Another proposition is that countries will do "best" if they specialize in producing those commodities for which their technology and institutional setup give them a comparative advantage. In this case, a country should specialize in those commodities for which it has the comparatively lower requirement for factors of production. These important insights are the essential products of—and the reasons for constructing— analytical engines.

Analytical engines can yield insights beyond those discussed here. For instance, an assumption can be added that introduces transportation costs. Yet another assumption can introduce different regimes of export and import taxes in one or more countries. In each instance we can discern (predict) how trade patterns will change, how relative comparative advantages will shift, and how patterns of gains and losses will be shared between consumers and owners of the various factors of production. Notice that an analytical engine allows us to introduce different assumptions for the purpose of exploring the logical implications of the simple case that is based on fewer assumptions. This property renders analytical engines capable of generating testable hypotheses. Each additional assumption elaborates the case.

It is important to recognize, however, that at this stage an exercise in pure deduction cannot result in a general theory because the insights to arise from an analytical engine are necessarily restricted—quarantined—by the constrictions inherent in the logic of the system. That is, the insights of analytical engines are nothing but artifacts of the assumptions and logical structure of the system that has been constructed. Belief derived from an analytical engine is structurally dependent belief. This follows from the fact that an analytical engine is simply a logical syllogism whose validity depends on its internal coherence, but whose truth content depends on the factual basis of its axioms and assumptions. We see that analytical engines concern how things work, or how they can be expected to work under different assumptions. But such questions (how) can only be addressed within the specific structure of the particular analytical engine built to shed light on those questions. That is, at a conceptual level, how does trade affect prices, factor use, product prices, wages, and national tendencies in production? Of course, one can always reframe the question to say, "Why do countries specialize?" but that new framing is still embedded in a set of assumptions and structural parameters that show how specialization is, hypothetically, beneficial.

An analytical engine cannot become a source of theoretical belief—that is, it cannot provide us with a theory—until we add applicability postulates to the case. Indeed, it is common to encounter stories that are called by their author "pure" theories. These are deductive accounts with only axioms and assumptions, but without any applicability postulates. In a strict sense, a coherent theory of trade requires the following components:

AXIOMS + ASSUMPTIONS + APPLICABILITY POSTULATES

A theory of international trade would, therefore, bring together: (1) the core axioms of neoclassical economics; (2) assumptions regarding differential factor endowments, technology, consumer demand, and wage rates; and (3) applicability postulates. We can think of the applicability postulates as maintained hypotheses or premises that render the analytical engine applicable to a particular trade setting. Only with these three components can we say that we have a chance of developing a theory of trade in the particular circumstances defined by the applicability postulates that are appended to the analytical engine. An analytical engine can help us to describe and understand patterns of international trade, but a theory of international trade requires the addition of applicability postulates to the analytical engine. That is, theories are context dependent, and experience with and replication of these varying contexts permit us plausibly to claim that we have a credible (general) theory of international trade.

Notice that the applicability postulates consist of empirically derived and verifiable propositions and relationships from the countries we seek to encompass in our theoretical story. Particular applicability postulates give the analytical engine empirical content and render it capable of producing belief of the sort: why does country X produce more wine than country Y? Or, why does country Y produce much more wine than it does cheese? Notice that a theory allows us to suggest that particular countries, with specific empirical circumstances, will be likely to specialize in particular trade goods. Under particular circumstances, the theory allows us to ask *why*, not merely *how*. Notice, however, that answers to "why?" questions must be predicated on more than the structural and axiomatic nature of the analytical engine. The answer, to be credible, must incorporate the empirical reality of the various countries under study. Our theory of international trade is still grounded on an analytical engine—the particular deductive structure that consists of axioms and assumptions—but with the addition of applicability postulates, we can do more than explore structural dimensions. We can also do more than simply generate structurally dependent hypotheses.

We see that the applicability postulates impart particular belief about production technology in the countries under study (perhaps econometrically derived cost and production functions), the structure of wages in those countries, the elasticities of demand for various products in these countries, the patterns of consumption in those countries, and other empirical aspects necessary to render the theory applicable to the trade situation under study. Notice that the three components of a theory—the axioms, the assumptions, and the applicability postulates—all contain (or consist of) "assumptions." The axioms are, as indicated previously, the foundational assumptions (presuppositions) of economics. The assumptions proper are necessary to render the analytical engine appropriate to understand issues of international trade. The applicability postulates are assumptions derived from careful empirical work concerning the economies and the sectors under study. Again, the assumptions and the applicability postulates comprise the case.

Explicating this structural dimension of deduction allows us to understand one particularly contentious proposition in economics—that as long as a theory can predict, we need not worry excessively about the "realism" of its assumptions. It should now be apparent that the issue turns on the answer to the question: which assumptions need not be realistic? Certainly the assumptions that comprise the applicability postulates must be realistic or our explanations and predictions cannot possibly be correct. And, of course, the general assumptions must be realistic because, together with the applicability postulates, these comprise the *case* of the argument. When we come to the axioms of the analytical engine, realism becomes less of an issue. There are, in fact, two views of this matter. Consider the axiom of "rationality." We allege that people are rational and then proceed to study their behavior without the slightest idea as to whether they are behaving as the strict definition of rationality requires. As Herbert Simon might put it, "Who needs rationality?"

The second option is to modify one or more unrealistic axioms by incorporating specific assumptions that override—in fact, replace—one or more of the axioms. For instance, if we think that "perfect knowledge" is an unrealistic axiom of neoclassical economics, we can, following Joseph Stiglitz, introduce an assumption that incorporates asymmetric information. With this modification, it is possible to test whether a particular theory is better at explaining (and predicting) behavior than it was without the new assumption of information asymmetries. Similarly, if the axiom of zero transaction costs (costless information, costless contracting, and costless enforcement) seems unrealistic, then we can modify that particular aspect with a new assumption about transaction costs. If we believe that commodities are not one-dimensional but rather entail a number of attributes of interest to the consumer, then we can follow the lead of Kelvin Lancaster (1966) and unpack commodities into their constituent parts (attributes). This insight—an assumption that allowed the generation of new testable hypotheses—opened the door to hedonic price analysis.

The schematic structure of deduction can be repackaged to think of it in terms of axioms, assumptions, and postulates leading to testable empirical claims that result in theoretical propositions. That is:

(6.1) AXIOMS, ASSUMPTIONS, POSTULATES →

(6.2) TESTABLE EMPIRICAL CLAIMS →

(6.3) THEORETICAL PROPOSITIONS

The analytical engine (axioms plus assumptions) augmented by applicability postulates is contained in (6.1), and from this conjunction we create testable empirical claims (6.2). Ideally, these empirical claims are checked (tested) against known empirical situations to allow a refinement of the assumptions and applicability postulates with the purpose of generating more general theoretical propositions (6.3). Sometimes, if there is reason to suspect that the empirical claims will not be found consistent with reality, this testing will not be very aggressive, and it is here that critics of neoclassical economics focus their attention. They argue that certain theoretical propositions are simply too convenient—or too essential to the survival of the reigning canon—to risk impeachment by testing.

So far we see that deductive belief is descriptive. That is, everything so far has been dedicated to the task of explication and clarification of pertinent relationships. Even the theoretical propositions are conjectures in that they retain the basic logic of "if. . . , then . . . " Deductive belief arises from an analytical engine and is, therefore, of a tautological kind. As I indicated previously, deduction produces a result from axioms and the case, and those committed to deduction are too often content to rest their case on logical validity rather than on actually confronting the result to see if, indeed, these beans are white. Deduction can be a powerful way of fixing belief, but it is not the only way.

ABDUCTIVE BELIEF

> *Result:* These beans are white.
> *Rule:* All the beans from this bag are white.
> ∴ *Case:* These beans are from this bag.

Abduction is a class of inference that yields explanatory hypotheses for observed phenomena. In contrast to deduction, abduction is not the result of the deductive application of a rule (axioms) and a case (assumptions and applicability postulates) to produce a result (an empirical claim). Whereas deduction produces empirical claims that might result in theoretical propositions, abduction starts with particular observed empirical circumstances (the result) and then invokes specific axioms (the rule), and the case (assumptions, and applicability postulates) to produce propositions (testable hypotheses) with the intent of explaining those observed circumstances. That is, abduction concerns a process of going from result and rule to case. Some prefer the term *diagnosis* for this way of fixing belief, and it is indeed the very process engaged in by those whose task it is to diagnose empirical phenomena—physicians, automobile mechanics contemplating an engine that will not start, and forensic pathologists who perform autopsies. Charles Sanders Peirce often referred to abduction as the "method of hypothesis." We engage in the quest for abductive belief when we observe certain empirical regularities (or newly observed irregularities) in the world around us and seek to construct plausible explanations (the case) for those observed phenomena.

Consider again the example of an airplane crash. Now, however, the investigator has a different problem. Rather than searching for the lost plane, the first indication of a problem is that a ship captain radios to authorities that an oil slick (and some small floating debris) has been spotted on the high seas. This is the empirical phenomenon that triggers the quest for abductive belief. To the pragmatist, this is the "surprise" or the "irritation of doubt" that triggers the process by which we seek to fix belief concerning why the plane crashed. Presumably friends or family will contact authorities about the missing plane and its passengers, but in the absence of survivors there will be no way to know why the plane crashed. There are, to be sure, competing explanations (some individuals may refer to these as competing hypotheses or competing theories) for the crash. Working backward from the observable phenomena—spot of impact, nature of recovered debris—investigators attempt to generate assumptions and applicability postulates that would be consistent with the known empirical data. The purpose of the research task here is to construct the *case*. Peirce would put that matter as:

> *Result:* The surprising fact, C (the crash), is observed.
> *Rule:* But if A were true, C (plane crashes) would be a matter of course.
> ∴ *Case:* There is reason to suspect A is true.

And so the search begins for A. What exactly are the constituents of A? As previously, some of the axioms would constitute covering laws— gravity, aerodynamics of the aircraft (if a known type). The same assumptions noted earlier would be pertinent to the behavior of this particular kind of aircraft under conditions of engine failure, mechanical problems that compromise particular steering mechanisms, instrument failure, fuel level, and resiliency in the face of pilot error. An additional assumption would concern ocean currents in the crash zone so that adjustments might be made to locate the exact point of impact with the water. If there are good data on this phenomenon, then such data become part of the applicability postulates; if not, the investigators must construct some assumptions. Other applicability postulates would consist of the observable data surrounding this crash, such as weather in the immediate area, the experience of the pilot, weight of the plane at takeoff, duration of the flight when it disappeared from radar, last known speed, elevation and heading, visibility. Notice that now the task is not to find the aircraft (and possible survivors) but to determine the reasons for the crash. As we saw previously, the feasible explanations would include engine failure, sudden incapacitation or disorientation of the pilot, or perhaps sabotage. The problem here is to generate (often) unobservable events that are consistent with the axioms, assumptions, the applicability postulates, and the known phenomenon (the crash) requiring explanation.

We see that abduction concerns the quest for an answer to the question of *why* did the plane crash, as opposed to deduction that concerns the quest for an answer to the question *how* did the plane crash? Of course, the two often go hand in hand. In the first illustration, where deduction was used to help guide the search and rescue mission, abduction would be used, once the plane is found, to try to explain the reasons for the crash—the "why" question. If investigators succeed in recovering remnants of the airplane, they might more successfully formulate a set of hypotheses to explain why the plane crashed. But notice that the process here is one of diagnosis—what assumptions (case) and axioms (rule) plausibly explain the crash (result)?

In economics we find an example of the quest for abductive belief in the notion of an environmental Kuznets curve. The original Kuznets curve concerned the hypothesis that as poor countries became more developed, the gap between rich and poor widened at first and then narrowed. That is, income distribution became more equal as the development process evolved. The environmental Kuznets curve is thought to capture the general observation that as countries undertake the development process, environmental quality at first declines and then improves as countries become richer (Selden and Song 1994). The empirical case, at least to some, seems clear. But the problem comes in whether we can find a theoretical explanation for this phenomenon. Or, as it is jocularly put, "it may be fine in practice—but does it work in theory?"

The economist interested in this problem starts with several assumptions. One is that environmental quality is a luxury good—the demand for which increases in some elastic relationship with rising income. Another assumption is that governments and public decision makers are reluctant to allocate scarce resources to pollution control and enforcement until other more basic needs have been met. A third assumption is that poor nations cannot afford to be fussy about which industries they support and attract. If polluting industries are made to feel unwelcome in the industrialized world, then they are certainly welcome in the developing world; they will be forced to clean up only when the country becomes richer. Fourth, it might be assumed that the industrial composition of developed nations, differs from that found in the poorer nations and so there will be a natural progression toward cleaner industries and economic activities.

These propositions constitute the assumptions of the heuristic template that is the core of abduction. Notice that the assumptions arise from a combination of economic theory, general economic intuition, and some practical empirical knowledge concerning the developing world. When these assumptions are combined with some axioms from the core of contemporary economics (perfect knowledge, individuals as price takers, mobile factors of production, zero transaction costs), we can construct a heuristic template that may (or may not) offer some plausible support for the empirical regularities that prompted the research in the first instance. But the work will be improved—that is, its explanatory power will be enhanced—if some applicability postulates are appended. These applicability postulates might concern elasticities of demand for various goods and services in the countries under study, they might concern wage levels and data on expenditures, and they might contain empirical data on pollution-control expenditures over time. Finally, the applicability postulates might suggest that urban air quality will improve first because: (1) urban air quality is more critical to public health concerns; (2) reductions of pollution in urban areas may be more cost effective; (3) rising land costs may drive polluting industries out of urban areas; and (4) urban residents, by enjoying incomes that rise more rapidly than rural residents, will be the first to clamor for reductions in air pollution.

When these assumptions and applicability postulates are combined into a structured account or heuristic template, the expectation is that some plausible theoretical propositions might be derived. The schematic structure of abduction can be presented as empirical phenomena suggesting appropriate assumptions, axioms, and applicability postulates that then result in theoretical propositions. That is:

(6.4)   EMPIRICAL PHENOMENA →

(6.5)   AXIOMS, ASSUMPTIONS, POSTULATES →

(6.6)   THEORETICAL PROPOSITIONS

Notice that the generation of abductive belief starts with some known empirical phenomenon (6.4). A plausible explanation of that phenomenon starts, if one is an economist, with the same structured thought process that we use for the generation of deductive belief (6.5). That is, some axioms will be augmented by some assumptions and by a few applicability postulates that will be consistent with some theoretical propositions (6.6) that might explain the particular phenomenon under study. Put somewhat differently, axioms, assumptions, and applicability postulates combine to suggest theoretical propositions that are checked for consistency with the empirical phenomenon requiring explanation. If there is a high level of consistency, then we might say that we have a "theory" of the particular empirical phenomenon under study. That is why I call the core of abduction a heuristic template.

We can regard Ronald Coase's (1937) pioneering work on the nature of the firm to be an example of abduction. In this instance, Coase was clearly motivated by surprise—the existence of firms in the face of deductive belief from classical economics "proving" that the efficiency properties of markets would render firms inefficient and therefore unnecessary. The reigning classical theory held that it was not possible for arenas of command (and firms are nothing but arenas of command) to be more efficient than arenas of maximizing action driven by prices. Yet Coase looked around and, seeing plenty of firms both large and small, asked the obvious question: "If firms are so inefficient, why do we observe them?" His answer, familiar to us now, is that firms exist because of the transaction costs of using markets for some kinds of activity. Coase offered a theoretical explanation (that is, an explanation congenial to economic theory) for the existence of something that everyone knew existed—yet the existence of which was denied by the accepted body of theory. Indeed, adherents to the accepted belief of the day might well have defended their view by insisting that, while the idea of firms might be fine in practice, did they work in theory? Coase showed that they indeed "worked" in theory.

We see that abduction is an important aspect of our search for economic insights. An economist who observes particular human behaviors—or particular economic outcomes—and then attempts to explain those behaviors or outcomes employs abduction.

A third way to fix belief is induction. With induction the purpose is not to explain observed phenomena or to offer theoretical propositions of general applicability. Rather the purpose of induction is to develop general rules of association between (or among) observed phenomena. From these associations, abduction and/or deduction might then be employed.

INDUCTIVE BELIEF

> *Case:* These beans are from this bag.
> *Result:* These beans are white.
> ∴ *Rule:* All the beans from this bag are white.

Induction is a process whereby a rule, or a constellation of rules, is derived from the application of some specific assumptions and applicability postulates (case) to some particular observed phenomena (result). We say that induction concerns the process of going from case (assumptions) and result (observed phenomena) to rule (general proposition). In a strict sense induction is "to lead into the field of attention a number of observed particular facts as ground for a general assertion" (Runes 1983, p. 161). *Perfect induction* is an assertion concerning all the members of a class on the basis of examination of each possible member of the class: "All tomatoes in this basket are overripe." Notice that the conclusion— the rule—captures members of the class observed but does not (and cannot) go beyond that exact class. For this reason induction is not a class of inferential belief.

In a world in which all members of particular classes cannot individually be observed, perfect induction is impossible. In ordinary usage, induction concerns properties of all members of a class based on examination of a subset of that class. The classic inductive proposition—all swans are white—captures this idea. Unfortunately, swans in Australia are black. Or perhaps we should say that the Australian bird that is called a swan happens to be black in color. Induction is not inference, nor can it be regarded as a form of argument consisting of premises and conclusions.

Rather, induction is a perception of relations not subject to any rules of validity. Induction

> represents the gropings and tentative guessing of a mind aiming at knowledge. Intuitive induction is therefore not antithetical to deduction, because it is not a type of inference at all; and the discovery of the implications of a set of premises requires very much the same sort of guessing and groping. *There can be no logic or method of intuitive induction.* (Cohen and Nagel 1934, p. 275)

Contrary to popular notions, induction can be useful, especially in the early stages of a particular scientific pursuit when "groping and tentative guessing" is very much in need. The example is often given of Kepler searching for a rule regarding the orbit of Mars, or Boyle seeking a relationship between the pressure and the volume of a gas at a constant temperature. To the untrained eye, a forest may at first seem to be an undifferentiated mass of identical objects (trees). Upon closer examination, however, one will begin to see that in fact there are both conifers and deciduous trees in the forest, and that within these two classes there are in fact, subclasses. Indeed, the classification work of Linnaeus can be seen as fixing belief through induction (Broberg 1992).

Is there a role for induction in economics? Suppose an economist suspects a connection between the degree of democracy and the rate of growth across a class of countries—say, those still considered to be "developing" countries. This economist may observe that countries A, B, C, and D, all of which are, on the surface at least, highly democratic, have also experienced double-digit rates of growth in per capita income over the past two decades. The resulting hypothesis might then be that the more democratic a country is, the higher its rate of growth will be. Here is a form of induction that establishes a universal proposition on the basis of an examination of but part of the pertinent instances. But the veracity of this proposition requires that we establish the truth of an additional proposition: what is true of A, B, C, and D is true of all developing countries. Notice that this reframes an inductive process in the form of a deductive proposition. That is:

> *Case:* Whatever is true of A, B, C, and D is true of
> all democratic countries.
> *Result:* Rapid growth in per capita income characterizes
> A, B, C, and D.
> ∴ *Rule:* Rapid growth characterizes all democratic countries.

The well-known problem of induction is evident here. There is an additional problem associated with induction, however, which entails contamination by the introduction of value judgments. With deduction and abduction, the truth content of the argument is easily checked by ascertaining the veracity of the assumptions and the axioms. Because induction is not a form of logical argumentation, it is more difficult to pinpoint the flaws, and so induction is more susceptible to the introduction of bogus associations.

IMPLICATIONS

> By induction, we conclude that facts similar to observed facts are true in cases not examined. By hypothesis [abduction], we conclude the existence of a fact quite different from anything observed, from which, according to known laws, something observed would necessarily result. The former is reasoning from particulars to the general law; the latter from effect to cause. The former classifies, the latter explains.
> —Charles Sanders Peirce, *Essays in the Philosophy of Science* (1957)

Deduction, the dominant way of fixing belief in economics, relies on an analytical engine whose strengths are confined to explicating the structural nature of models constructed for precisely those reasons. From this particular structure, most economists fix their belief about how the world works. But deductive belief can be no better than the empirical pertinence of the axioms (covering laws) and assumptions that represent the core of the analytical engine. If the economist remains dedicated to those covering laws and assumptions, and treats the applicability postulates as reassuringly adequate for validation of the analytical engine, yet somehow never quite sufficient to discredit that analytical engine, then theoretical progress is virtually impossible. Of equal importance, explanation is often sacrificed by an unwillingness to recognize that the axioms and assumptions preordain the particular theoretical propositions to flow from deduction. Validationism is all too common. This means we do not explain events—we justify them. Deduction can readily find confirming evidence for its theoretical discoveries, and the avid deductivist will then declare satisfaction.

On the contrary, abduction is devoted to the task of fixing belief about observed phenomena. The difference is profound. The abductivist cannot merely offer universal theories that would be true in each particular case *if only* the data were a little better. Rather, the abductivist must produce plausible reasons for—explanations of—the results. If my automobile engine will not start, I am not interested in theoretical propositions about high altitude, cold weather, and faulty vaporization. This car, at this time, in this place, will not function as it is expected to. There are many deductive explanations for dysfunctional automobile engines. There is only one reason why mine will not start right now. Abduction is dedicated to explicating that reason.

CHAPTER SEVEN

Explaining

> I wish he would explain his explanation.
> —George Noel Gordon, Lord Byron,
> *Don Juan*, Dedication (1818)

The Urgent Necessity of Explanation

If one believes, as many economists do, that the essential purpose of economics is to offer predictions, one must acknowledge that explanation, being essential to prediction, is central to the practice of economics. Moreover, if one believes that the essential purpose of economics is to offer useful and valuable advice for solving particular social problems, one must acknowledge that explanation, being essential to prescription, is central to the practice of economics. In short, it is impossible to predict economic outcomes—and it is impossible to offer coherent prescriptions for perceived economic problems—without first developing plausible explanations of past, present, or future economic circumstances and outcomes.

When the rule under which a diagnosis is made consists in a law of connection—by which we mean a proposition of the sort "if X, then Y" that can either be logical ($2 + 2 = 4$) or causal (gas expands when heated)—the diagnosis explains the observed fact from which it started. However, if the rule is a law of conjecture—a hypothesis—that is a mere statistical uniformity, the diagnosis does not explain the observed fact from which it started. From the observation that an animal has cloven hoofs, one can frame, diagnostically, the hypothesis that it ruminates under the (inductive) statistical law that all known ruminants have cloven hoofs. But that diagnosis, correct or not, does not at all explain the cloven hoofs. All that happens here is that cloven hoofs are predicted from (and validated by) the statistical law. The fundamental question remains, Why do some animals have cloven hoofs? Obviously, the answer cannot be "because they ruminate." Equally, one cannot explain why some animals ruminate by reference to their cloven hooves.

Explanation requires apprehension of reasons. That is, if we are to explain particular economic phenomena, then we must be able to find reasons for particular actions and outcomes and not be content with mere causes. Although economics claims to be concerned with individual and collective choices, we often show little interest in the important distinction between causes and reasons (Lewin 1996). Or, if reasons must be adduced, many economists will deploy that all-purpose "reason": the particular choice was one that maximized utility. The obvious problem is that "reasons" for particular choices can be whatever individuals happen to say, and "causes" can easily be confused with "reasons." Assertions that one made a particular choice because that choice maximized utility is not to offer a reason but rather to offer a rationalization. Utility is not a reason.

When a cold breeze enters a room under control of a thermostat, a process is triggered that will bring the temperature in the room back to its predetermined level. Did the cool breeze cause the furnace to come on? Is that the reason for the furnace coming on? Or did the cool breeze act on specific parts of the thermostat to cause it to adjust, thereby causing the furnace to be activated, and eventually restoring the temperature to its predetermined level? What is the reason for the furnace coming on? The cool breeze? The suddenly activated thermostat? The sudden deviation between desired and actual room temperature? Here the process is automatic—purely mechanical. There is an important distinction to be drawn between actions that are mechanical and actions that are purposeful—one constituting a cause, the other constituting a reason.

Reason makes an action intelligible by redescribing it (Davidson 1963). Why is John's porch light on? Because he flipped the light switch? Because he is expecting guests? Because he thinks his house looks better when the front is lit? Because he is afraid of vandals? Because all his neighbors do the same? Because his parents turned their porch light on every evening? Because his wife asked him to turn it on? If so, what are her reasons? John made a clear choice, and by flipping the switch he caused the light to come on, but his reasons are quite another matter. In economics we often regard human behavior as analogous to flipping the switch—choosing X rather than Y—while the reasons for action remain suppressed under the excuse that doing so was consistent with preferences.

This is not much comfort for those who seek to be useful to the diagnosis of economic problems, and useful to the making of economic policy. For economic policy is often concerned with individual choice—individual behavior—as well as with the reasons for, and the effects of, the behavior of groups. For this we cannot be content with mere choices; we must understand reasons. That is, we must be able to explain why particular outcomes; themselves the result of thousands (perhaps millions) of individual behaviors; are or are not observed. And we must be able to explain what steps are necessary in order that particular outcomes will be more or less likely to occur in the future. That is precisely the purpose of economic policy. We see immediately the inextricable link between explanation, prescription, and prediction.

The urgent challenge in our need for warranted belief about economic phenomena is the acquisition of a basis for successful explanation. "Explanation consists in the supposition of something that would have been sufficient to the existence of the observed fact under a given known law" (Ducasse 1925, pp. 152–53). Explanation is, therefore, concerned with the identification and explication of sufficient reason. If we are to understand the meaning of economic institutions, and if we are to build a theory of institutional change, then we must ground our work on the concept of sufficient reason.

SUFFICIENT REASON

The fixing of belief is an evolutionary undertaking, with the starting point being one of searching for general patterns in observable phenomena. At this early stage, induction plays a valuable role. Recall that induction is a process whereby a general rule is advanced from the examination of sets of seemingly related yet quite specific phenomena. While induction is concerned with a perception of relations, it is not subject to any rules of validity. This means that there is no way to dismiss inductive propositions on logical grounds. Inductive propositions can only be evaluated in terms of their apparent "truth" content. For example, in the early stages of medical science we can imagine that a curious and astute practitioner began to systematize a large number of observations about people with fevers. At some point, and with a fair record of pure empiricism having been compiled, the individual might well have asserted:

> I have observed perfect correlation between the fact of fevers and the fact of open pestilential wounds. Every subject I have examined who had open wounds accompanied by ulceration has also been fevered. I conclude that fevers and open ulceration are coincident. I cannot, however, be certain whether ulcers cause fevers, or whether fevers cause ulcers.

Where does this observation lead us in terms of explanation? Notice that with this inductive proposition in hand, fevers seem to explain infections and infections seem to explain fevers. Notice, as well, that fevers predict infections and infections predict fevers. But the observer lacks the basis for a sufficient explanation because there is yet no way to tell whether fevers cause infections or infections cause fevers. The observer can only declare that:

TABLE 7.1
The Process of Induction (a)

Empirical Claim	*Case*: F
Mode of Connection	if Case, then Result
Conclusion	*Result*: I
Axiom	*Rule*: if F, then I

TABLE 7.2
The Process of Induction (b)

Empirical Claim	*Case*: I
Mode of Connection	If *Case* then, *Result*
Conclusion	*Result*: F
Axiom	*Rule*: if I, then F

> *Case:* Whatever is true of these people is true for all people with ulcerated wounds.
> *Result:* All of these people have fevers.
> *Rule:* Therefore, all people with infections have fevers (see table 7.1).

However, the observer might have as easily declared that:

> *Case:* Whatever is true of these people is true for all people with fevers.
> *Result:* All of these people have open ulcerated wounds (infections).
> *Rule:* Therefore, all people with fevers have infections (see table 7.2).

We see that the value of induction in establishing associations and relations is quickly dissipated when it comes time for explanation. It is here that deduction and abduction enter the picture. These two forms of logical inference are characterized as shown in table 7.3.

In producing deductive belief, we proceed syllogistically from general axioms (rule), assumptions and applicability postulates (case), to the thing requiring explanation (result). Notice that the explanation is not found in the result (the explanandum) but in the conjunction of the rule and the case (the explanans). That is, the axioms, the assumptions, and the applicability postulates combine to offer the deductive basis for a spe-

TABLE 7.3
The Structure of Logical Inference

	From		And		To
Deduction	Rule	→	Case	→	Result
Abduction	Result	→	Rule	→	Case

TABLE 7.4
The Process of Deduction

Axiom	Rule
Mode	If Case then, Result
Empirical Claim	Case
Conclusion	Result

cific result—either factual or hypothesized. Under the axioms, assumptions, and applicability postulates we can predict that country X will produce more wine than country Y (the result). This will happen because country X has a clear comparative advantage over Y in wine (the case made by the careful use of assumptions and applicability postulates). Deduction employs the mode, "if case, then result" (see table 7.4).

> *Axiom:* Countries produce according to their comparative advantage.
> *Mode:* If country X produces wine more cheaply than country Y, then it (X) has a comparative advantage in producing wine.
> *Empirical claim:* Country X produces wine more cheaply than country Y.
> *Conclusion:* Country X has a comparative advantage in producing wine.

Deduction is concerned to establish general explanatory propositions for specific phenomena that may or may not be directly observable (such as comparative advantage). In this situation the empirical claim can be observed (and confirmed), and the question then becomes "Why does country X produce wine more cheaply than country Y?" The answer, the explanation, is that country X has an economic advantage in wine production as compared to country Y. Notice that comparative advantage is not an observable phenomenon, and hence the economist deduces that country X has a comparative advantage in wine production from observations about relative input and output data (and relative factor prices). In fact, the term comparative advantage is simply a shorthand economic term for a set of conditions and relations pertaining to a particular region- or country-specific production possibilities set. We see that the notion of comparative advantage is a concept by postulation rather than a concept by intuition. Concepts by postulation are concepts whose meaning is designated by the postulates of some specific deductively formulated theory in which they are embedded. Concepts by intuition, on the other hand, are concepts whose meaning is immediately apprehended by the senses (Northrop 1967).

The deductivist says, "Can I establish general correspondence rules and axioms that allow us to deduce the explanation for particular phenomena?" To return to the medical example, the process may start with some basic well-established laws—perhaps offered up through a process of induction—that are the product of prior research. This may concern the fact that the human body has been previously observed to produce antibodies to fight infections. This process would then be studied, and it might be learned that when this antibody reaction occurs in humans rather than in laboratory experiments, the process is accompanied by a fever. From this work would emerge an axiom (a "law"). That axiom would say, if physicians encounter patients with a fever (F), it may suggest (imply) an infection (I) because antibodies attack infections and this is associated with a fever in humans. The deductive rule is "if fever, then infection." The deductive rule is the product of the following thought process: "How can I predict the presence of infections when that circumstance is not yet manifest in the form of an observable pestilential wound?" The inquiry does not concern itself with diagnosing a particular patient's maladies but rather with establishing general principles (rule and case) concerning the connection between infections and their symptoms (fever).

The deductivist would then say, because we now know that infections are associated with fevers, we can—with some considerable confidence—say that fevers "predict" infections in patients. In other words, the infection appears to explain the fever and our overriding interest is not in the fever but rather in the reasons for—the causes of—the fever. Because infections are known to cause fevers (through the intermediation of antibodies), we can say with some confidence that a person with a fever has an infection (see table 7.5).

Notice that in deduction the challenge is to develop the necessary arguments that will stand as the reasons for the case. The reasons for the case are, it will be noted, the rule (axiom) that says if there is an observed fever there will be an infection. Notice that the attention is on the case, and that one predicts from the case, via the rule, back to the result. The logical inference in deduction is from *case to result*. The power of deduction is

TABLE 7.5
The Process of Deduction in Medicine

Axiom	*Rule*: If F, then I
Mode of Connection	If *Case*, then *Result*
Empirical Claim	*Case*: F
Conclusion	*Result*: I

seen in the fact that one need not observe the infection; it can be deduced from the axiom and the case. But we can pay a high price from exclusive reliance on deduction. Specifically, deduction can lead to false predictions by its exclusive reliance on the connection between the rule (axioms) and the case (assumptions). This fact exposes economics to the criticism that we never really test our theory—the axioms and assumptions—by appeal to the real world (result). That is, our theory predicts a particular result, and if that result is not observed, we can always blame the assumptions, or we can blame the data—the applicability postulates—that are a central part of the case. Drawing on the medical analogy, if a patient is found to be fevered without an infectious disease, the earnest deductivist might doubt the accuracy of the thermometer that indicated a fever. In essence, the committed deductivist would seek to shift the focus from testing the explanation that if there is a fever, there will be an infectious disease, to a call for better thermometers to show that a "real" fever is indeed explained by an infectious disease.

Notice something else here. The infection explains the fever, but the fever does not explain the infection. That is, the body produces antibodies to fight an infection, and this gives rise to fevers. So the fever predicts the infection but does not explain the infection. The infection must be explained by an event outside of the fever-infection analytical engine. We must develop an understanding as to why the patient has an infection, and the answer to that question is most assuredly not that the patient is observed to be fevered.

This brings us to the other form of logical inference, abduction. Here, in contrast to deduction, the process runs from result and rule to case (see tables 7.6 and 7.7).

In producing abductive belief, we proceed syllogistically from the known phenomenon (result) and the axioms (rule) to particular assumptions and applicability postulates (case). Notice that the explanation (the explanans) in abduction is the same as with deduction. That is, explanation resides in the case (the assumptions and the applicability postulates), not in the thing to be explained. But there is a fundamental difference

TABLE 7.6
The Process of Abduction (a)

Empirical Claim	*Result*
Axiom	*Rule*
Mode	If *Result*, then *Case*
Conclusion	*Case*

between abduction and deduction. We saw in deduction that the focus was on discovering the reasons for the case (the fever). One might even say that the scientist is trying to justify or to build support for the case, and it is too easy to stop once an infection is found that constitutes the alleged reason for the fever, forgetting that the necessary scientific challenge is to work out the reason for the infection, not the reason for the fever. In this setting the scientist can easily become protective of the case—the assumptions and the empirical claims of the situation at hand. Indeed, critics of orthodoxy insist that this is precisely the problem.

In abduction the scientist is concerned with discovering the reasons for the result (the fever), but unlike in deduction the scientist is not committed to the case as the explanation. Returning to the medical example, the physician would start with the well-known axiom in medicine that says: infections (I), by mobilizing antibodies, will cause a fever (F). But the physician is more interested in diagnosing the patient with a fever—explaining the result—than in testing the case. The abductivist would, therefore, be open to an alternative set of axioms, one of which might be that acute leukemia (L), by interfering with the body's ability to dissipate heat, is known to bring on a fever (F). Abduction induces the physician to be open to several plausible explanations for the fever.

Her approach might be characterized as: if I see a patient with a fever (F), check first for an infection (I) and then, if that produces negative results, test for leukemia (L). The logic is: if I can explain this fever then I will know what is wrong with my patient—that is, I can predict the cause of the patient's fever. Using the primary axiom (if F, then I), the physician infers that the patient has an infection. She orders clinical tests for that hypothesis, and the test returns negative, so the physician cannot affirm that this patient has an infection. With the failure of this hypothesis in hand, the physician then turns to the alternative hypothesis—the fever is caused by acute leukemia. Again the physician orders a laboratory test, this time for leukemia. This test confirms that the patient has leukemia. We see here important lessons for explanation.

TABLE 7.7
The Process of Abduction (b)

Empirical Claim	*Result*: F
Primary Axiom	*Rule*: If F, then I
Mode of Connection	If *Result*, then *Case*
Conclusion (false)	*Case*: I
Secondary Axiom	*Rule*: If F, then L
Conclusion (true)	*Case*: L

Did the fever explain (predict) the disease? No, because there were two possible diseases associated with the fever—an infection and leukemia. Did the disease explain the fever? Not in the case of the infection, but yes in the case of leukemia. Recall that the disease explains the fever, not conversely. Patients can have a fever without an infection (and indeed without leukemia), but they cannot have an infection without a fever (unless their immune system is impaired as with HIV/AIDS). The presence of some disease explains the fever, while the fever merely alerts us to the presence of some disease but does not predict the particular disease. The process of abduction provides an answer to the question, Why does this person have a fever? In other words, abduction helps the physician to search through the plausible (as determined by the canonical axioms of medicine) causes of this person's fever until the true reason has been identified. The physician could then tell the patient:

> I can now explain why you are feeling feverish. I inferred from my diagnosis that you have acute leukemia. I ordered laboratory tests on the basis of that hypothesis and the laboratory tests seem to confirm that hypothesis. Or, more correctly, the tests do not allow me to rule out the hypothesis that you have leukemia.

Recall that the logic of abduction is found in:

> The surprising fact, C, is observed:
> But if A were true, C would be a matter of course,
> Hence, there is reason to suspect A is true.

Here the surprising fact is the fever. So we search for the reasons for the fever (A) (see table 7.7).

The deductivist operates with the mode of connection, if case, then result, while the abductivist operates with the mode of connection, if result, then case. Notice that the deductivist is trying to predict the unobservable result (I) from the observable case (F). The abductivist, on the other hand, is trying to predict the unobservable case (I or L) from the observable result (F). The deductivist seeks the reason for the case, whereas the abductivist seeks the reason for the result.

Unfortunately for the deductivist, the case (F) has two possible explanations, an infection and acute leukemia. The deductivist trap arises from a commitment to the axiom, "if F, then I." Or, in practical terms, the axiom is not complete, and the cause of (F) is not unique. The axiom is not complete because it can predict either an infection or leukemia, and it is not unique because a fever can arise from two possible causes, an infection and leukemia. The difference between deduction and abduction might be thought of as the distinction between two attitudes toward fixing belief. The deductivist regards the basic generalizations as immutable with the only problem being to figure out how to apply them to all situations. The abductivist, on the other hand, considers some of the necessary generalizations still to be discovered and formulated. In essence, the abductivist is more open than the deductivist to a variety of explanations.

Notice, as well that once the disease has been correctly identified, the next challenge is to explain the disease. Why does this person have an infectious disease (or leukemia)? Abduction carries us forward to the next level of surprise, then plausible hypothesis, and then perhaps to the correct explanation.

CAUSES AND REASONS

With a better concept of explanation in hand, it seems appropriate to address the common confusion between reasons and causes (Hands 2001; Rosenberg 1995). To many economists, "reasons are causes" (Hands 2001, p. 336). This issue brings us to the need to focus attention on the distinction between explanations that are mechanical (as in the relationship between fevers and infections) and explanations that are purposeful (as in human relations). In making that distinction, I will now confine the notion of cause to mechanical explanations, while the notion of reason will be reserved for instances of purposive explanations. Economics, because it addresses the human will in action, concerns purposeful behavior, and in that sense we are primarily concerned with reasons for actions.

To be able to speak of an act or an event as *purposeful*, it is neither necessary nor sufficient that the act be such that unless it (the act) occurs some specified result will not occur (Ducasse 1925). In the standard telling, what is required for *purposeful* action is that the following elements be present:

- *belief* by the performer of the act X in the law "if X, then Y" (call this the *epistemic premise*)

- *desire* by the performer of the act X that Y (the outcome) indeed occurs (call this the *volitional premise*)
- *implementation* by that desire and that belief jointly, of the act X (call this the *practical necessity for action*)

Notice that the explanation of the dependence of Y on X enters not as something that is true but simply as something believed by the actor. In contrast to purposeful explanations, the storage of nuts by a squirrel lacks both belief and desire. The squirrel is not moved by the belief that unless she stores nuts now she will starve next winter. Nor is it reasonable to suppose that while gathering nuts the squirrel desires not to starve next winter. The squirrel's actions are of a class called *positive regulation* (Ducasse 1925). As with the thermostat, the nut-gathering actions of the squirrel are automatic; they are mechanical in nature. By way of contrast, when a prospector digs over there for gold, we must suppose that he believes that is where gold is most probably to be found, and we must also suppose that he very much desires to find gold. The squirrel has causes; the prospector—as with John of the porch light—has reasons.

This approach helps us to apprehend the idea that the explanation— the reason—for a purposeful action is to be found in some outcome in the future. But, aren't all causes antecedent and all outcomes consequent? Not exactly. Only mechanical causes are antecedent to the outcome. Final causes—reasons—concern future states. The prospector is moved to dig by the prospect of finding gold; that is his reason for digging. To find gold in the future—not the distant future but perhaps in just ten minutes—he digs now. In this light, it would certainly seem odd to suppose that there is some antecedent condition that "caused" the prospector to dig. Does he dig because he just pulled on his pants? Because he has now finished his breakfast? Because the sun is now up? Because he just fetched his shovel? So the idea of some future state (finding gold) serving as the motivation for an action now—technically the reason for the action—is not as novel as it may at first seem. Explanations must be considered differently depending upon the context of the action to be explained (Hulswit 2002). Mechanical causes are those that precede the action to be explained. Final causes—reasons—are those that entail belief and desire on the part of an agent who looks to the future and acts accordingly. A belief is that upon which we are prepared to act. I call this prospective volition— the human will in action, considering possible outcomes in the future and acting accordingly.

Notice that explanations by mechanical cause consider the future in terms of the present. The thermostat, preset to some level, reacts when the current temperature deviates from that controlling the future (the next instant). The action of the thermostat (triggering the furnace) is predicated upon evaluation of the future in terms of the present, and when a discrepancy emerges, action ensues. This is the essence of mechanical cause. The squirrel is not moved to gather nuts by some prospect of the future but by the automatic imperatives of the present. To be a squirrel is to gather nuts. That is what squirrels do.

On the other hand, the human will in action—prospective volition—considers the present in terms of the future. Indeed, we are pleased to differentiate ourselves from the lower orders of life by our ability to "reason backward," as it were. Reasoning backward is precisely the act of understanding the present in terms of the future, and deciding how we wish the future to unfold for us. Final cause—reason—is concerned precisely with this idea.

IMPLICATIONS

As we seek to fix belief about why things happen (or fail to happen) it is essential to understand that such belief—such explanations—in economics can arise from either deduction or abduction. Deduction seeks to provide reasons for the assumptions and applicability postulates that constitute the case. In that sense, deductive explanations tend to be self-referential. The deductivist would say that certain results are not possible based on the analytical engine that constitutes the core of a particular deductive model. Or, the deductivist would say that her analytical engine provides clear "theoretical" support for certain general propositions. Deduction is protective of the rule and the case.

Abduction seeks to provide reasons for the observed phenomena that are referred to as the result. In that sense, abduction is not self-referential but is instead externally grounded on the world it seeks to explain. The abductivist would say that there are several plausible reasons for the observed result. Or the abductivist would say that her heuristic template suggests that this particular phenomenon is the plausible result of certain reasons.

In economics, both ways of fixing belief—both forms of explanation—must be concerned with prescription and prediction.

CHAPTER EIGHT

Prescribing and Predicting

> "Contrariwise," continued Tweedledee, "if it was so, it might
> be; and if it were so, it would be; but as it isn't, it ain't.
> That's logic."
> —Lewis Carroll, *Through the Looking Glass* (1872)

CAUSES AND REASONS AGAIN

Pragmatism suggests that economics must concern itself with explaining the reasons for observed action (phenomena) rather than with finding theoretical justifications for those phenomena. Once explanation is on sound footing, prescribing and predicting logically follow. If we know why certain results exist (or fail to exist), then we can plausibly prescribe what is needed to alter those observed phenomena should they be found to be undesirable. Or, we can plausibly prescribe what steps might be sufficient to induce different outcomes. Prescription therefore constitutes prediction about future states. Pragmatism also suggests that the central issue in prescription (and therefore explanation) is not which future states are the most desired. Rather, the central challenge concerns how to consider which future states, among many, we have the best reasons to pursue.

I earlier suggested that economics must concern itself with fixing belief about how societies organize themselves for their provisioning. Related to this, economics must concern itself with gaining an understanding of why different societies choose different provisioning strategies. That is, economists must seek to understand and to explain economic institutions and their implied human action. This intellectual agenda cannot succeed if it proceeds from an epistemology of deductive validationism central to much contemporary economic thought. Instead, from pragmatism and abduction we encounter an open-minded epistemology that offers hope in this regard. And from the quest for explanation springs the notion that when we understand why certain outcomes occur (or might be induced to occur), it is inevitable that we will pause to reflect on the desirability of both the phenomena being explained, as well as the reasons for—the explanation of—those phenomena. As Daniel Hausman has noted,

> The fact that explanations in economics involve both reasons and
> causes of the action to be explained has far reaching consequences,

because reasons, unlike causes, can be appraised. There are good reasons for action and reasons that are not so good. If the causes of an action are also good reasons to do it, then one has justified as well as explained the action. If the causes are not good reasons, then one has raised doubts about whether the action was justified. The evaluation here is rational or prudential, not moral. (Hausman 2001, p. 22)

When Hausman refers to the "reasons and causes of the action to be explained," we come immediately to the core of pragmatism's conception of individual action. Because any willful human action requires (presumes) reasons, we see that a view of the propriety of the action necessarily implicates the reasons for the action. But clarity here demands that we think about causes and reasons as two fundamentally distinct ideas. As previously, I reserve the use of the term *cause* for those explanations that are mechanical. If a particular disease plausibly explains a fever, then the disease is a plausible cause of the fever. When John flips the light switch, his physical act is the cause of the light coming on, but his *reasons* for flipping the switch constitute the central issue here. Although some historians consider the 1914 assassination of Archduke Francis Ferdinand in Sarajevo by the Serbian nationalist Gavrilo Princip to be the cause of World War I, the reasons for that war go far beyond this single violent act. That is, the assassination cannot possibly be the reason for the war, though we may well regard the assassination as the cause of the war.

Reasons concern the realm of purpose, whereas causes relate to the realm of mechanism. Consider the following situation. A person (Alpha) is discovered to have assaulted a neighbor (Beta) and to have inflicted physical harm on the latter. One might presume that the apparent judicial solution (a prescription) for this attack is to visit some punitive action on Alpha. But before that is undertaken, it is prudent to consider the realm of possible reasons for Alpha's violent action against Beta. Suppose it is discovered that Beta poisoned Alpha's dog? Given this, the problem then turns on understanding Beta's reasons. Perhaps Alpha's dog was menacing Beta's children? Did Alpha's dog bark incessantly, finally driving Beta to this immoderate act? The probable resolution of this situation reinforces the idea that in the human realm sufficient explanation demands finding the origins of actions, and here only reasons will do. We should therefore not be surprised to notice that the law in practice (jurisprudence) is concerned not with causes but with reasons. There is, after all, "justifiable" homicide, and there is "innocence by reason of insanity." These legal prescriptions, leading to particular action or nonaction against certain parties, remind us that all prescriptions must be predicated on reasons, not causes.

In economics, reasons come in various guises. The pursuit of efficiency is offered as a reason for many actions. Many economists are satisfied to assert that when individuals make particular choices, their reasons are to be found in their preferences—why else would individuals choose as they do? Rationality, after all, is defined as choices consistent with preferences. And to deal with the inconvenience of having little knowledge of individual preferences, we content ourselves by observing choices—and then are pleased to insist that choices reveal preferences. We may then declare individuals to be rational economic agents. Surely rational individuals would never choose what they do not prefer? The circularity here is comprehensive.

If economics is to gain credibility as a science of choice, then pragmatism suggests that we must find a more honest and realistic way to think about individual and collective choice. That is, economics cannot hope to be regarded as *the* science of choice as long as it persists in its claimed explanations of behavior derived from choices masquerading as preferences. To believe that choices explain (or reveal) preferences is simply a play on words. The challenge in economics is to offer explanations of particular human action, not rationalizations for particular human action. Saying that choices reveal preferences is simply to rationalize (justify) actions that have been taken. Rather, the necessary first step in a quest for explanation is to ask about the reasons for human action (where choice constitutes an action). The question we must ask is: "What things count as reasons for actions?" To economists the immediate response might be: "That particular action was undertaken for the sake of maximizing utility." A slight variation on this answer would be: "That action made the actor better off than any other feasible action available at the moment. After all, if the individual did not imagine that she would be better off acting as she did, why would she have acted in that fashion?" Notice that this alleged explanation is incomplete, because it justifies action in terms of utility rather than explaining action in terms of reasons. Utility is not a reason. Indeed, the idea of utility (and the term itself) is a convenient scientific fiction that merely allows us to label a functional relation in an analytically convenient way. A similar flawed logic appears in many accounts of public policy. Economists will compute the "welfare gains and losses" of various actions and, on the basis of this, will offer prescriptions regarding which policy actions are "optimal" or "socially preferred." Public policy—institutional change—is too complex to be captured by such reductionist maneuvers.

Finding Reasons for Institutional Change

The affinity for reductionism reflects the standard perspective from which many economists consider new public policy. Such consideration starts with the idea of a system otherwise in equilibrium—said equilibrium presumed to represent something necessary and inevitable called "the market." When there arises public recognition of, and expression of concern about, some particular social outcomes—environmental pollution, threats to human health, a desire for greater safety in the transportation system, inadequate housing—the economist may well be moved to ascertain, using the doctrine of welfare economics, whether a solution (or several possible solutions) to this problem will be efficient and, by implication, "socially preferred." Several aspects of this framing are worth consideration.

First, note that the aggregate outcomes of millions of atomistic choices, such choices informed and parameterized by the status quo institutional setup, have produced one or more social or economic results that a nontrivial share of the citizenry now seems to find unacceptable. Second, in response to this expressed desire for new and different outcomes in the future, several new policy initiatives (new institutional arrangements) will be proposed with the expectation that one of these alternative institutional setups will rectify these unacceptable future outcomes. At this point, the policy-oriented economist may well insist that the proposed institutional changes must be subjected to a benefit-cost (welfaristic) test to determine whether they are indeed efficient (or optimal or "socially preferred") to correct the existing problem(s). After all, if we are not careful, so-called government intervention in the market will bring us undesirable (inefficient) outcomes (Arrow et al. 1996; Cropper 2000; Palmer, Oates, and Portnoy 1995). Finally, notice that welfare economics is used here not to determine the most cost-effective means (policy initiative in the form of new economic institutions) to fix the recognized problem. Rather, welfare economics is used to determine whether it is appropriate —"socially preferred"—to solve the particular problem at all. In applying this decision rule, we are urged to rely on existing (or likely future) prices and perhaps hypothetical valuation exercises in the quest for a prescriptive truth claim that will reveal whether it is "worth it" to correct the flawed institutional setup so that the perceived problem is mitigated.

If the institutional change is not revealed to represent a Pareto improvement, then the unwanted outcomes, of obvious concern to an important share of the citizenry, are declared to be Pareto irrelevant (Bator 1958; Baumol and Oates 1988; Buchanan and Stubblebine 1962; Dahlman 1979; Mäler 1974). The obvious problem in this traditional approach is that a noneconomic problem is subjected to an *economistic truth rule* to determine whether it is economically efficient to correct the noneconomic problem. It is precisely here that prescriptive consequentialism can be inimical to the interests of democratic societies. It is important to recognize that the presence of economic implications from existing (and possible new) social outcomes is not sufficient grounds to render collective action the exclusive province of economics and Paretian (welfaristic) economic analysis. Surprisingly, this fundamental point has been lost in the rush to impose some vision of contrived "economic optimality" into public policy.

This does not mean that the economic implications of the status quo situation, or of the proposed solution, are immaterial to the informed consideration of institutional change. But to say that economic implications are pertinent to collective choice is not to give economics the decisive role in collective choice. Nor does it authorize the denunciation of politicians for implementing institutional change in the absence of evidence of a positive net present value from some action. We will often hear that a particular institutional change could not be defended on economic grounds and therefore was "mere politics"—the odious pleadings of special interests. Such logic seeks to deny the centrality of politics to policy. We must keep in mind that there are many legitimate reasons for particular actions, only a few of which pertain to economic efficiency and Pareto optimality (Bromley 1990; Mishan 1980; Tribe 1972).

Second, we must revisit the issue of causes and reasons. The existence of a serious—or merely annoying—social problem is quite a legitimate reason for the citizenry to seek relief. After all, if governments do not protect us from such things, then who will? Nations are often eager to mount military operations against foreign threats; surely a serious environmental or public health threat is a legitimate reason for action on the part of governments. We see that the reasons for collective action reside in, indeed originate in, the citizenry; individuals have a quite plausible (rational) wish to be free of threats to their health and well-being. On the other hand, we often see calls for careful study to determine whether it is "efficient" to change the existing institutional setup responsible for the apparent suffering of parts of the citizenry. Notice that in offering a decision rule for a particular public policy problem, there is an insistence to invoke quite a different reason for taking action. To the citizenry, the plausible reason for institutional change is to solve a very specific problem. To the economist, the plausible reason for institutional change concerns whether it can be declared a Pareto improvement (Cropper 2000). Can there be any mystery why our presumed "optimality" prescriptions are often met with bewilderment?

Some economists claim to "know" what will cause nations to experience high growth rates ("efficient" institutions) (Olson 1996). Or we "know" what is needed for African farmers to become more productive (private property) (Besley 1995; Feder and Feeny 1991). Or we "know" what steps are required to make sure that the level of environmental quality is socially optimal (benefit-cost analysis) (Cropper 2000). And we are certain that public policy must be held to the discipline of economic rectitude lest public policy become the exclusive province of the politicians, the manifest dangers of which are not to be underestimated. To hear some tell it, public policy in the hands of politicians is most assuredly much inferior to public policy guided by—indeed, disciplined by—good economics (Arrow et al. 1996; Buchanan 1972; Palmer, Oates, and Portney 1995).

Recall that public policy is collective action in restraint, liberation, and expansion of individual action. Notice, therefore, that public policy is nothing but a modification of the institutional structure of an economy that redefines choice sets (fields of action) for individuals. If you are restrained from harming or destroying parts of nature, then those individuals previously harmed or offended by your actions are thereby liberated by the adoption of new institutional arrangements that restrain your field of action—your choices—with respect to nature. If I am liberated from your unwanted behavior, it means that I am suddenly free from unwanted costs being imposed on me. If my field of action is expanded by collective action (a new policy enacted by the legislature), it means that I may now call on the collective power (the authority system) to help me do what it was previously difficult, expensive, or impossible for me to do. That is, an *expansion* in my field of action means that the state has agreed to stand ready to assist me in some new activities now rendered feasible by the fact that the state suddenly becomes my ally in some desired action on my part.

Some will choose to look at only one side of these new institutional arrangements and consider them to constitute "regulatory interference" with what they are pleased to presume is some "natural" state of affairs. Indeed, government intervention in the market seems to be the accepted term of art for such situations. Notice, however, that this account is a self-serving framing (and linguistic artistry) invoked by those no longer able to shift costs elsewhere. If food manufacturers are restrained by new laws (new institutions) from processing food in unsafe settings and circumstances, then consumers are liberated from the fear of eating contaminated food. If employers are forced by new laws to provide medical insurance to their workers, then those same workers are liberated from the necessity to undertake expensive self-insurance. If owners of coal mines are forced by collective action (new laws) to improve the safety conditions of their mines, then coal miners are liberated from the serious dangers of working in unsafe settings.

It bears mention that in the absence of these new institutional arrangements—so readily called "government interference in the market"—few would say that those exposed to unsafe food, or those without medical insurance, or coal miners whose lives are at grave risk were being interfered with in the status quo ante. There is not, in our usual lexicon, a term called "market interference." There is something called "market failure," but this does not carry the same burdensome implications as does the term "interference." The pertinent issue here is whether an unwilling exposure to the unwanted actions of others is regarded as an imposition— as interference? Rarely is it so regarded. The usual way to characterize this situation is that it is merely what exists at the time. Many will even insist that this status quo ante represents "the market" at work. We see, in other words, that the language of economic policy bestows special advantages on—privileges—the status quo ante. Indeed, it is common to see the status quo ante as somehow "natural" and therefore to insist that any alteration from that position must be justified on economic grounds (Buchanan 1972). In this conventional approach to public policy, deduction is deployed to justify particular approaches to policy.

We will be told that the Coase theorem "proves" that it is better to let those disadvantaged by the status quo ante institutional setup attempt to bargain their way out of their unwanted position (Baumol 1972; Burrows 1980; Fisher 1990; Hartwick and Oleweiler 1986; Pearce and Turner 1990). The standard approach to the economic analysis of institutional change assures us that institutional arrangements will change when it is efficient for them to change, and in the absence of that finding the existing institutional setup must be regarded as optimal. Notice that this usual approach seems devoted to the proposition that institutional change cannot possibly be in the public interest unless the aggregate willingness to pay for a change in the institutional arrangements is found to be greater than the costs of that proposed change. The justification will be that this economic approach assures us of policies that are socially preferred. In response to this, E. J. Mishan (1980) insists that it is impossible to rely on welfaristic calculations of the sort $\Sigma V_{II} > \Sigma V_I$ (where ΣV = the sum of individual monetary valuations over alternative social states) to reveal anything at all about whether social state II is socially preferred to the status quo ante (social state I). Others have argued similarly: "One cannot reasonably evaluate policies, institutions, or states of affairs exclusively in terms of their success at satisfying the interpersonally non-comparable preferences of individuals. For welfare is not preference satisfaction, and it seems that things such as freedom, equality, and justice also matter" (Hausman and McPherson 1996, p. 99).

A recent attempt to overcome the conceptual flaws in the standard approach to institutional change requires yet new value judgments (Coate 2000). It is odd that, despite fundamental problems with various welfaristic (prescriptive) truth rules, many economists persist in their efforts to hold public policy hostage to discredited ideas about how to judge which institutional structure is socially preferred.

Is the deficit too high? If so the marginal tax rate may need to be adjusted upward (a new institution), or perhaps certain public spending programs need to be reconsidered, the practical result of which might be their elimination or their scaling back (both of which are new institutional arrangements). Is the air too dirty? If so a new institutional arrangement may be needed to alter the rate at which automobiles and factories discharge their emissions into the atmosphere. Are millions, without health insurance, exposed to the possible financial ravages of a serious illness? Is urban sprawl destroying green space? Are motorways clogged with automobiles while mass transit programs cannot achieve a critical level of service and convenience? Are children growing up in unspeakable poverty and hopelessness?

Regardless of the ultimate disposition of these issues, conversations about them are properly considered as conversations about the instrumentality of existing institutional arrangements. By *instrumentality* I mean, Do the current institutional arrangements induce the socially desired behaviors on the part of all of us? Put somewhat differently, are the prevailing working rules of the going concern we call society (or the polity) defining choice domains (fields of action) that, in the aggregate across all individual behaviors and over time, seem likely to produce outcomes that are plausibly acceptable? The presumption of market apologists is that what exists must be socially optimal, for if it were not, then it would be changed. These would be the same people who would insist that any change in the existing "market" can only be justified if it can be shown using welfaristic truth claims that a change represents a Pareto improvement. The incoherence is complete.

Clarity here is enhanced by recalling the core axioms of contemporary welfare economics, but particularly those axioms attributable to Pareto. Recall that there are two value judgments at the core of Paretian economics. The first value judgment is that only individuals count. The second value judgment is that individual valuations (assessments) concerning any two possible states (policy outcomes) are sufficient to insist that the state with the highest sum of individual valuations is Pareto optimal (or Pareto preferred). This commitment to methodological individualism—the view that the individual is the sufficient unit of analysis—is then projected into the realm of economic activity through the celebration of atomistic action in arenas called "free markets" where bargaining over price and quantity occurs. This process implies transactional value judgments. I call these transactional value judgments because they convey a normative prescription concerning how individuals ought to interact with each other in matters with economic content. In fact, the transactional value judgments are nothing but the direct and indirect "theorems" of welfare economics:

1. Every competitive market equilibrium is Pareto optimal (PO).
2. Every Pareto-optimal (PO) state can be sustained by a market in competitive equilibrium, given some initial assignment of property rights and under some existing institutional setup.

To call them "theorems" is to disguise the fact that they are simply value judgments. If we consider the first transactional value judgment, we see that one can explain (and justify) various Pareto-optimal states by the existence of competitive markets. That is, competitive markets are not the reason for Pareto-optimal states; they are simply the mechanical cause of such states. A Pareto-optimal state can therefore be mechanically explained by a competitive market, and to the extent that a Pareto-optimal state is regarded as ethically good (economists certainly regard it in this light), then competitive markets are, ipso facto, good.

Now consider the second transactional value judgment. Notice that reasons and causes are not reversed in this converse approach to optimality. That is, competitive markets still mechanically cause a Pareto-optimal state, while that optimal state obtains its justification by the deployment of an assumption—given some initial assignment of property rights and under some existing institutional setup. This second transactional value judgment is properly stated as: name some (any) initial property rights regime and accompanying institutional setup, including the associated distribution of income and wealth, and a competitive market will then produce and sustain a Pareto-optimal state. We see, on this reading, that now the explanation for a Pareto-optimal state, the cause of that state, remains the competitive market, but that any possible constellation of initial conditions will generate such a state when run through the mechanism of the competitive market. Suddenly a Pareto-optimal state is seen as merely an automatic and inevitable outcome of a machine process whose initial conditions can be anything at all.

And precisely what are these initial conditions? They are the existing institutional setup and the income and wealth streams entailed therein. For any possible initial setting, we can rely on a competitive market and the associated atomistic bargaining therein to produce and sustain a Pareto-optimal state, by which we mean that there is no change that would improve the situation of one individual without at the same time harming at least one other person. Because we are unable—as "objective" scientists—to comment on the merits of such direct gains and losses, the situation cannot be "improved upon" using the Paretian criteria. Although the earnest welfare economist may well feel a certain heady exhilaration at the magnificent sweep of this idea, it is, in fact, a nullity. As Gertrude Stein would say, "there is no there there." Of what possible normative significance—of what possible recommendatory power—is

Pareto optimality if there is one of them for any possible set of initial conditions? Indeed, because there exists an infinity of such starting points, it follows that there is an infinity of Pareto-optimal states. What shall the eager prescriptive economist do? Most probably, indeed necessarily, there will be an immediate appeal to the status quo institutional setup on the grounds that it is the one that exists. And from this arbitrary choice springs the equally arbitrary truth claim that any institutional deviation from this quite arbitrary state must be shown to be superior on efficiency grounds or else it is "inefficient" and thus not socially preferred (Buchanan 1972). And what does one make of efficiency predicated on an arbitrary fundament? Logic would suggest that it too is arbitrary. The prescriptive certitude of Paretian (welfare) economics is seen to be arbitrary in all of its emanations.

This approach to solving particular policy problems, invariably called "market failures," in particular ways is all too familiar. Interestingly, such prescriptions—and the economistic justification for those recommendations—are very often ignored by public decision makers. One explanation among economists for this unpleasant snub is that politicians are not terribly astute. It is not unusual for us to characterize politicians and other public decision makers as engaging in the most bizarre behaviors as they presume to "go about the people's business." Many economists regard politicians as simple shortsighted vote maximizers. How is it possible that they might wish to know the rational thing to do, let alone recognize it when it is presented to them in the clearest possible terms? We might think of this as the *dimwit conjecture*. The dimwit conjecture suggests that politicians, by definition, are not amenable to reason and rational thought about important social problems. It is, therefore, unreasonable to expect the acceptance of economists' prescriptive truth claims from a class of individuals who are so misguided—even duplicitous. The general acceptance of this view leads to statements and actions that serve further to reinforce decision makers in their rejection of our prescriptive assertions about what is best to do in the public policy arena. Our derision of their obduracy in the face of clear economic "truths" becomes a self-fulfilling prophecy. This then leads to more aggressive efforts on our part to convince them of their misdeeds. Down this road lay serious disengagement and little good economic input into important questions of public policy.

There is a competing hypothesis for why the assured prescriptions of welfare economics are resisted. Perhaps our particular ways of fixing belief do not lend themselves to the production of reasons, explanations, prescriptions, and implied predictions that resonate with those charged with the task of determining our collective future. Notice that I do not suggest that the particular solutions and prescriptions are inappropriate, although that is implied. Rather, I seek here to call attention to the particular ways in which we generate those solutions and to the manner in which we advance them. Perhaps our framing of the collective choice problem is wrong, not because of the answers that framing generates, but because that framing fails to accord with reality. If the questions we pose are flawed, then it is only by the very smallest of chances that the answers we thereby produce could possibly be pertinent. We might think of this as the *cognitive conjecture.*

If the cognitive conjecture is a plausible reason for the rejection of our Paretian economic prescriptions for many important public policy problems, then perhaps it is time to reconsider how it is that we claim to know what we think we know. This focused contemplation might well challenge our various ways of fixing belief—our received epistemology. That is, how do we know what we presume to know? How do we gain the belief and the associated confidence to pronounce, with such evident conviction, the truths we so readily advance about the correct—we would call it the "optimal"—solution to a wide range of public policy problems?

The answer, of course, is that we acquire these durable verities from the way in which we structure the choice problem. It is not surprising that "optimal" choices should follow ineluctably from the way in which we structure various choice problems. Indeed, we create our models of choice for precisely that purpose. What remains surprising is that many economists persist in their apparent innocence of this circularity and seem genuinely puzzled (indeed often resentful) that others might find the premises and structure of our choice algorithms tendentious. More curious, perhaps, is that the structure of choice problems considered appropriate for the individual is adopted quite unmodified in the realm of collective choice. Here some metaphorical "social planner" is conjured whose task it is to maximize social welfare. And we are surprised that others are surprised?

In many respects, the central problem of fixing belief that will then provide the basis for policy prescriptions arises from the complexity in human affairs. In this regard, Brock and Colander write that

> complexity . . . takes away the reference point for theory's defense of the market. In the complexity vision there is no proof that the market solves problems. There is no unambiguous way of stating what is and what is not an externality, and there is no guarantee that the market leads to the most desirable equilibrium. Thus deductive theory cannot provide a basis for the defense of laissez faire. (Brock and Colander 2000, p. 82)

Complexity in human affairs denies to us the essential tractability and predictability we need in order to advance tendentious Paretian prescriptions about what is optimal to do in the realm of human action. Models of optimality bring nothing compelling and necessary to the realm of human action, either for individual action or for collective action.

PRESCRIPTIVE AND PREDICTIVE BELIEF

If we could but move away from a preoccupation with the claimed optimality prescriptions of standard welfare economics, there is hope for being able to offer coherent policy advice. Recall that when we deploy deduction in the quest for plausible belief, a specific behavioral norm is imposed onto the system that converts the simple analytical engine into an optimization algorithm with the intent of deriving putatively desirable (socially preferred) outcomes. We see this most frequently when some situation of alleged "market failure" is identified and then the optimality conditions are imposed on the structure so that the economist can prescribe what ought to be done in the name of correcting the alleged inefficiency. That is, we will identify a maximization problem—where utility or "social welfare" is the maximand—and then derive (deduce) the logical entailments from the solution to this optimization problem. More often than not, the economist will be pleased to discuss the "policy implications" that flow logically and thus necessarily from the analytical engine. This is prescriptive belief because it presumes to solve the identified problem, and it indicates what steps must be taken if there is an interest in solving the problem at hand. Notice that these policy implications are often derived from the application of deductive procedures in an axiomatic setting without benefit of empirical data. That one can label these descriptive and illustrative insights "policy implications" indicates just how the idea of policy implications has been transformed from clear and coherent suggestions about how to solve a specific economic problem in a very particular setting, into a fancy way of saying that this particular analytical engine reveals that under these specific conditions it would be optimal to do X, Y, or Z.

Examples of alleged "policy implications" to flow from standard (deductive) analytical engines include the ubiquitous claim regarding the beneficial efficiency properties of atomistic bargaining (the Coase "theorem"), the merits of a Pigovian tax to solve pollution problems (a contrary finding to the Coase theorem), the employment-limiting properties of a minimum wage, the work on labor markets and "natural" rates of unemployment (and agency problems), the "optimal" depletion of natural resources, intergenerational equity and resource depletion, and the mandatory comparison of social benefits and costs from pollution control. Deduction starts with a general class of similar phenomena and seeks to derive general implications for other situations that appear to fit the axioms and assumptions of the analytical engine.

Abduction starts with "the irritation of doubt" concerning a particular empirical phenomenon requiring explanation, say, Why did this plane crash? Notice that both means of fixing belief are explanatory as well as predictive. That is, they will—if done well—suggest an explanation concerning where to concentrate the search, and they will suggest an explanation as to why the airplane crashed. Both classes of inference will also contribute to the development of predictive belief. In the course of answering the question, How did this plane crash? (so that we might determine the best place to look for possible survivors), and Why did this plane crash? (so that efforts might be undertaken to preclude a future crash), the scientist will introduce and consider a large number of auxiliary assumptions and applicability postulates. The more of these one introduces into the research effort, the more quickly it will be possible to reach a plausible explanation. This follows from the fact that the more data points—even if in the form of maintained hypotheses (assumptions)—there are, the more easily we can rule out flawed candidates for the best explanation. But, of course, over time, as the community of investigators—a discipline—works with a large number of events to be explained, members of that discipline will tend toward a general methodological consensus that certain assumptions, and certain types of empirical data, have more explanatory power than other assumptions and other types of data. With this emerging consensus, it then becomes possible to pare down the explanatory models (of either a deductive or abductive kind) to allow the generation of plausible explanations in a more parsimonious fashion. We could say that Ockham's razor is periodically applied to produce the most parsimonious explanations.

Once we feel reasonably comfortable with the explanation of particular phenomena, the economist can then make the transition to prediction. In fact, it may be noticed that explanation entails a certain (though limited) category of prediction: "I predict that the best place to search for the missing airplane is in this particular Cartesian space"; or, "I predict that this airplane crashed because . . . . " Notice that the word *predict* is used here as a synonym for *hypothesize*. More generally, we would say that prediction from deductive belief entails the following class of statements: "In the future, if the following conditions obtain, then this kind of airplane will follow this specific trajectory to hit the water in this specific Cartesian space." Prediction from abductive belief entails the following class of statements: "In the future, if the following conditions obtain, then airplanes of this particular type are likely to crash."

If the precepts of comparative advantage are the reason for—the theoretical justification for—free trade, then it is the concept of comparative advantage that demands scrutiny and evaluation, not free trade. Advocacy for free trade is explained by the alleged efficiency properties of pursuing the logic of comparative advantage, and therefore the logic of comparative advantage is the reason why free trade is regarded as desirable. The question must then become, Is pursuit of the imperatives of comparative advantage a sufficient reason for advocating free trade? Put another way, Is the concept of comparative advantage sufficiently robust both logically and ethically to carry the entire burden for free trade? What if comparative advantage is itself an artificial construct? What then of free trade? Can the reasons for free trade—comparative advantage—be justified?

When we prescribe particular courses of action, we are inescapably endorsing the reasons for those actions and, as Hausman reminds us, "There are good reasons for action and reasons that are not so good" (Hausman 2001, p. 22). The problem then turns on the answer to the question, What things count as reasons for particular actions?

IMPLICATIONS

Prescriptions build on explanations and seek to ratify particular reasons why certain outcomes are (or are not) observed. That is, prescriptions are concerned with altering the institutional arrangements that at the moment define domains of choice—fields of action—for individuals and groups of individuals. Prescriptions are also predictions in the sense that we say, "Enact this particular policy and different (putatively desired) outcomes will ensue in the future." But just as there must be good reasons for particular outcomes, there must be good reasons for particular policy initiatives—institutional changes. To that subject we now turn.

CHAPTER NINE

Volitional Pragmatism

> The economic life history of the individual is a cumulative
> process of adaptation of means to ends that cumulatively
> change as the process goes on, both the agent and his environ-
> ment being at any point the outcome of the past process. His
> methods of life to-day are enforced upon him by his habits of
> life carried over from yesterday and by the circumstances left
> as the mechanical residue of the life of yesterday.
> —Thorstein Veblen, *Why Is Economics Not
> an Evolutionary Science?* (1898)

REASONS FOR ACTION

We are now ready to consider the general outlines of a pragmatic theory
of collective action. This theory will stand in contrast to the tendentious
and normative approach that now dominates much of the policy dialogue
in economics. The existing commitment to prescriptive consequentialism
constitutes the tenuous basis for truth claims (assertions) regarding definitions of the good, the socially preferred, and therefore the best thing to
do. When public decision makers find reasons to ignore these prescriptive
assertions, they are very often denounced for taking actions that are inefficient, politically motivated, irrational, or not in the public interest.

We see here a disjunction between the way many economists believe
public policy ought to be considered and implemented and the way in
which public policy is in fact considered and implemented. Who is right?
Do economists bring abiding truth to public policy through our regular
application of prescriptive consequentialism? Are the assertions (truth
claims) of economists of sufficient authority and disciplinary legitimacy
that they provide compelling reasons to alter the way democracies go
about the business of collective decision making? The issue under discussion here concerns a debate over who shall define for the members of a
particular political community what they ought to want, and how they
ought to evaluate what they ought to do. Common examples of such
claims from prescriptive economics would include the following:

- Policy X should be pursued because it will thereby increase social
  welfare.

- Policy Y should *not* be pursued because its net present-valued benefits are negative.
- Policy Z is socially desirable because it can be shown that the gainers from that policy could compensate the losers from that policy and still retain for themselves an economic surplus (although actual compensation need not occur and, of course, never does occur).
- Economic institutions will change when it is efficient for them to change. If it is not efficient for them to change, then they will not—and should not—change.

The question before us concerns the legitimacy—the warrantability—of such assertions. As we shall see, the matter of legitimacy has two components, one of which is internal to the community advancing these assertions, and the other of which concerns the intended audience for these assertions. The first component concerns the provenance, veracity, and coherence of such claims as judged by the shared standards of disciplinary practices from which they spring. That is, are these claims internally legitimate? The second component concerns the coherence and pertinence of such claims (assertions) as determined by the standards of the community whose decisions and actions they presume to inform and to judge. That is, do economists bring *justified* policy prescriptions to the arena of public choice? These questions concern the two core principles of volitional pragmatism: warranted belief and valuable belief.

Warranted Belief

A *warranted belief* (and its more active entailment *warranted assertions*) is a benediction—a judgment—that is bestowed by the larger (entire?) disciplinary community out of which particular disciplinary assertions emerge. The entire community of disciplinary practitioners (the full epistemic community) stands as the arbiter of assertions emanating from a particular subset of its disciplinary adherents. Notice that the judgment of warranted assertion is not the exclusive province of that subset of a discipline responsible for advancing those assertions. Although it is usually the applied economists who regularly advance such claims (policy prescriptions), it is the theorists within the broader discipline who stand uniquely qualified (and sufficiently detached) to help the rest of us decide if the assertions from one branch of the discipline are indeed on solid conceptual footing. The implication here is that no discipline can entirely trust the creators of, and thus the advocates for, particular scientific claims. After all, such individuals have a vested interest in the findings and prescriptive assertions they wish to advance. The practical import of this means that assertions advanced by, say, environmental economists, labor economists, health economists, development economists, or macro-economists must be accountable to the economics discipline in its entirety and not just to the minority who practice the same specialized craft—with its likely self-reinforcing and harmonized view of prescriptive propriety. In this way, the full complement of economic theorists and applied economists stands as the ultimate arbiter of belief (assertions) advanced by some subset of the discipline. This does not mean that all stand in perpetual judgment of the works of others within the same discipline. But it does mean that the views of others within the discipline (especially the theorists) must be taken seriously. We see an illustration of this with respect to Pareto optimality, a favorite truth claim of many applied (prescriptive) economists:

> As an example, consider the question: Do free markets and well defined property rights make society a better place? In the complexity approach, the answer to this question becomes . . . [an] empirical, not a deductive theoretical, question as it is in conventional theory. It [the complexity approach] does not approach the issue: given assumptions X, Y, Z can we prove that competitive equilibrium is "Pareto optimal"? Instead, it approaches it as an empirical issue whose answer may lie in areas totally untouched by simplified general equilibrium theory. As another example of how this does not change sophisticated economists' worldview, consider Frank Hahn's . . . favorite challenge . . . "How can you tell if the economy is in a Pareto optimal state or not?" Such a challenge demonstrates an understanding of the limits of a deductive approach, and the existence of a more sophisticated worldview. (Brock and Colander 2000, pp. 78–79)

Here Brock and Colander use the doubt and incredulity of Frank Hahn, a renowned general equilibrium theorist, to make the point about warranted assertions concerning Pareto optimality, a device of great importance to welfare economists.

Volitional pragmatism accords the status of warranted assertion only to the settled deliberations of a community of scholars—by which I mean a discipline (an epistemic community). When a discipline speaks with clear consensus on a particular matter, volitional pragmatism suggests that the rest of us would be well advised to regard these claims as constituting warranted assertions. On the contrary, when that disciplinary consensus is absent, or when it once existed but is now beginning to dissipate, those associated assertions lose their warrantability (their legitimacy). In the present context, and in light of widespread doubt concerning consequentialist welfarism, it is now impossible to regard prescriptive assertions predicated on welfarism as comprising warranted belief. For those seeking evidence of the sweeping discredit now bestowed on prescriptive consequentialism of the welfaristic type, the following literature might be useful: Blackorby and Donaldson (1990), Boadway (1974, 1976), Boadway and Bruce (1984), Bromley (1989, 1990, 1997), Chipman and Moore (1978), Coate (2000), Cooter and Rappoport (1984), Diamond and Hausman (1994), Field (1979, 1981), Gillroy (1992), Gorman (1955), Graaff (1957), Lewin (1996), Little (1949, 1950), Mishan (1969, 1971, 1980), Samuels (1971, 1974, 1989), Samuelson (1950), Sen (1977, 1982), and Vatn and Bromley (1994, 1997).

Indeed, evidence of the rather complete dissipation of warrantability is not confined to economists. Philosophers have long been troubled by prescriptive assertions predicated on consequentialist welfarism (Bromley and Paavola 2002). Legal theorists also have important things to say about welfarism and benefit-cost analysis (Posner 2003; Tribe 1972). In a comprehensive volume on cost-benefit analysis, legal theorists and philosophers combined efforts to contemplate the application of welfarism in benefit-cost analysis and did so without evident enthusiasm (Adler and Posner 2001). In a review of that volume, we see that:

> This is a magnificent collection of essays on cost-benefit analysis (CBA) written by economists, and by law professors and philosophers with some knowledge of economics. . . . Many will be surprised. . . . that the overall tone of a series of essays on this topic coming out of a law school very much influenced by economics, and by "Chicago-school" economics at that, is more questioning about CBA's use for regulatory policymaking for health, safety and the environment than would be mainstream discussions coming out of the prescriptive literature in economics or policy analysis. . . . it is fair to characterize their modal conclusions as follows: (1) policymakers should examine costs and benefits. . . . but the decision rule "maximize net benefits" is frequently problematic; (2) some of the most problematic issues CBA raises as a decision rule involve the use of existing private preferences as the sole raw material for public choices; (3) we should pay more attention than typically has been done to political considerations involving CBA. (Kelman 2002, p. 1241)

The early disciplinary consensus concerning welfarism in general, and benefit-cost analysis in particular, has deteriorated to the point that associated prescriptive truth claims no longer constitute warranted assertions. But even if that were not the case, that is, even if prescriptive consequentialism were a widely accepted truth rule among economists, this does not automatically imply its pertinence to the larger community into which such claims are regularly imposed. For that, we must turn to the individuals composing that political community.

Valuable Belief

Volitional pragmatism holds that a valuable belief is a benediction, a judgment, that can only be conferred by those who are the intended audience for specific assertions or truth claims directed to them. The implication is that audiences in a democracy are entitled to insist that particular authoritarian assertions (including the "authoritative" assertions from particular epistemic communities) be justified to them. This more interesting question concerns the general failure, already noted, of welfaristic assertions to be taken seriously by the political community—politicians, bureaucrats, citizens—into which they are projected as a guide to "rational" collective choice.

Recall that the internal acceptance of a theory (or a particular account) rests on the warrantability of its axioms, assumptions, prescriptions, predictions, and explanations. Internal acceptance implies that a particular discipline—an epistemic community—has reached a working consensus about a constellation of concepts, relations, and their implications. This working consensus is the necessary and sufficient condition for what I call warranted belief. This evolved and sustained scientific agreement is internal to the discipline and, as such, can be said to represent, at this time, the settled deliberations of a particular epistemic community with respect to the specific theoretical issue under consideration. In practical terms, the members of the discipline speak with one voice about particular matters under consideration. For the rest of us, we would be well advised to take a discipline's claims and assertions seriously. If cosmologists offer a warranted theory—a fixed belief—about the behavior of the planets, it is no doubt prudent for the rest of us to accept this account until a better one (a new fixed belief) comes along. But volitional pragmatism insists that this is not an inviolate requirement.

In particular, some warranted belief might be received by the community at large with justifiable skepticism. If musicologists tell us that the music theory and structure of a certain composer's work is the paragon of perfection, we are under no obligation to find that particular music compelling. If lawyers reveal to us the legalistic erudition and sparkling wisdom of particular judicial decisions, we are under no obligation to consider the decisions as correct, fair, or pertinent. If the received wisdom in psychology is that some categories of former prison inmates are not dangerous under particular circumstances, citizens may be excused for feeling anxiety if one or more such people are seen in their immediate neighborhood hanging about a children's playground. And if the world association of plant geneticists issues a proclamation declaring that genetically modified tomatoes are, to the best of their knowledge, really quite safe, many people will not be easily persuaded by this news and may choose to remain opposed to such genetic manipulation. The point here is that if the cosmologists get it wrong in their theory of planetary motion, few of us will notice or care. But if psychologists, or lawyers, or musicologists, or geneticists get it wrong, many of us will be affected in ways that we might find unacceptable. And so we see that the allegedly reassuring agreement of a community of disciplinary adherents—earnestly engaged in what Thomas Kuhn would call "normal science"—is not sufficient reason for the rest of us to stop what we are doing and instantly reformulate our belief about certain matters. After all, the citizenry has seen disciplinary claims revised with some regularity in the past; especially is this so in matters of diet, smoking, exercise, investment strategies, particular medicines, and the safety of observing nuclear tests during the latter phases of World War II.

The point is that the warranted belief of a community of disciplinary adherents is a necessary but not sufficient condition for the immediate acquiescence of the rest of us. Indeed, our acquiescence in its fixed belief and associated warranted assertions must rest on a separate set of arguments and reasons from those to which the discipline alone is privileged. Lacking this, disciplinary practitioners are not entitled to expect the rest of us to accept their particular assertions, even if they are deemed warranted by the discipline from which they spring. The pertinence of this point for public policy is obvious. The received wisdom—the fixed belief—of consequentialist welfarism is precisely concerned with telling the citizens of a political community which actions will enhance aggregate welfare, and therefore which actions are "best," "optimal," or "socially preferred." Why are most economists surprised and dismayed when the citizenry merely smiles at such conceit?

To be fair, welfare economists are not alone in being ignored from time to time. The point here is that any scientific community—indeed, any authoritative agent—must continually earn its way in democratic market-oriented societies where individuals are taught from an early age to think about and to challenge, rather than to accept on blind faith, what they are told. If scientists wish to be listened to, then they must offer valuable assertions—pertinent assertions—and justified claims about what they now suppose they know. This does not mean they must tell the rest of us what we want to hear. It means, instead, that they must give us good reasons to see the world as they see it. They must justify their assertions to us, not merely hand them out and expect us to fall in line. Thinking and discerning individuals will accept those assertions for which they find good reasons. William James (1907) regarded such assertions as having "cash value"—they were worth something to a particular audience. To paraphrase Joseph Raz, our deliberations concern the quest for what seem to be the best reasons to hold a particular belief.

This matter of valuable assertions is important because, as we saw earlier, the frequent disregard for welfaristic prescriptions among public officials or the citizenry is grounds for some Paretian economists to lament the irrationality, the inscrutability—indeed, the venality—of the political process in democratic market economies. But a richer and more realistic theory of public policy would provide an honest assessment of the grounds for such criticism. In other words, what if the alleged "irrationality" of the policy process is simply an artifact of the disciplinary predisposition into which some economists have been trained and socialized? Indeed, if the policy process in democratic market economies has its own logic and legitimacy, then judgments about, and indictments of, that process from any group of disciplinary practitioners will obviously lack justification. The question then becomes, Is there legitimacy to individual and collective choice despite what economists allege about those processes? Can individual and collective choice be considered coherent and rational if looked at, if considered, from a slightly different epistemological perspective?

Pragmatism offers a plausible description of how individuals and groups go about deciding what seems better, at the moment, to do. Without benefit of that alternative description, economists who criticize collective choice are relying on a self-serving disciplinary prescription for how choice ought to proceed. Obviously, it is intellectually more honest to seek a plausible description of how collective choice actually proceeds. With that description in hand, economists would then have an empirical basis for passing judgments on the alleged irrationality of the process. In other words, an intellectually compelling judgment concerning the coherence (or incoherence) of collective action awaits the formulation of a nontendentious account of that process. Only then can members of any particular discipline assess that process for its putative "rationality" or "irrationality."

But a new understanding of collective action requires a fresh analytical perspective. Recall that public policy is properly understood as collective action in restraint, liberation, and expansion of individual action. By way of contrast, collective action in economics is ordinarily concerned with individuals coming together voluntarily to accomplish that which they are unable to accomplish through individualistic behavior in markets. Indeed, many economists regard collective action as a sign of some market failure. The concept of collective action employed here is taken from John R. Commons, who saw that collective action occurred in the legislature (or parliament), the executive branch, and the courts (Commons 1924, 1934). The decisions of these governmental entities are demonstrably collective because these entities speak *for* and *to* the political community in their legislation, in their administrative rulings, and in their judicial decrees. All members of a nation-state are implicated in these decisions, and in that sense we are each restrained, liberated, and reconstituted by the actions of the collective authority of the legislature, the executive, and the judiciary.

With this fundamental redefinition of collective action in hand, I can now develop the core principles of volitional pragmatism in the service of outlining a general theory of human action, and a general theory of the process of arriving at settled belief. The theory to be worked out here draws its primary inspiration from John Dewey, Friedrich Nietzsche, William James, Ludwig Wittgenstein, Hans Joas, Charles Sanders Peirce, Robert Brandom, and Richard Rorty.

VOLITIONAL PRAGMATISM AS A THEORY OF HUMAN ACTION

I have suggested that we might come to understand an important aspect of public policy by viewing it as a syllogism of practical inference. Under this description, individual agents formulate volitional premises (desired outcomes in the future) and then develop epistemic premises that connect plausible belief-based actions to those desired outcomes. The conclusion of this syllogism of practical inference is a practical necessity (von Wright 1971, 1983). While this model holds certain intuitive appeal, it requires strong assumptions about the grounds for the a priori volitional premises that individuals identify and intend to act upon. That is, this formulation presumes that agents know what they want in the future as a precondition to their search for the appropriate epistemic foundations for necessary action. This linear process is seen as

DESIRE → BELIEF → ACTION.

In philosophy it is in fact called the desire-belief model of action. However, to pragmatic philosophers, and indeed to a number of philosophers who are not pragmatists, this model is now understood to be rather too contrived and mechanistic. The desire-belief model now lacks the property of warranted belief within philosophy. However, there is another theory of action available to us.

I hinted as much when I earlier insisted that we do not know what we want until we begin the task of determining—learning about—what we might plausibly have. We learn what we want by learning about what it is possible to have. And this brings us to another fundamental precept of volitional pragmatism: all action is a diagnostic undertaking in the quest for valuable belief—the only category of belief that provides a sufficient reason for human action.

Volitional pragmatism grounds human action in abduction. As we now know, abduction brings together particular observed phenomena (results) with particular axioms (rule) to suggest hypotheses and assumptions (case) that offer plausible reasons for the observed phenomena. Abduction is the only form of inference that introduces novel hypotheses into the search for reasons for particular actions or events. In economics, when we can identify reasons for actions or events, we have acquired a plausible basis for making predictions about, and for advancing explanations of, those actions or events. When individuals or collections of individuals face the need to choose (to act), abduction is the process we deploy to get a grip on the reason for the new surprise—that surprise (and its reasons) constituting the necessary precursor to choice and action. Diagnostic thought is deployed for the sole purpose of fixing belief. And a belief is that, and only that, upon which we are prepared to act.

Notice that abduction is not limited to scientists in need of hypotheses about cause and effect. As sapient beings, we are continually observing particular settings and circumstances (apprehended "facts") about the world around us. Coincident with this apprehension is a process of navigating our situatedness in those apprehended impressions of that apprehended world. Notice that this navigation is fundamentally a diagnostic (abductive) activity and that the observations and interpretations we form about that activity constitute the belief upon which we formulate abductive inferences about those settings and circumstances and our relation to them. Indeed, our observational and interpretive interest in those settings and circumstances is driven by the realization that the essence of living is incessant doing. At every turn we are presented with new "impressions," each of which stimulates, indeed demands, assessment, interpretation, and response. We are surprised.

In contrast to this diagnostic program, the more familiar Cartesian program is one of radical doubt about these impressions unless they can be empirically confirmed by independent testing. On this received account, to have fixed belief is to have accurate and indisputable mappings about—and descriptions of—the world "out there." To committed Cartesians, there can be but one "true" description and interpretation of the "facts" in the world, and it is the business of science to get in touch with that reality, to produce immutable descriptions and interpretations, and then to report back to the rest of us on what its practitioners have discovered about what is "really out there." On this view, scientific truth consists in getting that description and interpretation "right." Once this right mapping is obtained, it is possible to offer up universal truths about the world around us. Cartesians believe that if science is done right, the human mind becomes a flawless mirror of nature.

Pragmatists insist that this program of earnest representationalism is incoherent. Notice that the standard Cartesian story starts with the idea that there is but one reality. From this, human language—words, sentences, paragraphs—becomes the mediating tool that connects the alleged reality to the rest of us. Descriptions of that reality are true to the extent that they capture all of the pertinent information that is available to be captured. Subsequent descriptions keep adding to the thickness of the one abiding description until, at some point, it will become obvious to all who care that the *true truth* (the "real reality") has now been rendered. Once that has been settled, we can all move on to add to (or to become users of) the enhanced thickness of the description of a different piece of reality. Human history is seen as a continual process of getting the descriptions truer and truer—getting them right.

Pragmatism finds this conception to be quaint, futile, and teleological. Pragmatism insists that we formulate descriptions of what is called "reality" as we go about the need to reconcile ourselves to that reality. We never get it exactly right for the simple reason that there is no such thing as "exactly right." Or, we can never get it exactly right because we have no way to assess the "rightness" of competing descriptions. There is no independent authority to whom we might turn to help us judge rightness. There is no "other" to mediate for us. Instead, we stop writing new descriptions—we stop adding to the thickness of existing descriptions— when one description emerges that gains acceptance as being good enough for current purposes. Here is, at last, a description that works. This description has cash value. The extensive system of equations that deliver a tiny spacecraft, over the period of several years, to a far-off planet is not "correct" or "right" by the evidence of some external "other" who looks in on them and thus pronounces them to represent the "truth." That system of equations is correct because it delivered the spacecraft to its intended target. The engineers desired to hit a far-off target—an outcome in the future for the sake of which the equations were written down— and the equations did their expected task. The system of equations is the right system because it has shown itself capable of doing valuable (desired) work. What more is there to say?

Let us consider this general idea with respect to individual choice and action.

Volitional Pragmatism and Individual Action

Pragmatism starts from a fundamental denial that the human mind is a mirror of nature. Instead, pragmatists insist that our individual comprehensions of the settings and circumstances within which we are situated are necessarily limited to impressions of the world around us. And, most important, different individuals necessarily formulate and hold different impressions. There are, to be sure, objects and events "out there" in the world, but there are no universal and objectively "true" descriptions of the objects and events in that world; there are only impressions. Pragmatists insist that there is no single true and reliable report to be sent back by earnest observers and reporters who venture out into some singular reality. To put the matter another way, claims of "truth" about the world around us are a property of statements about that world. Truth is not a property of objects and events—the "thing in itself." Rather, truth is a property of statements about objects and events. Individuals do not discuss (and argue about) objects and events; they discuss and argue about statements about, and descriptions of, objects and events.

As sapient beings, each of us apprehends settings and circumstances within which we are situated, but especially as we move through new settings and circumstances. These apprehended phenomena become our impressions of those settings and circumstances. Such impressions are just that—acquired sensory signals (signs) as we contemplate our situatedness in a particular constellation of settings and circumstances. These impressions are the raw material of our understanding of our situatedness, but they are of little value until they have been transformed into coherent stories that we can express to ourselves and to others. When we describe these impressions to ourselves and to others, these descriptions and redescriptions constitute our expressions about the world around us. In other words, as individuals we create expressions of our situatedness from the impressions we have formed about that situatedness. To a certain extent, this idea accords well with Damasio's "autobiographical self" (Damasio 1999). These expressions are the stories we tell to ourselves and to others. More important, these expressions form the mental stage on which we live. This stage constitutes our individually perceived and individually constructed "reality." And that is all there is to say about it. It will not be your "reality," nor will it be my "reality." This particular reality "belongs to" the individual who created it. We might say that this particular reality is constitutive of the individual to whom it belongs.

We spend our waking hours apprehending impressions and formulating expressions of those apprehended signs. I earlier suggested that the essence of living is incessant doing. Following Peirce, the instigator of our impressions is surprise. *Surprise* is the necessary condition for us to take notice of the world around us and to process those received impressions. After all, if one fails to notice particular settings and circumstances, then this disregard implies familiarity, and hence the observation is fleeting and of little moment. Notice that certain settings and circumstances are either ignored (itself an action that dismisses the impressions without further action because they are not "surprising") or are processed as novel impressions. Those novel impressions become new expressions. Why is that car turning toward me? What does that house look like on the inside? I have never noticed those weeds before; why are they so profuse? Why is my roof leaking? We see that surprise triggers mental processes that confront settled habits of mind and induce us to form abductive syllogisms. Individual thought and action are abductively informed and animated. Surprise confounds our settled belief—our habits of mind—and brings about thought. And the sole purpose of thought is to remove doubt—to fix belief.

As we form abductive syllogisms about our constructed situatedness, we are at the same time negotiating our situatedness in the panoply of those impressions. From the conjunction of these impressions and inferences about the world being experienced, and our place in that world—and from the meanings we then attribute to these impressions, inferences, and situatedness—we abductively construct plausible inferences about the need to act and about the best actions to take in the light of the abductive belief just formulated. Here I find helpful Shackle's concept of "created imaginings" (Shackle 1961). Expressions are stories we tell ourselves about our present situatedness. Created imaginings are stories we tell ourselves about possible future situatedness.

Notice that the essential function of expressions is to constitute (to construct) the mental stage onto which we might then project our imaginings of future outcomes to see how they will "play out," how they will plausibly materialize. The central idea here is not just the positing of created imaginings in the abstract. It is, rather, our created imaginings projected onto the stage of our emergent expressions. It is here that we formulate the reasons that will come to provide the grounds for choosing among the array of plausible created imaginings. Individual choice and action are a contest, a struggle, between expressions and imaginings. We are necessarily situated in a constructed reality (an expression), and we continually reflect on alternative created imaginings. This deliberation consists in checking these imaginings against our expressions of the present and of the imagined future. Volitional pragmatism holds that we act when we find a feasible created imagining that satisfies expectations about situated outcomes in the future. And, of course, we also act when we reject all created imaginings (perhaps because they seem infeasible) and stick with our current action trajectory. To do nothing is to do something.

Volitional Pragmatism and Joint Action

With this account of individual action in hand, we may now focus on the problem of action involving more than one individual. The difficulty here should be obvious. The foremost burden in joint action is the necessity to deal with a multitude of contending expressions. It is in the nature of being individuals that we necessarily formulate and hold individualized expressions of the world around us; we are different autobiographical selves. Of course, most of us will agree that lamps are lamps, but the more pertinent issues go beyond this superficial identification of what the object appears to be. Is that lamp an antique? Does that lamp give enough light for reading? Why does that lamp tilt? Did that lamp cost as much as it would appear? How can he afford such a fine lamp? Is that lampshade dirty or is that its "real" color? Why would he have such an outrageous lamp in an otherwise tasteful room?

Notice the constituents of expressions in this string of questions: antique, light, tilt, income, cost, ambiguous lampshade, outrageous, and tasteful. We see that a lamp is not merely a lamp. Instead, a lamp is a series of effects constituting expressions to differentially situated observers. As Peirce insisted, the meaning of an object to us is nothing but the sum of its perceived effects (Peirce 1934). We create our expressions by collecting, sorting, and redescribing to ourselves the sum of our impressions of the effects of the subjects of our apprehended senses. Beauty is not a property inherent in certain objects, the thing in itself. Rather, to paraphrase Louis Menand, beauty is an effect produced by some objects (but not by other objects). And this produced effect will strike different individuals quite differently. Similarly, different individuals will ask themselves quite different questions about that lamp. In this sense, the lamp will create quite different expressions to different people. Is a lamp just a lamp?

The obvious difficulty in joint action is that everyone else is doing the same thing, although to quite different effect. It follows that each of us will apprehend a slightly different situatedness and thus that each of us will have quite distinct expressions about the world "as it is" and about our place in that world. It could not be otherwise because we are, by definition, different sapient beings. In the context of joint action, this means that there is not a single stage (expression) upon which our quite independent and disparate created imaginings are to be projected. Instead, there are as many "stages" as there are participants in the community whose task it is to ascertain but a single course of action for the future. And here, recall that the pertinent "community" could be a parliament, a legislative committee, a board of directors, a group of judges, a jury, a family, or a village council. This implies that there is an equally plentiful multitude of created imaginings being projected onto the multiple stages by those holding quite distinct expressions. And we wonder why collective action is contentious? Collective action forces all participants to agree on the many aspects (effects) of the lamp.

We see that the central challenge in collective action is for the pertinent decision group(s) to work out a reconciliation of the multitude of expressions and imaginings about the future. Notice that the issue here is not one of discovering the "right" expression out of the multitude of contending expressions. Nor is the issue to discover the "right" created imagining to fit the "right" expression. Indeed, as noted previously, the notion of rightness is precisely the wrong description of the process followed by those faced with the necessity of collective choice. The task, instead, is to focus on the various reasons for the disparate expressions, and for the disparate imaginings. Progress in such difficult matters is to be found in reasoned debate. Pragmatists put the matter as the asking for and giving of reasons (Brandom 1994, 2000). Those who come to the choice problem with their mind made up invoke absolutes where reasons are in order. And for some participants, those absolutes are precisely their reasons. However, the only thing to be said for such absolutes is that they give us a moral holiday from having to think hard about the difficult choices we face. Only in pragmatism are individuals forced to do the hard analytical work of figuring out what seems better, at the moment, to do. Absolutists know what is best (not merely better) by way of a priori revelations. Pragmatists insist that those who advance absolutist claims share with us the reasons for their convictions. To quote Hans Joas:

> In pragmatism, precisely because it considers all psychical operations in the light of their functionality for action, it becomes impossible to hold the position that the setting of an end is an act of consciousness per se that occurs outside of contexts of action. Rather, the setting of an end can only be the result of reflection on resistances met by conduct that is oriented in a number of different ways. Should it prove impossible to follow simultaneously all the various guiding impulses or compulsions to action, a selection of a dominant motive can take place which then, as an end, dominates the other motives or allows them to become effective only in a subordinate manner. . . . action is teleological only in a diffuse fashion. Even our perception is shaped by our capacities and the possibilities for action. (Joas 1993, p. 21)

We see here recognition of the many images of action, and we see that the setting of ends outside of the context of action is psychologically impossible. That is, the prior specification of created imaginings is impossible until those who must act are in a position (a context) to act. And for collective action, being in the context of action means being surrounded by others with divergent expressions, yet resolutely on the way to formulating their own unique and divergent created imaginings. Why would we assume that individuals should have identical expressions of the world in which they find themselves? Joint action is contentious, ab initio, because of the reality of contending expressions. Because joint action must ultimately result in but a single choice (coordinated and coincident action), contending expressions are inevitably confronted by contending created imaginings. Small wonder that collective action—public policy—is so difficult. The participants in that process bring differing expressions about the status quo ante, and quite different created imaginings about the prospects for the future.

Rather than dwell on the processes whereby a workable synthesis emerges from this expressional cacophony, let us instead recognize that such a synthesis does indeed emerge, for without that synthesis there could be no collective action. So the interesting problem here is not to question the existence of this or that emergent synthesis—the decision reached. The problem is how we might look upon that synthesis and how we might describe it. And this brings us to the benediction applied to that decision (to that synthesis). This synthesis, the emergent decision, has but one pertinent property, its acceptance by those charged with formulating a course forward.

What, precisely is signified by that acceptance? Would we say that the process, and the many participants, generated a decision that no one wanted? This is doubtful. Would we be right to discredit particular collective decisions because these decisions represented a "compromise"? On the presumption that there is nothing automatically despicable about compromise, the more likely description is that the decision represented the "consensus" of the body charged with reaching a decision in this particular matter. And what exactly is meant here by *consensus*? The pragmatist would suggest that this word is simply another way of saying that the decision seemed, to all (most?) participants, to be the best thing to do under the circumstances. Is this but another way of saying that this particular act seemed, at the moment, the right thing to do? If this action is the "best" and it is "right," then what is left for us to say about it? The pragmatist would suggest, without irony, that we might as well bestow the ultimate benediction on the decision. On the way to doing that, the pragmatist might well regard the decision as evidence of the emergence of settled belief about what ought to be done. Recall that truth is not a property of objects and events in our situatedness. Truth is, instead, a property of propositions and claims about the objects and events in that situatedness. We have, in other words, the emergence of a collective commitment to a way forward, the truth content of which is no longer in dispute.

Can we therefore call this decision "the truth" concerning the best way forward? We can certainly refer to it as a truth claim. That is, this decision and the action it entails is claimed by the participants in the decision to be a good thing to do. Because truth is a property of propositions and statements, the claim that this act is (or seems to be) the best thing to do under the present circumstances constitutes a statement *about* something. It is a proposition with truthful content. Pragmatism suggests to us that truth is the compliment we pay to our settled deliberations.

VOLITIONAL PRAGMATISM AS A THEORY OF SETTLED BELIEF

> [O]ne may say that truth is a matter of collective judgment and that it is stabilized by the collective actions which use it as a standard for judging other claims.
> —Steven Shapin, *A Social History of Truth* (1994)

The foregoing account suggests that the collective choice (decision) process is one of reconciling contending expressions and imaginings and that this is an essential activity leading to the formulation of what seems best, in the eyes of the individual (or of the group), to do. Individuals and groups work out what seems best by working out what seems possible as they work their way toward what they will come to realize seems best. The process entails not only working out the best means but also the best ends. Notice that this account is at odds with the decision process as envisaged by many economists. In that standard approach, individuals (and groups) start with a clear end (goal) in mind, they gather evidence of the costs and efficacy of alternative means for reaching that end, and they then select the most advantageous means for achieving that predetermined end. The "best" means is the one in which the net economic value (benefits of the end minus costs of the means) is as large as possible. Notice here the naive presumption of a clear distinction between ends and means, and notice that ends and means do not change in the course of calculating the "best" means to reach the predetermined end. On this account of the choice process, economics is strictly instrumental to optimal choices over ends that remain unexamined and beyond the ambit of economic analysis. This approach is consistent with the insistence of Lionel Robbins (and others who accepted his word for it) that economics is the science of allocating scarce resources among competing and limitless ends—the assessment of which is not an economic matter.

Ironically, this process is not at all about choice; it is about calculation. As we have seen earlier, in assessing this realm of economics, G.L.S. Shackle was moved to comment that:

> The escape we have suggested consists not in abandonment of rationality, not in abandonment of the adoption of the means which will lead to the selected end, but in abandonment of the postulate that the avail-

able ends are given. The escape from necessity . . . lies in the *creation of ends*, and this is possible because ends, so long as they remain available and liable to rejection or adoption, must inevitably be experiences by imagination or anticipation and not by external occurrence. Choice, inescapably, is choice amongst thoughts, and thoughts . . . are not *given*. (Shackle 1961, p. 273)

Choice is choice among thoughts, and thoughts are not given but created from impressions and imaginings. Shackle's theory of choice, elaborated in his *Decision, Order and Time* (1961) is consistent with, and a central component of, the volitional pragmatism developed here. What remains is to extend that theory to address the matter of whether or not "correct" and "rational" decisions can be said to emerge. In other words, the problem now becomes one of judging the decisions reached—such judgment being essential before we will know if welfaristic truth claims can be (or ought to be) relied upon to rectify the allegedly flawed decisions that would otherwise emanate from individuals and groups. Those committed to consequentialist welfarism are quite certain that their prescriptive assertions (truth claims) are necessary to rescue individual and collective action from incoherence and irrationality. But, as we have seen, welfarism fails the necessary condition for coherence; it lacks general acceptance within the discipline from which it emerges. Moreover, it lacks legitimacy among some writers in philosophy, psychology, and law. In other words, its concepts, its relations, and its entailments are deemed incoherent by a significant portion of theoretical economists who have explored this particular body of economics. Welfarism and its policy prescriptions fail the test of warranted belief.

The second issue to be discussed concerns whether consequentialist welfarism, despite its lack of disciplinary coherence, is "close enough" that it might offer essential guidance to generate more "rational" decisions for individuals and for collective action by groups. Does consequentialist welfarism promise help in the nature of "second-best" decision protocols? To assess this question, we must explore the decision problem from a slightly different angle.

The standard economic approach is to identify the correct decision protocols for reaching the correct decision. The logic is that if the right decision protocols are followed, the resulting decision will, by definition, be correct. That is, correct decision protocols are the cause of correct choices (decisions), and correct decisions are the effect of employing correct decision protocols. While this would seem to resemble Simon's procedural rationality, this protocol is implicated in choice that is claimed to be substantively rational as well (Simon 1987). Pragmatists would suggest that many economists have cause and effect confused. Rather, pragmatism suggests to us that the identification of the correct decision is something that occurs after a consensus has been reached regarding what seems best to do. Here the cause of the correct decision is not some external truth rule (a "correct" decision protocol) but rather the assiduous working out of—the diligent searching for—what seems the better thing to do in the current setting and circumstances. Once that has been worked out, the emergent choice becomes the correct choice by virtue of having been worked out. After all, would it not be surprising to discover that an individual (or a group) decided to do something that had been identified as clearly not the best thing to do at the time? Peirce insisted that "The opinion which is fated to be ultimately agreed to by all who investigate, is what we mean by the truth, and the object represented in this opinion is the real. That is the way that I would explain reality" (Peirce 1934, p. 405).

The arrival at a consensus about what is better to do is always predicated upon a clear but evolving notion of the purposes of the future—an outcome in the future for the sake of which action must be taken today. Recall that this is what philosophers call *final cause*. Purpose is central to pragmatism, and settled belief about both purpose and how to get there represents the essence of "correct" thoughts and belief about the appropriate action to be taken. Richard Rorty insists that the right question to ask is, "For what purposes would it be useful to hold that belief?" (Rorty 1999, p. xxiv). He sees this question as rather akin to asking, For what purposes would it be useful to load that particular program onto my computer? Pragmatists insist that science and religion are each perfectly legitimate activities for acquiring and categorizing belief, though of course for quite different purposes. We see, at once, that the venerable struggle, often approaching hostility, between science and religion is a product of the frequently obstinate view from both sides that each alone possesses THE TRUTH. If it could be understood that truth is that which, at the moment, seems most useful to believe, and that all truths are dedicated to particular purposes, then religious belief and scientific belief could quite easily coexist without a fight. For the rest of us, the issue is straightforward: do not ask clerics to provide lasting relief from hemorrhoids and heartburn, and do not ask scientists to preside at weddings and funerals.

Let us return to the matter of valuable belief. When economists offer specific prescriptions about collective choice—indicating which decisions are efficient, correct, rational, best, and socially preferred—we see truth claims from a particular discipline projected onto the individual and collective stage of contending expressions and contending created imaginings about what is best for the future of those persons (and their descendants) responsible for these contested expressions and contested created imaginings. The pragmatist would challenge these truth claims by asking the following question: can those specific truth claims be justified to all members of that particular community? If that justification is possible, then the truth claims are valuable. They are valuable because the community into which they are imposed finds them helpful, useful, edifying, decisive, and instrumental to improving the working out of what seems best to do in the current setting and circumstances. If those truth claims cannot be justified to the members of the community, then such claims are counterfeit. They are counterfeit only because the community finds them to be impertinent to the task they currently face.

Again, the issue here is not truth but justified claims. The pragmatist would ask whether welfaristic truth claims are capable of being justified to an audience of individuals who stand to be affected one way or the other by our "socially preferred" or "optimal" policies. The pragmatist would want to discuss the sovereign nature of truth claims emanating from prescriptive economics. By *sovereign* I mean here the ruling nature of welfaristic truth claims. Specifically, the pragmatist would ask the following question: "Why, exactly, are the truth claims of welfare economics more pertinent to this particular choice setting than, say, the truth claims of psychology?" And the pragmatist would be quick to rule out of bounds the automatic reply from the economist that economics is "the science of choice." Such tendentious claims raise their own pragmatic challenge. Specifically, is it a true statement that "economics is the science of choice"? Could this particular claim be sustained before an audience of psychologists, sociologists, and psychiatrists? It seems quite unlikely that it could. On the other hand, a slight modification would enhance the odds of it being true: "Economics is *one* of the sciences of human decision making, along with philosophy, psychiatry, and psychology—and perhaps astrology." It is likely that this latter proposition could be justified to a large pertinent community.

Economists need not feel singled out for special abuse here. After all, there are a variety of disciplines and specialized practices that also have structured prescriptions about what is the best thing to do in that particular choice situation. We might imagine hydraulic engineers, biologists, planners, lawyers, and water chemists each offering particular disciplinary prescriptions about what is best to do in matters of water pollution. We might imagine lawyers, sociologists, historians, social workers, and psychologists each offering particular disciplinary prescriptions about what is best to do in matters of poverty alleviation. However, because most economists have come to regard the discipline as *the* science of choice, having our truth claims ignored by decision makers strikes deep into our collective confidence, and often leads to charges of inscrutability on the part of policy makers. Of course, there are economic issues at stake in pollution policy and in poverty alleviation, just as there are in all policy matters. But the presence of economic implications does not, by that fact alone, authorize economics to become the dominant realm of reason.

We have here a debate about the true and the quest to justify claims about the true. I have earlier pointed out that pragmatism insists that the word *true* does not apply to events and objects in the world around us; rather, it applies to statements about events and objects in that world. In other words, truth is not a property of perfect correspondence between propositions (words) and particular events and objects to which those propositions (words) refer—between language and things (signs and objects). Truth is not denotative. Truth is, instead, a property of particular statements (words) about specific events and objects—between contending linguistic claims. Truth is connotative.

With this in hand, we can reconsider the truth claims about policies that are optimal, rational, efficient, or socially preferred. The pragmatist would ask whether those terms are properly denotative of present or future states in the world? That is, can one stipulate that there is a clear and valid connection between specific descriptive words such as "optimal" and specific events (new institutions) that might be predicated on that prescription? My earlier arguments insist that there is no such correspondence. Such terms of art cannot possibly describe actual outcomes in the "real" world. Instead, these terms (optimal, efficient, rational, socially preferred) refer to properties of the analytical engines (deductive models) constructed to divine the optimal (or the efficient or the socially preferred) policy. Such truth claims are entirely reflexive; they are self-referential.

IMPLICATIONS

Human choice and action is properly characterized as prospective volition—the human will in action, looking to the future, trying to determine how that future ought to unfold. As this process evolves, individuals (and groups of individuals) bring contending expressions and imaginings to the task of choice and action. Individuals (and groups) do not know precisely what they want until they are able to work out what they seem able to have. Surprise motivates action. This process of working out plausible futures entails the consideration of plausible imaginings in conjunction with existing expressions about current and future situatedness. Group action is more complicated than individual action because it requires reconciliation of disparate and contending individual expressions and imaginings until a consensus emerges, the properties of which are that this consensus is regarded as: (1) feasible, and (2) the best thing to do at this particular time. This process can be thought of as an exercise in pleading, resistance, persuasion, cautious acquiescence, and eventual emergence of a consensus.

The two properties of that consensus—feasible and best at this time—represent judgments reached by those individuals who are responsible for collective action. Notice that this judgment is something that can only emerge as individuals and groups contend with the need to reconcile disparate expressions and disparate created imaginings. The first step in this process of working out an emergent consensus is necessarily confined to legislators, administrators, and judges. In a democracy, the second step is to justify this agreement to the political community whose individual actions will be restrained, liberated, and expanded. In the absence of this justification, collective action will lack legitimacy. This justification to the larger political community necessarily entails the giving of reasons for the decision reached. The process of giving reasons must be carefully crafted so that the reasons given match as closely as possible the *asking for reasons* that is expected from the political community to whom the collective action is directed (Brandom 2000). This activity is properly thought of justification in the service of emergent consent.

This theory of choice (and action) stands in contrast to the deterministic and linear model that characterizes standard rational choice theory. Given the criticism of rational choice theory (Bowles 1998; Field 1979, 1981; Hodgson 1988, 1998; Rabin 1998), and the failure of coherence in consequentialist welfarism, it cannot be said that there is settled belief in the broader discipline of economics about individual and collective choice. Pragmatists insist that disciplinary belief that fails to satisfy minimal coherence standards from within that particular epistemic community cannot be the source of credible or compelling truth claims emanating from that discipline and subsequently directed at the larger community. Pragmatists further insist that, even if the proffered truth claims are deemed coherent by the discipline from which they spring, the projection of those truth claims into social choice situations is always tentative and contingent unless and until there is widespread acceptance on the part of those to whom the truth claims are directed. Sapient individuals retain the authority to reject, for their own reasons, the truth claims from any source. The status of valuable belief is a property bestowed upon assertions and claims by those to whom such assertions are directed. Valuable belief is not a property that can be claimed for disciplinary truths by those who produce that belief and advance correlated assertions. All that the producers of such "truth claims" can justifiably assert is that this particular belief enjoys wide agreement within the epistemic community out of which it arises. Even then, warranted belief is a benediction bestowed by the wider members of a discipline, not simply by those responsible for producing those assertions.

We see that prescriptive welfarism applied to public policy fails the pragmatist's conditions on both counts. First, welfare economics fails the test of coherence within economics; that is, Paretian economists do not bring warranted belief when they prescribe welfaristic claims to problems of collective action. Second, the truth claims about "optimal" or "socially preferred" policies are usually ignored by those to whom they are directed. These truth claims are ignored, I suggest, because decision makers find themselves either dubious or, if not dubious, quite unable to offer sufficient justifications to the broader citizenry to whom they are ultimately—in a democracy—accountable. Decision makers know that citizens demand justifications based on grounds that matter to them, and few citizens are waiting to be told that particular policies are Pareto optimal, or that they can be proved socially preferred by the application of potential compensation tests. To most listeners, this strategy fails the test of sufficient reason.

This does not mean that economic concepts and relations cannot provide valuable information to the process of working out what seems best to do (at this particular time) about specific problematic situations. But it does mean that economists must remain silent concerning what is best to do on the authority of Paretian concepts alone. And it means that economists must resist the temptation to criticize decisions for being irrational, inefficient, nonoptimal, or socially inferior to other more "welfare-enhancing" policies.

Volitional pragmatism insists that public policy cannot legitimately be held hostage to the prescriptive truth claims imposed on it by economists (or those from any other discipline). Volitional pragmatism employs abduction to uncover the reasons for particular policy choices. When we find reasons for choices, we will be on our way to the development of a theory of collective action and institutional change. That theory will require explicit recognition of the concepts of impressions, expressions, and created imaginings. That theory will require recognition that joint action in the policy arena entails the working out of contending expressions and created imaginings. It will require recognition that human agents cannot possibly articulate coherent and salient wants in isolation from the specific context of choice in which they learn about those wants as they learn about what they can have. Outside of this context, expressions of wants are mere cheap talk.

Public policy seeks to modify individual domains of choice by restraining, liberating, and expanding the opportunities and capacities of each of us to engage in particular activities. Policy is not some alien "intervention" into the otherwise wondrous "free market" of such appeal to some writers. Indeed, what some are pleased to call "the market" is simply the constructed artifact of prior collective action. Policy is nothing but a word we apply to a continual process of redefining—reconstructing—new realms of individual and group action. Public policy has been unnecessarily mystified by virtue of its having been embedded in the fictional logic of rational choice. If we could but see policy as a word that describes the incessant human quest for contending with surprise in the human condition, we would see that policy is not at all mysterious. Policy is simply choice and action in which groups of individuals work out what seems better, at the moment, to do. We do not need welfare economists telling us which of those plausible futures is socially preferred. We will figure that out for ourselves as we go about figuring out how to reconcile our contending expressions and contending created imaginings. Positivism is of no help here. Volitional pragmatism helps by reassuring us that it is perfectly acceptable—it is quite "natural"—to be confused about what seems better to want and to do. Confusion and surprise are the starting points of working out what seems better, at the moment, to do.

Volitional pragmatism forces us to confront the Myth of the Other. In the beginning, God was there to define for us what was good and right to do. Modernism pushed God aside, and High Philosophy quickly stepped in to provide guidance. Philosophy became our new Other. When philosophers became justifiably uneasy with this burden, the task was eagerly taken up in the middle of the twentieth century by welfare economists. Volitional pragmatism suggests that we have now outgrown our need for external truth rules to tell us what is the better thing to do. The Myth of the Other is precisely concerned with the idea that tough choices cannot usefully be turned over to God, or to philosophers, or to welfare economists. There is no Other—there is only us. And volitional pragmatism entails the working through of what we think we want by learning about what we seem able to have. Only then will we take responsibility for our decisions. When we have settled our deliberations, we will anoint those settled thoughts with the ultimate benediction—it seemed the best thing to do at this time. And we shall be happy with that decision, until the next surprise.

PART THREE

Volitional Pragmatism at Work

CHAPTER TEN

Thinking as a Pragmatist

> [T]he fundamental premise of pragmatism's theory of
> action . . . does not conceive of action as the pursuit of ends
> that the contemplative subject establishes a priori and then
> resolves to accomplish; the world is not held to be mere ma-
> terial at the disposal of human intentionality. Quite to the
> contrary, pragmatism maintains that we find our ends in the
> world, and that prior to any setting of ends we are already,
> through our praxis, embedded in various situations.
> —Hans Joas, *Pragmatism and Social Theory* (1993)

FINDING REASONS

Volitional pragmatism is concerned with the explanation of individual
and collective action and with economic outcomes. In that sense, volitional pragmatism concerns the asking for and giving of reasons. To illustrate what it means to think as a pragmatist and to consider public policy
from the perspective of volitional pragmatism, I explore here, in a very
general way, a selection of issues.

SMOKING IN PUBLIC PLACES

As we know, laws governing smoking in public places have undergone a
fairly pronounced change over a rather short period of time. Of course,
many laws change frequently, but the speed with which institutional arrangements governing such widespread (and addictive) behavior have
changed would seem to call for an explanation. Do we simply dismiss this
as a sudden shift in the relative "power" of smokers and nonsmokers?
Are there some "efficiency" explanations that might explain this rapid
institutional change? Are we any further toward an understanding of this
institutional change if we dismiss it as mere rent seeking behavior by nonsmokers? Or do we gain clarity on the matter by putting this down as a
mere redistribution of benefit streams (wealth positions) away from
smokers and toward nonsmokers? Pragmatism suggests a different and
more promising approach. Recall the abductive syllogism:

The surprising fact, C, is observed.
But if A were true, C would be a matter of course.
Hence, there is reason to suspect A is true.

Here the "surprising fact" is the fairly rapid change in the legal situation of smokers and nonsmokers. In virtually all public places, those who smoked were in a legal position of privilege, whereas the rest of us were defined by a situation of no right. If a nonsmoker had complained about the fellow at the next table puffing on a cigar (or pipe or cigarette), that person would have been informed by the manager of the restaurant that he—the offended diner—had no right to demand that the smoker be made to stop. The manager might have misspoken and informed the unhappy diner that the fellow who was smoking had a "right" to do so. We may forgive the manager for not knowing his Hohfeld, but the issue here concerns the rather pronounced rapidity with which—in America at least—smokers went from a situation of privilege with respect to smoking to one of duty (not to smoke in most public places). Those who objected to such behavior went from a situation of no right to one of a right (to be free of offending smoke). How might the pragmatist start the search for an explanation?

The "surprising fact" here is this rapid and widespread institutional change (C). Abduction brings us to focus on the constituents of A. That is, what hypotheses in A constitute the case for (reasons for and thus explanation of) the result? The search for A would start by a telling (a careful retelling) of the settings and circumstances surrounding smoking.

In the "beginning" (say, 1975), most smokers knew that their habit was not necessarily safe, but they seem to have weighed the supposed pleasures of their habit against the increasing volume of information about the heightened chances that lung disease would materialize in the future. By this time the "causal mechanism" (notice the mechanical nature here) was becoming rather well established by the scientific community. It would seem that there was an emergent warranted belief among those in the medical community, although there were certainly some doctors (perhaps smokers themselves) who continued to dispute the evolving body of evidence. The American Cancer Society was engaged in a major campaign to show smokers that lung cancer was a probable long-term implication of their habit. Were smokers following their preferences to the detriment of their welfare? This is thought by some economists to be impossible. Apparently, many smokers had weighed their "long-term welfare" and concluded that smoking was the better thing to do. The pragmatist would not invoke such mysterious notions as welfare and preferences. The pragmatist would simply say that, although the medical views concerning smoking and lung cancer soon came to represent warranted belief, many smokers apparently failed to find it valuable belief.

But there is more to the story, and in its elaboration we can begin to see volitional pragmatism at work with respect to an emerging theory of institutional change. Recall that there was a time when smoking was regarded as giving of high status and as an essential aspect of thoroughgoing social grace—such fixed belief and habit of mind having been largely created and perpetuated by major advertising campaigns by the industry. The rich and dandy flaunted their long cigarettes in elegant settings, while the poor grubbed about for cigarettes, even buying them individually out of a necessity to keep within a serious budget constraint. There could have been no doubt that smoking was the right thing to do. Social conditions, and that would include the institutional arrangements with respect to smoking, had both induced—and had become constituted by—the reigning belief, habit of mind, custom, and everyday practice. Smokers were doing what they believed in, and they believed in what they were doing. Notice that prevailing beliefs legitimize particular social practices, and these practices then provide a justification for particular institutional arrangements suited to those beliefs and practices. No one would have asked, "Why is that fellow smoking in the seat next to me (in this airplane)?" There was no irritation induced by doubt because doubt was never expressed (except, perhaps, by the occasional asthmatic).

But this situation of fixed belief would not last long. When public sentiment began to turn against smoking in public, the arguments were usually confined to the incompatible "interests" of smokers and nonsmokers. But it became apparent that one garners little support in public policy discussion by openly announcing specific interests in particular outcomes. Much better language is available. Specifically, those who smoked were quick to insist that they had a "right" to smoke and it was no one else's business (thereby denying the externalities associated with their habit). At the same time, nonsmokers insisted that they had a "right" to be free of unwanted smoke. What they should have said, and what they meant, is that they had an interest in not having smoke circling about their heads and getting into their nose and lungs. Suddenly, established habits of mind started to diverge.

The second phase of the struggle was joined when medical research began to suggest that "secondhand" smoke held plausible harm for nonsmokers. Suddenly the "mere" displeasure of nonsmokers became more difficult for smokers to ignore. Previously, nonsmokers could only complain that they did not enjoy smoky rooms and airplanes. But their discomfort was not taken very seriously. Only asthmatics and those suffering from related respiratory difficulties were able to take their discomfort beyond the simple loss of pleasure. Once secondhand smoke became recognized as a more general issue, not confined to those already afflicted with asthma, the former moral clarity about what seemed better to believe began to dissipate. Now, the presumed settled belief about the propriety of smoking was not so easily framed as the mere pleasure of smokers as against the mere displeasure of nonsmokers. New information scrambled fixed belief. The irritation of doubt set in.

The third phase in this institutional evolution was triggered by a few large wrongful-death lawsuits filed by relatives on behalf of longtime smokers who had died from various forms of lung and throat cancer. At this stage the strategy of the defendants (cigarette companies) was to frame the struggle as one of free choice exercised by smokers. The companies claimed that those who smoked were doing so willingly and therefore how could there be any legal liability? Warning labels on packages of cigarettes emerged at this time but not without a fight from the tobacco companies. That fact was used, as well by the defendants, showing that despite the warnings these individuals had continued to smoke. During this phase, however, new information emerged from the legal struggles: documents were discovered that implicated the tobacco companies in a decades-long campaign to make sure that smokers lost their ability to stop smoking. That is, great expense had been incurred to make cigarettes even more addictive than they might otherwise have been.

This evidence of a long-standing strategy to make cigarettes more addictive appears to have been decisive in further scrambling previous fixed belief. And that decisiveness is related to the pragmatist's emphasis on purpose—as in, "for what purpose would it be useful for cigarette companies to do that?" Stated in the language of final cause: actions are explained by the purposes they serve. Or, in more formal terms, that purpose is an outcome in the future for the sake of which a particular action today is found to be instrumental. Now we see that the new "surprising fact" in this story is not the speed with which a general ban on smoking in public places arose. Rather, we now have: what is the case (assumption or hypothesis) that might explain this new surprise (the discovery of efforts to make cigarettes more addictive)? What is the reason for this particular surprising result? A plausible hypothesis is that the cigarette companies wished to make it ever more difficult for smokers to abandon their habit of smoking. It seems reasonable to presume that the tobacco industry emerged, as with any consumer-goods industry, with the purpose of selling tobacco products to those who wanted them. But along the way the desire for yet more sales, and the desire to insulate current and future sales from an unwanted reduction, led to a series of practices that had as their purpose (their justification) the locking in of smokers to their habit. When it was discovered that the tobacco industry had lied about its product and had taken action to make cigarettes (more) addictive, outrage—and more legal claims—soon followed.

And this brings us to the final phase in this evolution toward new fixed belief. The central idea here is that the purpose of the tobacco industry was transformed from one of providing a product to those who desired it to a quite different purpose—to make sure that current and future customers lost their ability to control their consumption of that product. It seems that the tobacco industry was discovered to be selling addiction rather than a product. With that new information in hand, those who were opposed to smoking in public places suddenly had much better reasons than they had been able to muster at the beginning of the struggle over the institutions governing smoking in public places. And with those new reasons in hand, bans on smoking in public places spread very quickly. Suddenly smoking was not described as a situation of no law but became one of a right for nonsmokers to be free of unwanted smoke and for smokers to be under a duty to smoke only in a few places (mostly outdoors).

Human action is motivated by which reasons seem, at the time, the better ones to believe. Institutional change is, as Shackle might remind us, about competing thoughts, and thoughts can only be imagined. But the imagining of competing thoughts brings us immediately to the idea that institutional change concerns a contest over who is able to marshal the more compelling reasons for abandoning existing habits of mind (fixed belief). Institutional change starts with giving people new and more compelling reasons to work out new fixed belief. In the case of smoking in public places, the complicity of the tobacco companies was decisive in shifting beliefs. Institutional change was not far behind.

Mad Cows

News of "mad cow disease" in Britain, and apparent isolated outbreaks in Spain and Germany, precipitated public reactions that seemed extreme and irrational given the actual odds of a threat to humans. One infected animal in Spain and one in Germany were sufficient to spark the most intense display of individual and official outrage. Beef sales in Germany dropped by 50 percent when the news first spread, and remained low for an extended period of time thereafter. If this matter were approached in a traditional way, it might be easy to conclude that these reactions are overdone. What, after all, are the chances that someone will actually acquire new-variant Creutzfeldt-Jakob (nvC-J) disease by eating meat from a cow with bovine spongiform encephalopathy (BSE)? Conventional risk assessments would suggest that most people (and the governments of several European countries) were irrational in their overreaction to these minor events. However, what seems rational on the basis of simple statistics (often called the "risks") concerning the chances of infection leads us to a dead end in this situation. Something more is needed if we are to understand and to explain these immoderate reactions. We see here an example of "framing effects" from prospect theory (Kahneman and Tversky 1979; Tversky and Kahneman 1987). The pragmatist starts with the abductive syllogism:

> The surprising fact, C, is observed.
> But if A were true, C would be a matter of course.
> Hence, there is reason to suspect A is true.

Here, the surprising fact C is an immoderate reaction by governments to the very small odds of an outbreak of BSE and the associated exposure by the human population to nvC-J. What can possibly explain this extreme reaction? That is, what is the case (A) that, if true, would render C quite expected rather than anomalous? One hypothesis is that governments are unwilling to be seen as indifferent in the face of public health crises. Another hypothesis is that the integrity of a nation's food supply is not amenable to "ordinary" risk assessment. But there is more to the story, and here abduction invites us to persist beyond the obvious.

Specifically, in the course of uncovering information about the origins of BSE in cattle, it became widely known that a common protein supplement consists of ground up body parts from sheep and perhaps cattle. As we saw in the preceding section, the revealed and quite surprising behavior of the cigarette industry—working hard to remove from consumers the ability to exercise real choice over whether they continued to smoke—emerged as the plausible decisive factor in explaining the quick turn against cigarette companies (and smokers). In the present case, consumers were quite surprised (just shocked!) to learn that cattle had been fed the body parts of other animals. Are there no other protein sources available? What is the purpose of this? Is this really necessary?

When it became common knowledge that cows developed BSE after being fed infected sheep tissue, the question on many minds was: "And why, exactly, are cows—serious herbivores—eating body parts?" The answer to this question was, apparently, that doing so had something to do with the saving of money. Someone would surely point out that it was obviously "efficient" to do this or the industry would not have done it. While this approach (justification) apparently satisfied a few people, the rest of the general public was surprised and appalled. This surprise introduced a decisive element into the emergent mad cow policy debate. Suddenly members of the public, worried members of the medical profession, and angry politicians began to ask whether it was really necessary to feed unwanted sheep parts to cows? Some were prompted to ask questions along the following lines: what is the purpose of the food system, anyway? Is it to recycle otherwise superfluous sheep parts? The immoderate public reaction to the outbreak of mad cow disease reflected obvious horror at the prospects of unsafe food and outrage at the feeding of body parts to cows. With this new information in hand (this "surprise"), mad cow disease immediately moved from the realm of accident to the realm of scandal (Stone 1989). Are carnivorous cows accidental? Was this practice really necessary?

Of course, a number of institutional changes soon followed that immediately prohibited the feeding of animal parts to cows. Here is an institutional change that is quite easily attributable to the emergence of surprising information, such information quickly galvanizing collective action to redefine realms of individual action for members of the livestock industry. As a result, this particular industry was suddenly restrained in what choices it could take with respect to the diet of cattle, and the rest of us were liberated (we hope) from the likely prospect of acquiring new-variant Creutzfeldt-Jakob disease as we go about the business of enjoying our latest steak or hamburger. The food system still passes along risks, but the chances of getting nvC-J from eating beef have probably dropped somewhat. Is this "rational" public policy? Was a benefit-cost study undertaken to assess this collective action? The pragmatist would respond by suggesting that rationality is acting according to revealed preferences. And the evidence would seem to suggest that the expressed (revealed) preferences for the diet of beef cattle have suddenly undergone a dramatic change. The persistent economist might be expected then to ask whether it was "rational" for our preferences to shift so dramatically? At this point the pragmatist might gently point out that economists have no idea about preferences because we observe choices and then *infer* (economists would say "recover" as if there were something real out there to go looking for) preferences from choices. Finally, the pragmatist would insist that if one believes in consumer sovereignty, and if one believes that most consumers are reasonably alert to the information they receive and process, it is inconsistent for an economist to say anything at all. Indeed, the economist would be well advised to adopt the pragmatist's position that there is now a new constellation of settled belief about what seems better to do with respect to the dietary composition of cattle. And that is the end of the matter—until the next surprise.

JUGGLED GENES

The controversy over genetically modified organisms (GMOs) may be usefully viewed from the perspective of volitional pragmatism. In contrast to regulations over smoking or cattle feed, here we see technical possibilities and social wariness. The moral issue here is captured by the idea of, Ought we to do what we are able to do? The other idea central to this discussion is the presumption of social beneficence that inevitably accompanies the scientific enterprise. Few scientists embark on a career, and fewer still work long hours in the laboratory, motivated by the commitment to create something that will be seriously harmful to society. As with the prospector in search of gold, the scientist is motivated by the thought that every day she or he is getting closer to something both useful and valuable. So we should not be surprised to hear that the scientific community responsible for creating genetically modified products is quite convinced of the manifold benefits of such technology. We see this in how scientists talk about their own work, and how they characterize the scientific quest in general. Science is the search for new knowledge, and few can seriously doubt that new knowledge is wonderful and beneficial to all.

When new knowledge concerns better ways to do traditional tasks most people are open to those endearing prospects, particularly when these new ways are cheaper, easier, faster, and safer than the old ways. But when new knowledge comes embodied in a new object—a seed, a particular kind of electric generating station—then excitement is often replaced by ambivalence. Those responsible for the new discovery will claim overarching social benefit to almost everyone. Such claims are very often accompanied by assurances that there are no known risks associated with this new discovery. And, just as predictably, others will dismiss these assurances as yet another instance of technological optimism. In the case of GMOs, those who are wary of such technology will assert that the very novelty of it, and the long time span over which adverse effects can materialize, imply that there are no reliable means whereby the plausible risks can be measured and assessed.

Moreover, those wary of GMOs may reject a priori risk assessments of such technologies. For this they are criticized for refusing to accept the logic and the evidence of the scientific community. Those in favor of such technologies will claim to be dealing with the facts, while they will accuse the opponents of being Luddites and of appealing to nothing but mere emotion. Indeed, it is not uncommon to hear the advocates of new technology insisting that public policy about technical change should be guided by "the science" and not by emotion and political posturing that is the preferred retreat of the scientifically naive. It may also be noticed that the advocates for new technology will often talk in a way that the absence of proof of risk is suddenly transformed into proof of the absence of risk.

The issue, however, is not as straightforward as the technological optimists might wish. Skepticism about the manifold wonders of GMOs will not be resolved by the display of data about the lack of proof of risks. Nor will it be resolved by accusing the opponents of being Luddites. Those opposed to GMOs are sometimes held accountable for the persistent starvation and misery of millions of the world's most fragile individuals. This is surprising because the technological optimists usually accuse the opponents of such technology of engaging in emotional arguments, while the scientists (usually the advocates) claim that they "stick to the facts."

Let us consider two important aspects of this struggle viewed from the perspective of volitional pragmatism. First, notice the existence of two quite distinct families of created imaginings. I call these *families* of imaginings because the various aspects of each dominant view will be formulated so as to appear coherent and connected. Those responsible for the scientific discovery can be expected to formulate and to advance wonderful expressions of our current situatedness, and onto that stage they might then lead a marvelous array of connected imaginings that reveal this particular scientific advance to be related to many others that we know from the past, and ought to be excited about in the future. We would not be surprised to hear the names of Pasteur, Curie, Pauling, and Salk offered up as plausible predecessors in the inescapable march toward improving the human condition. On the other hand, the skeptic will be adept at developing a rival stage of expressions onto which quite different yet connected imaginings are led and portrayed—all of them having some known demerits, or promising quite unpleasant outcomes in the future. Notice that the two protagonists are not talking about any particular known future because, as Shackle reminds us, outcomes in the future cannot be objectively known except as thoughts and imaginings. Notice as well that the contending conversations will conform to the Peircean pragmatic maxim: "Consider what effects, that might conceivably have practical bearings, we conceive the object of our conception to have. Then, our conception of these effects is the whole of our conception of the object" (Peirce 1934, p. 1).

Here it is apparent that both sides to this contentious conversation will structure their imaginings in terms of the effects of the object under debate. To the scientist, all of the effects will be positive. To the skeptic, all of the effects will be unwanted. Where is the "truth" in this fight? Unfortunately, there is no truth in this fight. Both parties can be accused of exaggerating the "facts" and of twisting the "truth." But such assertions are of little avail. Pragmatists would urge us to get beyond the search for "truth," and this is especially important if there is a tendency to presume that the truth is to be found with one of the two contending positions. Rather, pragmatism asks us to focus on the question: "For what purposes would it be useful for the two parties to hold their respective beliefs?" This approach will not assure clarity of thought because we are still left with dramatically disparate created imaginings. But it might help. And pragmatism suggests that we must dig down beneath the two stories in a difficult quest for which of the two contending imaginings seems to offer us the most compelling reasons to fix our belief one way or the other. Each position will suggest, or will be suggestive of, new avenues of inquiry that might clear up particular confusions. But eventually the matter will be decided the only way that it can be decided—by one vision of created imaginings capturing the ground that seems better, at this time, to occupy.

Notice that there is, as always, a role for the idea of purpose. Those who are agnostic about the wonders of GMOs will speculate about the purpose behind their introduction. The controversy over the terminator gene—in which farmers would be unable to save and use genetically modified seed in subsequent years—reveals just how central the idea of purpose can be in economic policy. Skeptics were quick to speculate that the "real" purpose of the seed companies was to "hook" farmers on particular seeds, just as tobacco companies had done to smokers. Of course, the advocates of GMOs can find equally noxious purposes behind the opposition to those products. They are social pests looking for yet another way to cause trouble and impede progress. That is *their* purpose.

The issue is not whether GMOs are good or bad. The issue is that disputes such as this are the everyday stuff of public policy. Welfaristic calculations are not merely impertinent to such debates; they are counter-productive to the necessity of asking for and giving of reasons.

Toward Clear Thinking

Collective deliberation and action concerning the specific institutional arrangements pertaining to such social practices as smoking in public places, about the diet of cattle, and about the use of genetically modified organisms in the food system require honest conversations and the search for good reasons by which belief can be fixed. Volitional pragmatism insists that the rest of us listen to the assertions from the scientific community and find our own reasons to be persuaded, or to remain skeptical. It is difficult to marshal compelling reasons that can seriously challenge the presumed "authority" of science. In today's world, the assertions that emerge from the scientific community carry considerable social heft. Whereas the church at one time told us what to believe about the world around us, today it is the business—the purpose—of science to tell the rest of us what we ought to believe about obscure and complex matters.

But those who challenge the technological optimists in the scientific community deserve more than rude dismissal (being labeled Luddites) or ridicule for acting on something as unreliable as "emotions." Such conversations are not well served by reference to scientific "truths" trumping the flawed rhetoric of "mere opinion." Neither is the struggle for what seems better to do much helped by the fiction that all technical change is presumptively wonderful unless proved otherwise. Notice that this standard approach to controversy puts the burden of proof on those most handicapped in the quest for alternative compelling reasons. This handicap is compounded if advocates from the scientific community are allowed to define the terms of the debate—that is, to define what are and what are not "legitimate" reasons. This clearly privileges one side of the debate over the other. Of course, scientists can often advance warranted assertions. But pragmatism holds that others retain the obligation and the opportunity to consider warranted assertions and to judge those assertions in terms of the reasons that matter to them. Democracy is incompatible with the subtle yet pervasive authoritarianism of science. Volitional pragmatism insists that those who speak with the authority of science owe it to the rest of us to justify their assertions—their truth claims—in terms that we find compelling. In democratic market economies, the citizens retain the authority to decide if and when scientific assertions constitute valuable belief.

CHAPTER ELEVEN

Volitional Pragmatism and Explanation

> [P]rogress in economics does not come merely from the mechanical application of hypothesis tests to data sets. There is a creative act associated with the construction of new models that is also crucial to the process.
> —Paul Romer, *The Origins of Endogenous Growth* (1994)

FIXING BELIEF

A major theme here concerns how it is that economists come to "know" what we think we know about particular events or outcomes. Paul Romer captures, to a large extent, how many economists contend with the difficult matter of explanation. Ordinarily a deductive model is constructed based upon the axioms of economics, some plausible assumptions, and a few applicability postulates. The structure of this analytical engine is inevitably driven by what data the economist believes to be available from secondary sources. Notice that the choice of data, to a large extent, preordains the structure of the model (the analytical engine) and therefore the constituents of the "explanation" that will emerge from the empirical work. If the data are not ideal for the "explanatory" variables to be included, then it is necessary to redefine the variables so that they comport with available data or to use data that are less than ideal. Once the model is estimated, some of the variables (and we may think of these variables as hypotheses that are, in a sense, being tested within the confines of the model) are found to be significant and with the "right" signs, some are found to be significant but with the "wrong" signs, and some are found to be insignificant. Notice that the judgment of "right" or "wrong" signs is itself one that emerges from the theoretical model with which the economist starts. We build our models as formal axiomatic images of how we imagine the world to work—or how it should work if it conformed to the normative images we hold for it.

When this work is finished, the economist will be ready to announce that she has "explained" (or perhaps failed to "explain") what it was she set out to explain. Notice that this exercise has simply brought together some seemingly relevant hypotheses (independent variables) whose very presence in the same model structure (and the exclusion of other hypotheses) locks them in some inevitable relation. Relative to the other hypotheses in that structure, we may draw some comfort from the empirical findings. But have we explained phenomena out on the ground? Or have we built a contrived logical structure that lends itself to very great caution about its connection to the real world? Most economists with much experience in such things are the first to admit that this is an uncertain enterprise at best. They treat their findings and "explanations" with appropriate circumspection.

But others, often eager to produce something interesting, are more enthusiastic about their findings. The issue I seek to address here concerns this standard method of fixing belief, and how its application can often lead us away from, rather than toward, a full understanding—an explanation—of events and circumstances. More generally, the point is to think about this deductive exercise and compare it with how one would approach the challenge of explanation from an abductive perspective. Our ways of fixing belief in economics have been the subject of some speculation that economics is undergoing a long-overdue epistemological transformation. Indeed, an article in the *New York Times* portrayed the struggle as the "empiricists" versus the "theorists" (Uchitelle 1999). Unfortunately, this characterization fails us precisely because the issue under discussion is decidedly not one of "theorists" versus "empiricists." It cannot possibly be true that one group (the "theorists") uses theory while the other group (the "empiricists") does not. Nor can it be true that the "empiricists" use data while the "theorists" do not. Economic theory is essential to both ways of fixing belief, and detailed empirical work is an essential part of any scientific work. Terminology aside, the article went on to recount the creative interaction between those who are, in fact, deductivists and those who are, in fact, abductivists. That is, abduction is essential to the development of good deductive analytical engines, and deduction is essential to the development of the heuristic template that is the core of abduction. But the two ways of fixing belief must find points of mutual reinforcement, and this can often be difficult.

As indicated previously, deduction entails a potentially flawed precommitment to the established axioms and assumptions of economics. When the explanations and predictions from deduction seem not to describe or fit what economists believe to be the case, they will often struggle to find "better" data that will—at last—confirm their theoretical model (their particular analytical engine). As Romer puts the matter, this is a strategy to "enshrine the economic orthodoxy and make it invulnerable to challenge" (Romer 1994, p. 20). I have referred to this as *validationism*. The abductivist, not precommitted to a particular model (a specific epistemological structure of "explanation"), is at liberty to approach the problem from a more open and thus creative epistemology. We see this at work in the emergence of endogenous growth theory in the 1980s. In discussing endogenous growth Paul Romer writes:

> This work distinguishes itself from neoclassical growth by emphasizing that economic growth is an endogenous outcome of an economic system, not the result of forces that impinge from outside. For this reason the theoretical work does not invoke exogenous technological change to explain why income per capita has increased by an order of magnitude since the industrial revolution. The empirical work does not settle for measuring a growth accounting residual that grows at different rates in different countries. It tries instead to uncover the private and public sector choices that cause the rate of growth of the residual to vary across countries. As in neoclassical growth theory, the focus in endogenous growth is on the behavior of the economy as a whole. As a result the work is complementary to, but different from, the study of research and development or productivity at the level of the industry or firm. (Romer 1994, p. 3)

Romer's account of the interaction between adherents to neoclassical growth theory (predominantly deductivists) and those who introduced endogenous growth theory (predominantly abductivists) not only is an interesting story in the history of economic thought but shows the valuable contributions that can be made by the two dominant ways of fixing belief in economics. In this case, the stimulus to challenge neoclassical growth theory came from the "creation of new data sets with information on income per capita for many countries and long periods of time" (Romer 1994, p. 4). The new data were inconsistent with received wisdom—the reigning theory—at the time. To the abductivist, this constitutes the essential surprise that motivates the quest for a new explanatory model. The emergence of doubt suggested other research questions that might have been dismissed during the emergence—and certainly during the dominance—of the prior orthodox explanation. Standard neoclassical assumptions in the reigning model were necessarily modified or replaced to render them more consistent with the new empirical evidence. This process continued in successive efforts to produce more plausible explanatory hypotheses for observed phenomena. Some modifications were beneficial, whereas others were not. Here, macroeconomists had to abandon the deductive program that seeks to find reasons for the case and replace it with an abductive program that seeks to find reasons for the results.

But abandoning the neoclassical model was not easy for those who were heavily invested in it.

> The implication from this work is that if you are committed to the neoclassical model, the kind of data exhibited in Figures 1 and 2 [the basis for some to cast about for a new theory of growth] cannot be

used to make you recant. They do not compel you to give up the convenience of a model in which markets are perfect. They cannot force you to address the complicated issues that arise in the economic analysis of the production and diffusion of technology, knowledge, and information. (Romer 1994, p. 10)

Romer reports that there was remarkable agreement among all of the researchers with respect to the "basic facts. . . . The differences between the different researchers concern the inferences about models that we should draw from these facts. As is usually the case in macroeconomics, many different inferences are consistent with the same regression statistics" (Romer 1994, p. 10). He continues by placing the epistemological issue in its proper context:

Economists often complain that we do not have enough data to differentiate between the available theories, but what constitutes relevant data is itself endogenous. If we set our standards for what constitutes relevant evidence too high and pose our tests too narrowly, we will indeed end up with too little data. We can thereby enshrine the economic orthodoxy and make it invulnerable to challenge. If we do not have any models that can fit the data, the temptation will be to set very high standards for admissible evidence, because we would prefer not to reject the only models that we have. (Romer 1994, p. 20)

We see that the inevitable tension between the deductivists and the abductivists is often played out in ways that do not necessarily advance disciplinary coherence. But if one believes in the ultimate triumph of coherent understanding, then we remain dedicated to the pursuit of models and theories that seem to hold some hope of offering plausible explanations concerning observed phenomena (results) in the world around us.

To illustrate this issue in a practical policy setting, I now turn to an example in which rather standard deduction has clearly failed to offer coherent explanations of an important empirical phenomenon.

TROPICAL DEFORESTATION

Accelerated deforestation is a major concern throughout the tropical forests in the developing countries. Not only do such practices result in the wholesale degradation of large tracts of land; local livelihoods are often threatened by such practices, and global climate change is exacerbated by the loss of an important equatorial resource that can sequester greenhouse gasses. In efforts to bring a halt to such practices, there has emerged a serious commitment to understanding why these practices persist. That is, there is a quest for an explanation for the phenomenon of deforestation. Inevitably, the problem is laid at the feet of "slash-and-burn" agriculture, the spread of roads into remote areas, rapid population growth, the lack of viable economic opportunities in nonforested areas, cattle ranching, fuelwood gathering, the "frontier" and its weak property institutions, powerful logging interests, and often weak or corrupt governments.

The issue to be discussed here concerns how economists have attempted to fix belief about this important problem. The standard approaches are represented in a number of empirical investigations (Allen and Barnes 1985; Barbier, Burgess, and Markandya 1991; Deacon 1994, 1995; Deacon and Murphy 1997; Kaimowitz and Angelsen 1998; Sandler 1993; Southgate, Sierra, and Brown 1991; Vincent 1990). My purpose here is not to review this literature but rather to use the issue of tropical deforestation to illustrate the differences between deduction and abduction and to demonstrate how abduction helps us to understand and thus explain the plausible reasons for these unwanted behaviors and resulting devastation of tropical habitats. Without understanding the reasons for particular results, we are necessarily unable to offer meaningful policy prescriptions that might correct the situation.

Recall that when standard deductive approaches get underway, conceptual models are constructed that necessarily reflect readily available (and easily quantifiable) data. In the deforestation setting, this means that standard "explanatory" variables are likely to include rates of population growth at the national level, prevailing discount rates, incomes of households in forested areas (and perhaps elsewhere), access to markets (roads in forested areas), agricultural input and product prices, timber prices, rural wages, indices of technical change in agriculture, indices (perhaps as dummies) on property regimes, and foreign debt. The problem with such analyses is that they focus too quickly on what is imagined to be the antecedent conditions to deforestation. The pragmatist would insist that greater care must be devoted to a search for plausible reasons for deforestation. As we now know, this focus on antecedent conditions confuses a mechanical cause with a teleological reason (a purpose). Volitional pragmatism suggests that events and outcomes such as deforestation can only be understood—explained—by giving explicit recognition to the purposes that might be served by those particular outcomes. This is the idea of the human will in action, looking to the future. Put most explicitly, deforestation does not happen because of roads or the "wrong" prices. Deforestation happens because there are purposes to be served by deforestation. The intellectual challenge is to search for those purposes. Abduction can help us to ascertain the reasons for the result.

We see this most clearly if we consider population growth, often cited as a cause of deforestation. Obviously population growth is not intended to bring about deforestation. That is, population growth, or migration into forested areas, does not come about for the purpose of causing deforestation. Of course, population pressure may be related to the rate at which tropical forests are cleared, but population growth cannot possibly constitute a reason for tropical deforestation. Recall that reasons constitute outcomes in the future for the sake of which particular actions are undertaken today. The search for an explanation—the reason for deforestation—requires the establishment of a connection between particular events (deforestation) and the purpose to be served by those events. In contrast, the traditional search for causes of deforestation tends to look for antecedent conditions or circumstances that are mechanically related to the event.

Let us consider road building into remote forested regions, an activity that will, in many instances, be followed by deforestation. Can we therefore conclude that roads "cause" deforestation? Assume that the roads are built into remote forested areas precisely to gain access to timber. Here, the desire for access to timber is the reason for the roads, but notice that roads cannot possibly constitute the reason for timber being harvested, although roads certainly facilitate timber harvesting. The quest for timber constitutes a reason for roads to be built, so roads are the mechanical cause of deforestation, but they are not the reason for deforestation. Roads are merely instrumental to the easier acquisition of timber.

Now assume that roads are developed in remote areas for the purpose of allowing sedentary agriculture to flourish where trees now grow; this process of land conversion is of concern to many. Here, the establishment of sedentary agriculture is the reason for the roads. We now see that when it is said that roads cause deforestation, it is analogous to an assertion that roads cause sedentary agriculture. This seems implausible. Roads allow settlements in the forest, but the issue of the plausible reasons for the result, deforestation, must be more carefully considered. It will also be claimed that population growth and poor peasants cause deforestation by creating a demand for agricultural land whose access is denied by thick forests. Roads open up new territory, timber is cut off, and then sedentary agriculture can be established. But again these "explanations" confuse the mechanical explanation with the teleological explanation.

This emphasis on finding the reasons for the results (deforestation) reminds us that coherent explanation requires that we pay attention not just to proximate cause (the mechanical explanation) but to the purposes (intent) behind deforestation and land conversion. That is, we must investigate whose interests are served by deforestation and the conversion in land cover and land use, and how those interests manage to work the political system so that their purposes can be achieved.

The Standard Empirical Approach

The foregoing discussion suggests that analysis of the reasons for deforestation is plagued by a failure to distinguish between mechanical and teleological explanations. Economists have been much better at identifying the former than the latter. Robert Deacon, whose empirical work stands out for its clarity, writes that:

> [C]onsistent associations were found between deforestation and political variables reflecting insecure ownership. . . . The explanatory power of the model is fairly low, however, so firm conclusions would be premature. . . . The task of developing analytical models that better illuminate the fundamental causes of deforestation remains. Any such model must recognize that many, possibly most, of the factors taken as causes in popular accounts of deforestation are really determined endogenously. . . . The political indicators of insecure property rights examined here probably should not be regarded as truly exogenous either. . . . Unraveling this chain of causation is centrally important to any policy intended to control deforestation or the use of other natural resources. Absent an understanding of these causes, and a firm basis for separating causation from correlation, policy in this area will mistakenly treat symptoms rather than causes. (Deacon 1994, p. 429)

In a related paper, one year later, Deacon observes that:

> While knowledge of ownership issues is important for understanding the process of deforestation, this knowledge does not point to a straightforward fix. The sheer size, multiplicity of access points, and communal service flows of tropical forests make monitoring and enforcement very costly in some situations and virtually unimaginable in others. Redefining nominal rights in ways that appear to correct inefficiencies in the written law may yield gains in some instances, but an approach to environmental protection that leans heavily on this approach seems directed more at symptoms than causes. Similarly, policy approaches based on the use of Pigovian taxes or marketable permits can be expected to encounter the same monitoring and enforcement problems that keep the market from providing forest services efficiently. (Deacon 1995, pp. 16–17)

Another researcher, Todd Sandler, exhibits rather more confidence:

> Tropical deforestation is a complex problem stemming from a host of activities including forest farming, logging, cattle ranching, and large-scale infrastructure projects. The driving forces behind these activities are population pressures, highly skewed land ownership, and/or misdi-

rected government policies. (Sandler 1993, p. 232)

And yet for a less confident assessment, consider the following from a comprehensive survey of the large empirical literature addressing deforestation:

> We are sceptical of the value of the global regression modelling work done so far, and of some of the highly stylized general equilibrium models, based on rather artificial assumptions about economic behaviour and how the economy functions. We would like to see more studies that combine a realistic description of household behaviour and the regional/national dynamics, both in terms of general equilibrium effects (endogenous prices) and migration, as well as the spatial dimension. Micro-level models should attempt to better include aspects of poverty, social differentiation and institutions. . . . Finally, . . . this review's exclusive focus on quantitative models may have left some with the mistaken impression that we consider this approach is superior to others that have been used to understand deforestation. We believe qualitative analysis and studies using descriptive statistics are complementary to formal models. Qualitative models provide important insights that are difficult to capture in quantitative models and can inspire model builders to include new variables and causal relationships in their models. They are also particularly useful for adding a historical dimension to studies of deforestation and for highlighting institutional issues that have proved difficult to model. Quantitative models, on the other hand, are useful to check the internal logic of the arguments: What are the implications of a given set of assumptions, or what are the assumptions necessary for certain policies to work? Empirical quantitative models may also be useful to test hypotheses about causes of deforestation, and the relative importance of different factors. (Kaimowitz and Angelsen 1998, pp. 105–7)

Notice several things here. The standard deductive approach is said to result in "quantitative models," whereas the other approach is concerned with "qualitative models." Can there be any doubt that this particular terminology leads the economist interested in "rigorous" work to favor the allegedly "quantitative" model over the more "subjective" qualitative model? Interestingly, we see that the qualitative models provide important insights and invite researchers to include new variables in their models, and to pay attention to important historical and institutional issues that have proved difficult to model. From language such as this, the durable dichotomy arises between rigor and relevance. But, of course, the dichotomy is spurious because the categories "quantitative" and "qualitative" are seriously flawed in their portrayal, and thus in their labels. The issue is not one of quantitative—and thus rigorous and objective—models as opposed to qualitative models that are subjective. Rather, the issue is between deductive and abductive ways of fixing belief. The problem with conventional studies of deforestation is not that they are quantitative but that they have looked in the wrong place for the wrong thing to be explained. These models may be quantitative and thus may bestow an aura of rigor, but it is a misplaced rigor. The problem with standard explanations of deforestation is that those who build deductive models of the process have mistakenly regarded deforestation as the end state requiring explanation and have therefore focused analytical attention upon the antecedent circumstances that appear, at first glance, to "cause" deforestation: population pressure, road building into remote areas, land-hungry peasants, insecure property rights. But if we would come to see deforestation not as the end of the causal chain but as an intermediate step along the way, then we would be better situated to find much-needed clarity in the quest for an explanation of—the reasons for—deforestation.

The pragmatist would start the search for an explanation by asking, What event or circumstance in the future is served by deforestation? When we locate that event or circumstance, we will have discovered the reason for (not the cause of) tropical deforestation. Lacking this, the conventional deductive explanations are mechanical in that they focus on antecedent circumstances. When we understand that deforestation is an event serving some subsequent purpose, it becomes logically necessary to conclude that there are only two possible explanations for deforestation that can constitute reasons: (1) to earn revenues from harvesting trees; and (2) to convert forest land to other uses. The first of these regards trees as a source of income for the state (and those able to poach on such income streams), whereas the second of these regards forested land as having an unacceptably high opportunity cost if it remains under forest cover. Indeed, perhaps the two reasons really collapse into one—the high opportunity cost of forested land, the conversion of which will provide access to scarce land, with the costs of conversion being partially (or fully) covered by the selling off of the forest cover (Deacon 1995).

The obvious conclusion from this sequence would seem to take us back to population growth as the real cause of the high social opportunity cost of land remaining under forest cover. But this would be too simple. Perhaps the reason for the felt need to clear land (deforest it) for settlement is the unwillingness of many governments to formulate and implement other actions that would relieve the apparent shortage of land and thus drive down the seemingly high opportunity cost of land remaining under forest cover. Such lands now considered off-limits are, perhaps, politically unavailable for settlement by poor farmers and those now crowded into peri-urban slums. In other words, perhaps forested land has a high opportunity cost in its current use because of the failure (unwillingness) of the government to address the issue of land scarcity elsewhere in the economy. If most of a nation's rural nonforested land is owned by a rich and powerful minority of the population, and if the government is unwilling to address the land scarcity brought on by this particular ownership structure, then the opportunity cost of forested land is artificially inflated. Perhaps this is a plausible reason for government support of other activities that inevitably entail deforestation. It is quite possible that many governments find it much easier to allow the clearing of the forest than it is to confront the political and economic heft of those who now own much of the land that might otherwise be made available through land reform programs to the landless and to those trapped in urban slums.

Suddenly we see that willful intent (purpose) forces us to admit that in many instances, so-called population pressure against scarce land cannot be a plausible reason for tropical deforestation; it only looks that way because governments wish for that perception to persist. Indeed, it is quite plausible that some governments find large financial benefits accruing if they can convince others that population pressure is the reason for deforestation. Doing so may allow them greater access to foreign financial assistance to address the serious "problems" of population pressure, a problem that may be mostly of their own creation (Ascher 1999). Many international environmental groups might find this "explanation" to their liking since it serves their interests as well.

We see that the issue is not easily characterized as a choice between quantitative and qualitative models. Rather, the central issue here is the great difficulty of building coherent deductive models that offer some hope of actually explaining observed economic phenomena such as deforestation in widespread and highly divergent economic and social circumstances. The empirical problem is obvious: it is difficult to get governments to admit that they are unwilling—or unable—to take actions that will solve the problems associated with landless people. It is equally difficult to get some governments to admit that they need (or want) the revenue from the widespread harvesting and land conversion activities that deforestation entails. That is, the intentions of government policies are difficult to include in an econometric model. Though difficult, it is not impossible to undertake quantitative research under this alternative framing. If the economist follows the logical chain suggested here and begins to see that the problem is properly framed when we look at deforestation as an activity that many governments promote or tolerate, it is quite possible to test that hypothesis with some good quantitative models. Explanatory variables might include: (1) extent of landlessness; (2) extent of the inequality of income and wealth; (3) dependence of local, regional, or national governments on revenue from extractive industries; and (4) balance-of-trade position with other countries. Unlike the deductive models, we might see that deforestation is not the result of—is not explained by— "bad policies." Deforestation is explained by "good" policies. Here we need to remember that the judgment of good and bad is always in reference to an objective. Given the objectives of government, its promotion of deforestation is perfectly rational. Some may not like the implications for forests, but that is a separate issue. The job of the economist is to explain—to find the reasons for—a particular outcome (deforestation). Our job is not to defend the forests (as much as we might personally revere them).

Notice that while the empirical work may have started with the idea that deforestation required explanation, switching from deduction to abduction induces the researcher to keep pursuing the reasons for the results. Recall the Peircean concept of abduction:

> The troubling fact, C, is observed.
> But if A were true, C would be a matter of course.
> Hence, there is reason to suspect A is true.

Here C can be thought of as tropical deforestation. The task of explanation is to fix belief about the content of A. That is, what are the constituents of A that would render C explicable? Peirce called this the method of hypothesis, and we see that the constituents of A are indeed hypotheses. In earlier chapters, these were referred to as assumptions and applicability postulates. Abduction concerns a process of going from result (a known empirical phenomenon) and a rule (axioms) to case (assumptions and applicability postulates). These assumptions and applicability postulates comprise hypotheses, or we may think of them as theoretical propositions. Someone might be expected to say, "I have a theory about why deforestation happens." Another person might be expected to say, "I have a hypothesis (or a set of hypotheses) about why deforestation happens." Someone else, more cautious about universal claims but still convinced of the soundness of her analysis, may declare: "I know why deforestation happens in Indonesia." Regardless of the terminology, the listener is put on notice that an "explanation" of deforestation is about to be advanced—an assertion (a "truth claim") is on the way. The speakers may well regard the forthcoming assertions as warranted belief. Others from within the same discipline may be excused for regarding these assertions as plausible but as yet insufficiently ripe (tested by others) to constitute warranted belief.

The key here, however, is to keep in mind that explanations pertaining to human action are incoherent without explicit reference to intent. All other alleged explanations are merely mechanical and, as such, provide no insights about policy reform. That is, the prescriptions to flow from mechanical causes will inevitably address symptoms of the problem—observed phenomena—rather than the reasons for those phenomena. As long as a particular government is driven by a desire to earn revenues from harvesting trees, and as long as landlessness—itself the result of other specific policy choices—induces governments to promote the exploitation of remote forested areas, then very little is to be gained by suggesting that nations stop building roads, or that property rights be made more secure, or that population control be implemented, or that government corruption be rectified, or that the powerful logging interests be reined in. The only way to confront deforestation is to focus on the plausible purposes it serves now and in the future.

We also see that deforestation is often but a part of a suite of activities out on the ground (surprises, perhaps) that include active road building into forested areas, settlement programs to help poor landless people move into the forests, legal arrangements that reward title to cleared land, and formal credit policies that induce particular behaviors. On this recognition, we see that it is not deforestation that requires explanation but rather the existence of roads, particular legal arrangements, credit policies, and settler programs. It is no longer adequate to blame deforestation on bad policies, or weak governments, or the insecurity of property rights. Indeed, the identification of final causes allows us to see that governments must intend that deforestation occur; otherwise they would stop it. The abductive approach allows the researcher to posit that deforestation serves the purposes of the government. It is not a matter of bad policy, or of innocence as to why deforestation occurs, or even of incapacity to change deforestation practices. Rather, deforestation serves the purposes of the state and its government. Those other purposes are the reason for (the final cause) of deforestation, as well as a number of other outcomes (roads, settlement projects).

For some social scientists, this new clarity in explanation may not be welcome. We usually operate with two maintained hypotheses: (1) that most governments generally seek to do what is right by their citizens; and (2) that the only impediment to improved public policy is careful analysis and the provision of new information upon which improved policies can be based. The implication, in the case of deforestation, is that governments surely wish to be told that deforestation is caused by insecure property rights, road building, population pressure, powerful logging interests, and other bad policies. If this is believed, we can then help governments to correct these circumstances that are thought to cause deforestation. That is what prescriptive economists do. This approach is misguided, however, precisely because it is predicated on a false explanation of deforestation. Careful assessment of deforestation in the developing world would reveal that most governments know what they are doing with their forests, and they know exactly why they are doing it (Ascher, 1999). If this is the case, then it is a very different challenge to tell governments that they should stop seeking to earn revenue from their forests, or that they should not try to solve the land hunger problem. On the other hand, this realization opens up other avenues for assisting governments to deal with deforestation. Perhaps land hunger can be addressed by other policy reforms. In other words, perhaps deforestation is less about forestry and rural land use than it is about economic policy in general?

Prescriptions for the Right Reasons

If we start from the realization that deforestation happens not by accident or neglect but because governments intend for it to happen, then we gain considerable clarity on a problem that has been blamed on a number of disparate and dubious causes and circumstances. Again, it certainly brings a different perspective to discussions with government officials who may be understandably reluctant to admit the obvious. If we assume that some governments genuinely seek to reverse decades of deforestation, then it will be necessary to insist that these new intentions must be accompanied by a serious change in de facto and de jure circumstances. That is, we may well find that governments have, in the past, expressed concern about deforestation but have been unwilling or unable to do much to stop it. This disjuncture between words and deeds is not lost on most observers and generates, in time, a level of cynicism that must be rectified.

Implications

The discussion here opened with reference to the use of deduction in neo-classical growth theory—problems exacerbated by the tendency in deduction to undertake empirical research with a strong precommitment to the reasons for the *case*. As Romer points out, this commitment induces the economist to lament the lack of sufficient data to allow the generation of theoretical results that would be found consistent with reigning theory. In this research program, the economist can always find "good" reasons to defend the received assumptions—the conventional wisdom.

We see a similar problem here in the context of deforestation. Although most researchers admit that the standard deductive approach is not edifying as to an explanation of deforestation, they are reluctant to move beyond the standard model—in part because of the fear that to do so is to abandon rigor (quantitative models) in favor of something that is subjective (qualitative models). Starting with Peircean surprise, however, we see that abduction can be helpful in diagnosing particular outcomes in a manner that seems to offer some promise. In this enhanced pursuit of the reasons for deforestation, the economist can bring clarity to the controversies over natural resource use in the developing world. The reasons for deforestation can no longer be a mystery, and it is no longer credible to blame deforestation on the uncontrollable avarice of millions of poor and scattered peasants and loggers throughout the tropics. When we realize that tropical deforestation occurs because governments wish for it to happen, we can begin a policy dialogue with a much more focused set of participants. If those in the developed world wish for tropical deforestation to cease, then it is clear to whom the necessary political pressure and economic incentives must be directed for that to happen. And it is no longer credible for the governments in the tropics to wring their hands in frustration, protesting that they know not what to do about the persistent problem of forest destruction.

CHAPTER TWELVE

Volitional Pragmatism and the Evolution of Institutions

> Only those economic advantages are rights which have the law back of them . . . whether it is a property right is really the question to be answered.
> —Justice R. Jackson, *Willow River Power Co.*,
> 324 US 499, 502 (1945)

CONTESTED PROPERTY RELATIONS

I have suggested that we will be unable to gain clarity on the content and meaning of economic institutions without first accepting the idea that the subject matter of economics is properly understood as the study of how societies organize themselves for their provisioning. At the moment, much of economics is taught as if the subject concerned mere economizing behavior from within a set of institutional "constraints." Even the new institutional economists regard institutions as "constraints" (North 1990). The new institutional economics also seeks to make institutional change endogenous and thus mechanically driven by the same price-theoretic algorithms that are often thought to explain individual rational behavior. There are two flaws in this research program: (1) it ignores the centrality of purpose in human affairs; and (2) it fails to acknowledge that the economy is always in the process of becoming. If we are to understand economic institutions, then we cannot possibly ignore the idea of purpose and its evolution. And if we are to understand why the economy is always "becoming," then we must understand how the necessary evolution of purpose is ineluctably played out in the continual process of redefining how it is that democratic societies attend to and implement their necessary provisioning.

Of the three classes of institutions—norms, working rules, and property relations—the last-named category is generally thought to represent the clearest and most durable class of institutions. That is, norms can evolve without the need for collective action to agree on the direction and substance of that evolution. And working rules can be modified by various forms of democratic processes—legislatures, administrative rulings, and courts. But the existing structure of property rights (what I call *property*

relations) is usually regarded as reliably immutable. Indeed, property relations are thought to be so durable that any change in such institutions is
inevitably accompanied by calls for compensation from the government.
This durability of property relations is claimed to underlie concepts of
individual liberty, and also to be the fundamental legal foundation of capitalism.

A careful reading of the legal history in most democratic countries
would reveal, however, that property relations have undergone considerable change and that such change has not always been accompanied by
government compensation. At one time slaves were the private property
of their owners, and wives were considered the property of their husbands. These changes in presumed property rights were unaccompanied
by compensation, although American slave owners tried their best. As
an example of the presumed sanctity of the institutions of property, the
American Constitution contains a "property clause" (the Fifth Amend-
ment) that declares, in general terms, that private property may not be
taken for public use without the payment of just compensation to the
owner. Here is an entitlement at the very highest level in the American
system of governance. The reason for this particular rule seems obvious.
First, the rule prevents government entities from taking arbitrary and ca-
pricious action against the assets of the citizenry. Second, the rule forces
governments to pay for what they say they need to carry out their various
civic functions. Finally, this particular institutional arrangement insures
that no single person is made to bear the cost of the necessary functions
of society. That is, compensation serves to spread these necessary costs
among the taxpayers in the pertinent jurisdiction.

The central idea here is that the U.S. Constitution calls for compensation when private property is taken for public use. However, notice that
this declaration leaves unspecified the precise empirical content of three
key ideas: (1) private property; (2) taken; and (3) public use. It should not
surprise us, therefore, that the courts have had to struggle with precisely
these three concepts in sorting out the conflicts before them. How can
courts "protect" private property rights against incursions for public use
if the very concepts at the core of this idea are themselves contested and
unclear? This approach probably seems odd to many observers. We are
sure we know what property is; it is that to which one holds title. We are
also sure we know what constitutes a "taking" (this is a diminution of
market value), and we know that a public use is an economic loss to the
owner that shifts some economic gain elsewhere. While it is very clear to
us, it is not always clear to the courts. And this lack of clarity might be
thought of as an economic problem in that uncertainty can stifle productive activity. With risk-averse agents, institutional uncertainty is said to
represent a welfare loss. From a quite different perspective, however, all

rules—even property relations—are simply one more element in the reality that the economy is always in the process of becoming. Entrepreneurs are constantly on the lookout for unexpected changes in a variety of economic variables and parameters. Why should they not be expected to remain alert to changes in the economic institutions that are so central to their fields of action—their opportunity sets?

Normally, we construct models with prices and quantities as the endogenous variables that are codetermined given stable preferences, technology, and endowments. As Alexander Field asks, do such models explain the solution (prices and quantities)? His answer is: only to the extent that they are simply products of the parameters (Field 1979). That is, different boundary conditions will necessarily produce different "solutions" to the consumption problem, and hence there will be a different constellation of prices and quantities. The two fundamental theorems of welfare economics capture this idea when we say that for every set of initial conditions (endowments, preferences, and technology) there is an allocation that is Pareto optimal (the second—or indirect—theorem), and that this allocation can be sustained by a competitive equilibrium (the first—or direct—theorem).

Institutional change can enter such models in two possible ways. Market clearing prices reflect agents' expectations of the present value of a stream of future values embodied in their consumption choices. To the extent that new institutions alter the future net benefits associated with the consumption of an object, altered prices can be thought of as one way that new institutions alter consumption outcomes. In essence, the Walrasian auctioneer announces a price vector reflective of the new institutional arrangements that differs from the price vector pertinent to the old institutional setup. For instance, the auctioneer might announce a price vector in which the price of automobiles reflects an anticipated change in the pollution attributes of cars that will hold implications for their gas mileage performance.

Second, the idea of "endowments" represents the asset position each agent brings to the auction. If owners of assets face the prospect of some institutional change that will alter their endowment, then the solution to the process (a vector of consumption and prices) will differ. In essence, the deus ex machina of the market—the Walrasian auctioneer—calls out a rule vector r (with prices fixed), and individual consumption decisions will be made with that new institutional setup in mind. Either way, we need to recognize the difference between institutions that change often and unpredictably and institutions that change in response to new social settings and circumstances. To the extent that we believe agents are well informed and rational, it seems difficult to argue that they do not know, for instance, that certain environmental standards are currently under redefinition. Few landowners can, today, credibly invest in land covered with wetlands and claim innocence about the prospects for draining said land. Nor can owners of land including critical habitat for endangered species plausibly claim ignorance of evolving social ideas about biodiversity and ecological integrity. In a similar vein, owners of industrial plants cannot plausibly claim innocence about the ongoing evolution in health and safety matters on the shopfloor.

This brings us back to the idea that because the economy is always in the process of becoming, the institutional arrangements of society change in accordance with new scarcities, or they change in accordance to new ideas about what now seems better to do. In the earlier chapters, I mentioned a number of institutional changes that have been driven by evolving social norms over the past two centuries. And this brings us back to land and the presumed clarity of the social idea of ownership. It seems historically unmistakable that individuals own and control assets in a political entity, whether land or otherwise, only at the implicit consent of all others in that particular society. This is what political philosophers mean by the "problem of consent" (Christman 1994). On the subject of consent with respect to the holding of private property, consider the comments of the English historian R. H. Tawney:

> Property was to be an aid to creative work, not an alternative to it. . . . The law of the village bound the peasant to use his land, not as he himself might find most profitable, but to grow the corn the village needed. . . . Property reposed in short, not merely upon convenience, or the appetite for gain, but on a moral principle. It was protected not only for the sake of those who owned, but for the sake of those who worked and of those for whom their work provided. It was protected, because, without security for property, wealth could not be produced or the business of society carried on. (Tawney 1978, p. 139)

Here one sees the basis for understanding the evolution of institutions in a society—with particular reference, in this instance, to the most durable of institutions. Historically, rights in land have been granted to individuals by the civic community because of the larger social benefits to arise therefrom. It serves all of us that a few own and contribute to the social provisioning that secures a better life for the rest. But that grant of ownership—that consent—is always predicated upon the continual benediction of the larger social good. Property relations are a social construct and thus objects such as land and associated assets are not protected because they are "property." Rather, those things (such as land) that are protected become—by virtue of that conscious social action—"property." The direction of causality is important here. The epigraph opening this chapter captures that idea well—"whether it is a property right is really the question to be answered."

The period of great philosophical debates about individualism, what we now call the Enlightenment, coincided with the formative years in the New World and very much informed the American idea. Small wonder that individuals will claim that any redefinition of their land-based actions requires that they be compensated from the tax receipts of the public purse. And yet others, equally adamant, insist that this cannot be. Why does land excite such emotions? Obviously land symbolizes some idea of freedom. Indeed, the idea of land and property rights is a static and durable one to many. Some merely wish to be left alone on what they imagine to be "their" land. Others hope to get rich from it. Part of the enduring appeal of the idea of property rights in land is that many people seem to imagine that while other things may change, property rights have not changed, will not change, and indeed cannot change. Of course, this is not true. Most of us live in a neighborhood that is stabilized by zoning laws, and zoning itself was a profound institutional change found acceptable by the courts. Moreover, landowners once imagined that they controlled everything to the core of the earth, and to the heavens above. If that were true, air travel would be either impossible, or very expensive as airline companies tried to negotiate with each landowner along various flight paths.

We can learn something useful about institutional change by considering several landmark property rights cases. Litigation concerning Grand Central Terminal in New York City provides an illustration of the difficult choices in land-use conflicts (*Penn Central Transportation Co. v. New York City* [438 U.S. 104 (1978)]). The Penn Central Transportation Company (the owner) sought to construct a high-rise office complex above the terminal. The proposed office tower would have destroyed the historic character of Grand Central Terminal and filled up one of the last remaining areas of "airspace" in mid-Manhattan. There were, therefore, two new scarcities at work—a historic structure (the terminal) and open space in a canyon of very tall structures. Penn Central was prevented from constructing its planned office complex above the historic structure, and the courts (it was appealed all the way to the U.S. Supreme Court) would not require that it be compensated for this inability. At one level this seems unfair to Penn Central, which was, in effect, being required to save a building of some significance to the larger public (because of its historic value), and to preserve open space for the benefit of surrounding building occupants. The economist might be inclined to look at this dispute and observe two forms of externalities. The first, the preservation of a historic building, would continue to bestow benefits on a number of people who would not need to pay for such positive externalities. Indeed, the dispute was in the court precisely because of the existence of a New York City Landmarks Commission whose writ included assuring that historic structures were preserved. The second externality shows up in the form of preserving open space in the area above the terminal, space that would otherwise be filled up with yet another tall building. Neighbors would benefit from this open space, and the resulting absence of yet more office space in the neighborhood might have kept rental rates high in surrounding buildings.

How could a court possibly deny, without compensation, Penn Central the "right" to build a tall building in a city of many very tall buildings? The financial setback to Penn Central must be enormous. Pragmatism asks us to consider the possibility that Penn Central got caught by shifting attitudes about historic structures and open space in a crowded urban center. In a process reminiscent of early court findings regarding air rights and the overflight of aircraft, the U.S. Supreme Court simply found that the Penn Central Transportation Company did not own the air rights above Grand Central Terminal. Note that the Court did not say that Penn Central once "owned" those rights and that they were now being taken away. The Court simply said that, looking to the future, the air rights were not available to Penn Central to use as it wished. And because Penn Central did not own the space into which it sought to build, the Court saw no reason to tax the residents of New York City to fund a compensation scheme to pay Penn Central for its inability to take away a historic site and the associated open space. Of course, Penn Central retained the considerable economic asset of the terminal, but it was not able to pursue a new income-earning opportunity above that structure.

Obviously Penn Central argued that it was being made to provide the benefits of open space (and a historic structure) to its neighbors and was not being paid to do so. This, or so they pleaded, was most unfair. And, again, economists might look at this situation and announce it both unfair to Penn Central and "inefficient"—said inefficiency arising from the fact that Penn Central was being made to provide uncompensated public goods to the city of New York. But looked at in another way, the public-good benefits of open space and a monumental historic structure were already being provided, and Penn Central was merely being denied the opportunity to impose harm on others by destroying those benefits. Notice the subtle linguistic distinction here—being made *to provide* a new public benefit versus having the inability *to cease providing* an existing public benefit. What one "sees" depends on how one looks at a particular issue.

This important distinction is central to another case concerning nature conservation. A landowner in Wisconsin sought to drain and fill some wetlands on the shores of a lake for the purpose of constructing dwellings (*Just v. Marinette County* [56 Wis. 2d 7, 201 N.W. 2d 761 (1972)]). The act of filling the wetland would impair the nutrient processing that is an important (and quite recently understood) ecological function of wetlands. The county denied the owner a permit to drain the land, and subsequently the owner sued the county. Eventually the Wisconsin Supreme Court upheld the county's permitting requirement, and the owners were enjoined and not compensated. The Wisconsin Supreme Court ruled that the owners originally bought wetlands and, after being denied the permit to drain that land, they still owned what they had bought. The county, in its refusal to issue a permit to destroy the wetland, did not take from the owners something that they once had. The owners were, indeed, prevented from realizing a higher income from modifying the wetland, but the court saw no reason to force county taxpayers to remunerate the landowners for the latter's inability to realize some development scheme that would require the destruction of nature. As with *Penn Central*, the landowners insisted that they were being made to provide the benefits of water purification in their wetlands and that they should be compensated for this service. On the contrary, the county insisted that the filtering attributes of wetlands were as old as time and the owners, by their hoped-for action, would actually destroy those valuable services. Why should they be compensated for their inability to destroy what nature had freely provided?

The economist might ask about the incentive effects of decisions such as these. In both cases, we see that the courts sought to determine (adhering to Justice Jackson's opening epigraph) whether there was indeed a property interest requiring compensation; in one case it was "air rights," whereas in the other it was "draining rights." In both cases we see a gradual and quite decisive shift in public understanding and perceptions about the assets under litigation. In *Penn Central*, airspace had become increasingly scarce and, in the process, became increasingly valuable. Had Penn Central sought to build its tall structure twenty years earlier, there would, we might suppose, have been no problem in its doing so. But eventually the new scarcity of airspace would surely have affected some party who sought to build a tall building. In the wetlands case, new scientific understanding revealed that wetlands were not mere swamps but in fact performed valuable environmental services. Had the owners sought to drain the wetland twenty years earlier, before this was understood, perhaps there would have been no problem. Indeed, we can interpret the existence of a permitting requirement at the county level as clear political (social) evidence of the evolved perception in the value of wetlands (Bromley 1993).

We see in these two instances quite clear evidence of certain settings and circumstances—material aspects of our surroundings—actually becoming valuable assets. Airspace in mid-Manhattan was not always scarce and valuable, but it certainly became so during the latter half of the twentieth century. Wetlands were not always scarce and valuable; indeed, for most of human history wetlands have been seen as impediments to agricultural production, as breeding grounds for mosquitoes, and as unwelcome barriers to the expansion of coastal cities. But changing perceptions, enhanced by new scientific findings, helped to convert—to redefine—wetlands from social liabilities into social assets. The economic question in these "takings" cases then turns on who should pay for this new economic situation? Should taxpayers be forced to indemnify Penn Central for its inability to eliminate assets (open space and an unsullied vista of a historic structure) that are now of great social value? Should taxpayers be forced to indemnify the owners of wetlands for their inability to destroy the filtering services of those wet areas?

At one level, it might seem that the answer to both questions should be yes. Didn't collective action (the courts) take something from them? At another level, however, both parties were left with what they already had—Penn Central still had its terminal, and the Justs still had their wetlands. All they lost was the possibility of new income from an investment that each sought to undertake, with said investment destroying assets that now had new social value. Pragmatism induces us to ask: does a market economy owe landowners an assured return from their plans and schemes? Clarity is gained by considering the counterfactual. In the *Penn Central* case, the company would either get the new income stream from the building, or it would receive compensation for the lost value from not being able to build the skyscraper. Now it seems that an interesting strategic opportunity appears. The payment of court-ordered compensation to Penn Central Transportation Company would presumably make the company indifferent between being allowed to construct the building (and thereby become the recipient of an income stream into the future), or receiving compensation from the taxpayers for the inability to construct the building (said compensation being determined by the monetary value of its alleged economic "loss" from being denied the opportunity to build). So Penn Central would receive a similar income stream under either situation. Surely this is an odd incentive to lay before economic agents. Unless the state proceeds with caution, all manner of similar extortion possibilities lies in wait.

If Penn Central should get reimbursed for not being allowed to fill up scarce open space in Manhattan, then what is to prevent another landowner, also with desires to increase income, to proceed to construct yet another tall building? Or, it might be asked, "why didn't the Court order compensation to be paid to Penn Central but then issue a decree that henceforth compensation would not be paid?" The answer is that courts do not set public policy; courts act on the facts before them and, in doing so, send a signal to others about what behavior is socially acceptable. Those seeking to destroy historic landmarks—or to fill up airspace—have certainly had their economic expectations modified by the *Penn Central* case. They have new fixed belief. Similarly, those seeking to drain and fill wetlands will, presumably, modify their expectations in light of the Wisconsin case. In this way, society moves forward and responds to new scarcities and new amenities (new "resources"). Of immediate pertinence, we see that the courts are charged with the task of fixing belief about whether owners really possess a property interest. This is the essence of a rationing transaction.

Recalling the pragmatic theory of action, we see that property rights are constructed (not found or discovered) in light of the emergent created imaginings presented to the courts in the context of a specific struggle over whose interests shall prevail in particular contentious instances. Courts must consider these possible but mutually exclusive futures and then figure out which of the claimants before it has the more compelling claim in light of those imagined futures. The courts are forced to fix their belief about which of the contending assertions about property rights are the better ones to believe. Immanuel Kant, certainly no pragmatist, had a profound concept of property that comes very close to that of the pragmatist's theory of "truth." Kant takes us to the nub of the matter when he insists that rights are not tangible empirical realities (*possessio phenomenon*) but rather noumena (*possessio noumenon*). Things that cannot be apprehended by the senses (seen, touched, heard, smelled) but are knowable only by reason constitute noumena. In an abductive approach, Kant asks what conditions (the case) are necessary in order that an individual might be able to make internal something that is, by its very nature, external (the result)? The key idea here is one of belonging—of *belonging to*. Something external to an individual (land and material circumstances) is made internal by understanding the idea of belonging to. And how is it decided that something external belongs to an individual?

An individual may simply declare, in classic Lockean fashion, that some particular object or situation belongs to her. Notice that this is a claim against all others to whom the object or situation might otherwise belong. Such claims are asserted by those who wish to persuade others that the speaker is the rightful (justified) possessor and controller ("owner"?) of the thing under discussion. Once asserted, something external has, by dint of unilateral proclamation, become internal to the speaker (at least in the mind of the speaker). But Kant noticed something important here. He recognized that such claims represent negations of the interests of others within the same community. And he suggested that while one individual may indeed announce and display physical possession of something external, this was not equivalent to the socially sanctioned authority to make that declaration binding on others who might wish to make internal that very same thing. That is, unless others to whom the possessor directs her assertion are predisposed to respect and honor those claims, the situation is unstable and therefore cannot be expected to settle the matter once and for all. Kant noticed that it is only from the consent of others that one can make internal that which is clearly external. For if that external thing can belong to anyone within the community, what mental work is required to allow it to become internal (to belong to) any particular member of that community? Why should others willingly accept binding duties on nothing more compelling than the self-serving assertions of those already in possession of (or seeking new control of) something of potential value to others?

Kant said that such assertions are nothing but the affirmation of empirical possession. And by being based on mere possession (*possessio phenomenon*), they confuse physical control with something much more profound. That more profound circumstance is one that Kant called "intelligible possession" (*possessio noumenon*). We see intelligible possession at work when a community of sapient beings reaches agreement that indeed it is both right (moral) and good (prudential) that someone among them should be able to make internal something that has hitherto been external. We see immediately that the essence of empirical possession is a dog with a bone. There is not, nor can there be, recognition among the community of dogs—all of whom covet the bone—that it "belongs to" the one in whose mouth it now resides. The most one can say is that dogs acknowledge possession. It takes Kantian reason to transcend empirical possession (Williams 1977). Dogs are as incapable of apprehending *possessio noumenon* as they are of the idea of yesterday.

On this account, what is mine depends not on what I say about it being mine. Rather, what is mine becomes mine in virtue of the assertions of all others who, by their declaration, acquiesce in their own disenfranchisement from the benefits associated with that object or circumstance. Others grant me *possessio noumenon*; I cannot take it for myself. Kant helps us to understand that the holding of land ("property") in the face of scarcity requires something very special. For scarcity raises the specter of deprivation and exclusion if Lockean acquisition and continued holding of land works against the interests of others in the community who, in virtue of coming late, find that all of God's commons has already been justly acquired. How are we to explain and thus justify holding of land ("property") once there is no more of it to be justly acquired?

Contemporary Lockeans have a ready answer to this question: let the latecomers buy it from those who have justly acquired it (or who have previously purchased it). We see that once the initial acquisition has been transferred to another for due consideration (a purchase price), the logic seems compelling and without end—all future acquisitions must be mediated by due consideration to the extant holder of land ("property"). And what is transferred in this way is, and must be, precisely what earlier acquirers obtained (Bromley 2004). The just acquisition and holding continues into perpetuity. This seeming escape from the grips of scarcity leaves one fundamental issue still to be addressed. What if the current holding results in land-use practices that, in the fullness of time, are found to lack continued social ratification—obscuring and fouling historic train stations, draining and building on scarce wetlands?

Given this possibility, on what grounds can payment then be justified in order to induce the current holder to stop using her land (her "property") in an antisocial manner? In other words, what is to preclude one or more holders of land from engaging in social extortion? We see that land justly acquired may evolve into land unjustly held—its current use no longer satisfies the condition that it seems the "best" thing to do. And the idea of "best" can be either moral or prudential. Here Locke joins Kant in admitting that under certain circumstances the presumed beneficial link between acquisition and holding might be severed. Recall that Locke presumed that land justly acquired would be used in a manner that redounded to the benefit of the entire community, and that fact was part of the justification for its acquisition and continued holding. But what if this is not the case? Kant answered with the proposition that the community itself must determine whether land justly acquired remains justly held. How is this to be done? It is accomplished through reason emerging from a *burgerliche Gesellschaft*—a civil society. The community itself must set the standards by which the continued holding of justly acquired land ("property") remains justified.

This brings us to a difficult pass. We are, it would seem, in need of a theory of holding. Such a theory must offer an explanation (justification) for difficult decisions about just and prudential holdings of valuable assets into the future. In more practical terms, this theory must address the issue of what to do when extant holdings are found to warrant just attenuation. Must payment using public funds be made for this attenuation? This is the essential "takings" question. The deductivist would start work on such a theory by invoking certain axioms, soon to be augmented with a few auxiliary assumptions, with the intent of producing a general theory about how one decides when extant holdings may be abridged in the absence of payment to the holder. We see one particular form of this deductive chain in play when some commentators produce a "theory" indicating that there are no circumstances in which actions on land ("property") justly acquired can be partially or completely attenuated by government without being accompanied by payment. Notice that we are here discussing the realm of regulatory takings, not per se takings in which the state physically removes a just holder from her land.

We see such a theory at work in the writings of Richard Epstein (1985). Epstein and others who see the law in this way deploy axioms and assumptions that allow them to conclude that *any* attenuation by the state of uses on justly acquired land requires payment from the public purse. And, of course, the central axiom in this line of thought is that "property rights" are antecedent to the state because they were acquired, Lockean style, in a "creation story" (Kreuckeberg 1999). Once property existed, a state became possible, and it therefore became the paramount obligation of the state to protect those property rights that underpinned the very legitimacy of the state.

Deduction is also the epistemology of choice of those who believe that there are plausible grounds to fashion an approach that is less absolute. That is, this group of legal theorists seeks to invoke axioms and auxiliary assumptions that will allow sharper distinctions to be drawn about justified and therefore uncompensated attenuation. The "theories" that emerge from this group of legal scholars invoke several assumptions (hypotheses) as may be needed to give their "theory" traction. Here we are likely to see assumptions (explanatory hypotheses) concerning: (1) reciprocity of advantage; (2) reasonable investment-backed expectations; (3) beneficial use; (4) proportionality; (5) the distinction between preventing harms and providing benefits; (6) legitimate public purpose; and (7) the extent of diminution of "all economic value." These deductivists apparently imagine that they have a more coherent and consistent theory of justified and uncompensated attenuation—a more nuanced theory—than the extreme position of, for example, Richard Epstein. Such theorists will dissect the facts of "takings" cases, and they will carefully read legal decisions, in an effort to discern which of these several "causal factors" can explain the particular findings. Sometimes one of these factors will be found sufficient. In other cases, several of them will be found necessary in order to "explain" the decision. But in most cases the legal scholars can resurrect enough hypotheses that they can then advance a "theory" of that particular case.

Careful thought reveals something quite odd here. That is, all posited explanations of this sort "explain" the particular decision under scrutiny, but they obviously fail to offer us a general theory by which we may understand the general idea and practice of property rights in the American experience. Each "theory" is of a very particular kind—and it is, therefore, not a theory at all. Each "explanation" merely redescribes the specific findings and, in doing so, tells us that one or more hypotheses are adequate to "understand" this particular decision. The cynic would call this ad hoc empiricism. I call it verificationism.

Notice that the deductivist asks: "Does this particular Supreme Court respect (protect)—or fail to respect (protect)—property rights?" The deductivist will then invoke hypotheses (assumptions) that will render a tentative answer to that question. Or, the deductivist will ask a somewhat subtler question: "What is the position of this particular Supreme Court with respect to property rights?" Notice that both of these questions start with an apparently clear and definitive idea of the nature of property rights, and the investigator then seeks to answer his or her own question by reading carefully and by parsing particular legal decisions (the law's "sacred texts"), paying particular attention to the footnotes wherein legal scholars seem to find the "real" meaning of what has transpired before the courts. The abductivist finds these two questions to be seriously flawed. The questions are flawed because they presume (axiomatically) the prior nature and scope of something (property rights) that is the very idea (concept) requiring explanation. It is akin to asking a two-year-old if she is telling the truth.

Again, the abductivist has a more promising epistemology. The abductivist would observe a series of Supreme Court decisions that, on their face, appear to hold quite different implications for the concept (the a priori idea) of property rights. Candidate cases—the empirical phenomena requiring explanation—might easily include a few of the classic "takings" cases: *Euclid v. Ambler Realty, Teleprompter Co. v. Loretto, Hadachek v. Sebastian, Mugler v. Kansas, Penn Central Transportation Co. v. New York City, Agins v. City of Tiburon, Lucas v. South Carolina Coastal Council, Keystone Bituminous Coal Association v. deBenedictis, Nollan v. California Coastal Commission, Pennsylvania Coal Co. v. Mahon, Palazzolo v. State of Rhode Island,* and *Tahoe-Sierra Preservation Council v. Tahoe Regional Planning Agency.* To the deductivist, the findings in these cases would appear idiosyncratic and without logical coherence. These cases are the stuff of long and tortured exegetical law review articles in search of some unifying explanatory thread. After all, the Supreme Court must have some guiding principles by which it resolves property rights disputes. Aren't there durable legal doctrines that inform decisions in such important cases?

In *The Legal Foundations of Capitalism* (1924), John R. Commons sought to formulate a theory of the evolution of institutional arrangements by studying how disputes and conflicts are eventually "worked out." Commons insisted that Adam Smith got it wrong when he offered a general theory of economic life predicated on harmony and mutual benefit from exchange. To Commons the very essence of daily life is one of conflicts over scarcity, and those scarcities are not mediated by mutually beneficial bargaining but rather by negotiations and struggle. Ultimately those struggles, many of which start out at a local level, or in a national legislature, stand a good chance of ending up in the courts. Indeed, a fraction of those disputes will find themselves at the Supreme Court. In essence, it is here—at the Supreme Court—that "disputes go to die." That is, the Supreme Court (indeed all courts) must pick a winner. Commons used the term "to pick a value." In essence, the decisions of the Court must look to the future and decide which possible future it seems better to endorse. All struggles are, after all, about the future. The members of the Supreme Court must imagine (must create) a future they find compelling, and they must then decide the cases before them in light of that future. Commons knew that the Court did not act on principles—legal doctrine—because timeless and universal principles inevitably fail under the confining particularity of each dispute. Courts decide cases in terms of what, at the moment, seems to be the more compelling reasons. In doing so, courts inevitably "pick values." Commons called this "reasonable valuing."

In essence, Commons was endorsing the insights of John Dewey and the emerging theory of pragmatism. In essence, conventional efforts to divine the idea of property rights in the American experience are flawed in their epistemology. If we employ abduction, we start with the surprising fact that the Supreme Court decides one land-use case as if it were determined to "protect" property rights, while in another decision it seems to decide "against" the protection of property rights. How is this possible? Aren't property rights clear and stable, merely waiting to be discovered when a dispute arises? Volitional pragmatism starts by asking us to imagine a hypothesis that would render these seemingly inconsistent decisions explicable. That is:

> The surprising fact, C (inconsistent decisions), is observed.
> But if A were true, C (inconsistent decisions) would be a matter of course.
> Hence, there is reason to suspect A is true.

If A is true, what must be the content of A such that inconsistency (C) is a matter of course? The only plausible content of A (the assumption or the hypothesis) is that rather than a property right being some a priori concept whose content awaits discovery by the courts, a property right is created as the courts struggle with the conflicting rights claims before them. In essence, courts listen to conflicting assertions about where the property right is said to lie, and must, ipso facto, decide which assertion seems the most compelling. The issue therefore becomes which party can marshal the best reasons for the court to take its side in the dispute? We see that property rights are not protected by the courts because they are property rights. Rather, those settings and circumstances that gain the protection of the courts become, by virtue of that protection, property rights.

The abductivist, rather than finding these cases perplexing, would use their very confounding nature as the starting point for working out a theory of property rights. That is, these cases and their findings are the results that require explanation (a reason). And there is a plausible explanation for these seeming disparate decisions by the Supreme Court. The only way to understand the idea of property rights in the American experience is to understand that this term is the benediction applied to those settings and circumstances that, when the dust of consideration by various levels of jurisprudence has finally settled, are found worthy of indemnification by the state. This proposition springs from the logic of volitional pragmatism. Notice that the term property right is not something known axiomatically, something whose essence is clear to us by intuition or introspection before the specifics of a particular legal struggle is joined. Rather, the idea of property rights is arrived at—created—in the process of resolving mutually exclusive rights claims before the court. That is, property rights are not a priori "essences" that exist and await discovery in a particular legal scuffle. Rather, property rights are created in the process of resolving disputes originating in conflicting rights claims brought before the courts. The American judicial system does not seek to discover where the a priori property right lies. Rather, the courts offer a necessary forum before which, from time to time, conflicting and mutually exclusive rights claims will be brought. When the more compelling rights claim has been determined, the courts will issue a decree to that effect. We see that property rights are made, not found.

This recognition follows necessarily from the meaning of "right." To have a right means that you have been granted the ability to compel the coercive power of the state to come to your assistance against the contrary claims of others. Rights allow an individual to enlist the wondrous powers of the state as your very special ally. The granting of a right by the state (and the courts are but the final arbiters of state action) does not imply passive support by the state. Rather, that grant bestows active assistance for those to whom the state has granted that status of a "right." That is, the state stands ready to be enlisted in the cause of those to whom it has granted rights. We say that rights expand the capacities of the individual by indicating what one can do with the aid of the collective power (Bromley 1989; Macpherson 1973; Commons 1924).

Notice that to have civil rights means that the state will come to your aid if, for instance, you wish to eat in a particular restaurant or enroll in a particular university. Federal officers, acting under a binding decree from the courts, stand ready to assist you in those acts, regardless of their personal views about the legitimacy (justifiability) of your demands. You have rights, and the state is your ally, the reality of which is the necessary condition for you to be said to have rights. Others—owners of restaurants unhappy about your desire for a meal there, governors intent on keeping you out of particular universities—have duties to comply with the wishes of the state on pain of police action (itself possibly coerced by the courts and, if necessary, the national militia).

We must also understand that property is not an object but is, instead, a value. When one buys a piece of land (in the vernacular, a "piece of property"), one acquires not some physical object but rather control over a benefit stream arising from that setting and circumstance that runs into the future. That is why one spends money (one benefit stream) in order to acquire a different benefit stream ("ownership" of a new benefit stream arising from the fact of ownership). Notice that the magnitude of that new benefit stream depends on the legal parameters associated with it. Can one build a tall office tower on it, or a mere bungalow? Is it now covered by water six months out of the year, and if so, will local ordinances allow it to be drained for some more remunerative use? The price paid to acquire that new benefit stream is none other than the expected discounted present value of all future net income appropriable from "owning" the thing. This is why property is the value, not the object (Bromley 1991; Macpherson 1973, 1978). And, of course, we put together two concepts—property and right—to arrive at the understanding that this pertains to the grant of authority by the state to a person now called an "owner." That authority promises that the state is a willing participant in the imposition of binding duties on all those in the class of individuals called "nonowner."

I insisted previously that the courts create property rights out of the disputes that come before them. This act of creation stands in contrast to the idea that the courts discover property rights as they dig into conflicting rights claims. What might this idea of creation entail? Here I draw on Louis Menand's *The Metaphysical Club* (2001), which concerns the origins of pragmatic philosophy in America. Central players in this story include William James, John Dewey, Oliver Wendell Holmes, and Charles Sanders Peirce. Of course, Holmes turned out to be one of the most celebrated of American legal theorists. Menand writes, "It was Holmes's genius as a philosopher to see that the law has no essential aspect" (Menand 2001, p. 339). What is meant here by "essential aspect"?

In philosophy, *essence* is the being or the power of a thing—its necessary internal relation or function. Essence is what a thing (including an idea) does for us or to us. For Locke, essence is the being whereby a thing is what it is. For Kant, essence is the primary internal principle of all that belongs to the being of a thing. For Peirce, essence is the intelligible element of the possibility of being (Runes 1983, p. 112). Indeed, Peirce insists that knowing is confined to the possibilities of being. As we saw previously, "Consider what effects, that might conceivably have practical bearings, we conceive the object of our conception to have. Then, our conception of these effects is the whole of our conception of the object" (Peirce 1934, p. 1).

Menand, in writing about Holmes and his famous book *The Common Law*, notes that this book—a compilation of twelve Lowell Lectures presented by Holmes at the Harvard Law School in 1880—was intended to trace and explain the evolution of legal doctrine. More important, the central purpose was to explain the remark that Holmes had made in his very first law review article in 1870: "It is the merit of the common law that it decides the case first, and determines the principle afterwards" (Menand 2001, p. 339). This is a paradox. If legal principles don't decide cases, what does? Holmes's answer to this paradox provides the basis of all of his later jurisprudence. Menand conveys Holmes's views as follows:

> A case comes to court as a unique fact situation. It immediately enters a kind of vortex of discursive imperatives. There is the imperative to find the just result in this particular case. There is the imperative to find the result that will be consistent with the results reached in analogous cases in the past. There is the imperative to find the result that, generalized across many similar cases, will be most beneficial to society as a whole—the result that will send the most useful behavioral message. There are also, though less explicitly acknowledged, the desire to secure the outcome most congenial to the judge's own politics; the desire to use the case to bend legal doctrine so that it will conform better with changes in social standards and conditions; and the desire to punish the wicked and excuse the good, and to redistribute costs from parties who can't afford them (like accident victims) to parties who can (like manufacturers and insurance companies).
>
> Hovering over this whole unpredictable weather pattern—all of which is already in motion, as it were, before the particular case at hand ever arises—is a single meta-imperative. This is the imperative not to let it appear as though any one of these lesser imperatives has decided the case at the blatant expense of the others. A result that seems just intuitively but is admittedly incompatible with legal precedent is taboo; so is a result that is formally consistent with precedent but appears unjust on its face. (Menand 2001, p. 339)

And Menand continues:

> Many years later, when Holmes was on the Supreme Court, Holmes used to invite his fellow justices, in conference, to name any legal principle they liked, and he would use it to decide the case under consideration either way. . . . When there are no bones, anybody can carve a goose. (Menand 2001, p. 340)

It seems that volitional pragmatism is pertinent to the core idea of American jurisprudence, and that volitional pragmatism offers a way to consider and understand the evolution of institutions under the collective control of the state. The challenge in property rights disputes is to fix beliefs about where the most compelling property interests lie. The most compelling claims will constitute the best thing to do in those circumstances. Truth is the very special benediction we bestow on our settled deliberations.

IMPLICATIONS

Property rights constitute one class of institutions that most of us imagine to be inviolate and secure. Some imagine that property rights constitute the bedrock of individual liberty and an efficient market economy. Indeed, since the fall of the eastern European economies, it seems that all manner of economic problems are laid at the feet of "insecure property rights." These discussions tend to confuse an economy with a secure and effective rule of law providing transactional security with one in which property rights are thought of as some durable and unchanging foundation for all transactions. Any economy in which legal relations cannot change, however, is an economy locked in a structure that, in the fullness of time, will end up strangling the very thing that makes a market economy adaptable to changing conditions. That adaptability is nothing but the ability to induce institutional change when the existing working rules and entitlements no longer seem instrumental to the evolving purpose of the nation state. And, as we have seen here, property rights undergo change when the courts, confronted with a new and perplexing fact situation, come to realize that the future would not be well served by preserving existing property relations. And so suddenly it seems better to allow for some malleability—some elasticity—in that class of institutions that, under ordinary circumstances, are most resistant to change.

Volitional pragmatism teaches us that the courts in the American experience (and surely elsewhere) struggle with the same problem that individuals must confront: when faced with surprise and doubt, we marshal created imaginings to help us sort out the future. Russell Hardin suggests, "What the judge actually does in the common law when a case arises in a new context is to establish a rule to guide *future* actors while treating the present litigants *as though the rule had been in place when they acted*" (Hardin 2003, p. 47). The renowned appellate judge Richard A. Posner tells a similar story in his *Law, Pragmatism, and Democracy* (2003). As individuals (and as justices in judicial chambers) come to grips with how they imagine the future might and ought to unfold, they will settle on a majority vision that now seems better to endorse. They will justify that consensus to themselves and to the disputants. And they will leave a legal record that will serve as a basis for their emergent thoughts about the putatively better future. And tomorrow a new dispute will emerge. The economy becomes.

CHAPTER THIRTEEN

Volitional Pragmatism and the Economic Regulations

> Equilibrium economics, because of its well known welfare
> economic implications, is easily convertible into an apologia
> for existing economic arrangements, and it is frequently so
> converted.
> —Frank Hahn, *Some Adjustment Problems* (1970)

THE ECONOMY AND THE POLITY

A frequent organizing principle in economics is that there is something identifiable and separate called *the economy*. Coincident with this perception is the related idea that there is something else called *politics*. That these demarcations happen to mirror the disciplinary turf of modern universities is not unrelated to this demarcationist vision of the modern democratic nation-state. Of course, at one time economics and political theory were united both mentally and structurally in the academy. But the advent of economics becoming both "analytical" and method-driven gave rise to the felt need to differentiate the "science" of economics from the mere "art" of governance and politics. Economics came to be about tight models of rational choice, whereas government and politics remained concerned with interest groups, logrolling, power, and contested visions about the purpose of government and society.

This demarcation, at least in the minds of the welfare economists who gained ascendancy in the latter half of the twentieth century, allowed the emergence of talk about market failure, government failure, and the emergence of a line of work that saw its main purpose being to pass judgment on when, exactly, so-called government interference in the allegedly separate workings of the economy would enhance or stifle economic efficiency and social welfare. Nowhere has this demarcationist program been more assiduously followed than in the literature on environmental regulations. To mainstream environmental economists, particularly that branch to emerge from the field of public finance (with its frequent resort to the standard concepts of distortions, deadweight losses, and the sacred trinity of efficiency, redistribution, and stabilization), the demarcationist world view is foundational. But is it coherent?

ENVIRONMENTAL REGULATIONS

The notion of market failure has been the dominant metaphor in the economic analysis of environmental policy. Environmental pollution, an example of externalities, has long been regarded as the essence of market failure. That is, atomistic choices in the status quo institutional setup (invariably called "the market") are found to produce outcomes—smoke, toxic fumes, pesticide-laden fruit and groundwater, noise, chemical discharges into rivers—that harm (impose unwanted costs on) others. These spillovers are then said to represent a market failure. But, of course, welfare economists will insist that this cannot automatically be called a market failure unless it can be shown that the benefits of correcting the existence of this harm exceed the costs of correcting the status quo institutional setup that produces the harm (the externalities). This logic is the essence of work attributable to Harold Demsetz (1967) and Ronald Coase (1960). According to this view, property rights will become more specific with respect to environmental spillovers when the benefits of doing so exceed the costs of necessary change. If the benefits cannot be shown to exceed the costs then it is efficient ("optimal") that the institutional setup not be changed. While the victims might very well be seriously harmed by the smoke, toxic fumes, or chemical discharges into rivers, their harm is deemed to be less than the necessary costs to change the existing rules (institutions) that allow the unwelcome discharge of these pollutants.

As standard Paretian economists often put the matter, something's economic benefit (or worth) is determined by how much people are willing to pay for it. If clean water or air (or a preserved wetland) cannot muster a sufficient willingness to pay on the part of those who find those things compelling, then it is socially optimal that the air or the water remain dirty (or the wetland be drained to make way for what these days passes for progress). It will then be asserted that no market failure exists in such cases because the costs of change are claimed to exceed the benefits of that change. In the terminology of environmental economics, interference with others in the form of costs shifted on to them (pollution or a wetland turned into a parking lot) that is not worth internalizing is regarded as a Pareto-irrelevant externality. Those exposed to fish they cannot eat, water they cannot drink, air not fit for breathing, and sunsets they cannot enjoy may not be amused to learn that the harms they suffer are Pareto irrelevant.

We see here the reigning deductive paradigm of that branch of environmental economics that is concerned with "market failure." If governments, under pressure from the victims of externalities, are going to alter the extant institutional arrangements (linguistically privileged by the label "the market") for the purpose of addressing the visitation of environmental harms on others, then those changes (linguistically prejudiced by the labels "regulations" or "government interference") must pass a benefit-cost test. In this field of applied economics, benefit-cost analysis stands as the definitive test of the rationality (the social optimality) of new environmental policy initiatives, and many economists are committed to its widespread (and required) use (Arrow et al. 1996; Palmer, Oates, and Portney 1995; Pearce 1997).

The obvious problem here is that these environmental problems (air and water pollution, destruction of waterfowl habitat, greenhouse gas emissions, toxic wastes) will inevitably result in calls by the citizenry for some resolution. Most environmental economists will be suspicious of such demands made on the political process. Indeed, many of them will blame environmental organizations for excessive environmental regulations. It will be said that those who demand a cleaner environment are seeking to free-ride on the political process by getting something through the legislature (new institutional arrangements leading to an improved environment) so that they can benefit without having to pay for it. After all, if they can free-ride on the political initiative of others, then those who favor less pollution might be able to get a cleaner environment without having to offer payments to polluters to cease their contamination of the water and air. These economists will assert that if we allow this sort of free riding to occur then society will end up with "too much" environmental quality—the air and water will be too clean, and the fish will have too few chemical residues in their edible flesh, and there will be too many hectares devoted to wildlife and waterfowl habitat. Left unaddressed in this complaint is precisely why those seeking to be free of pollutants should have to pay in order to change the offensive behavior of those causing that suffering. Why should not payment flow the other way? That is, why are polluters not made to pay victims of pollution for the ability to keep fouling the air or the water? The pragmatist would suggest that this is a policy initiative worth serious consideration. And the pragmatist would not be persuaded that the mere fact of historical use is sufficient reason to continue particular activities once we know they are harmful to the rest of us. Pragmatism induces us to ask for and to articulate reasons.

Among many environmental economists, we see frequent assertions about the harm to befall society from institutional change that is undertaken when the Demsetz-Coase condition is not met. That is, economists could not find benefits of institutional change that exceeded the costs of that change, and yet scheming politicians, ever mindful of the next election, bowed to the special pleadings from the environmental lobby. From this observation it will then be asserted that because the efficiency conditions were not met, the institutional change cannot possibly be *socially* preferred. And so many environmental economists, apparently unaware of the fact that positive net benefits of institutional change are neither necessary nor sufficient for a social improvement (and conversely), will lament the meddling of politicians in the economy (Bromley 1990; Mishan 1980; Vatn 2005; Vatn and Bromley 1994, 1997). We see, in other words, the world carved at the joints: on one side stands the "economy" while on the other side stands "politics."

This position derives from more than a failure to apprehend the incoherence of welfare theory. The flawed approach is predicated on a curious version of what we might call *political economy*. Specifically, environmental economists will complain that if an environmental problem is corrected in the absence of proof that the benefits of the policy change exceeded the costs of that change, then this is an egregious example of politics interfering with a rational economic decision (Palmer, Oates, and Portney 1995). But isn't this a little odd? The appeal of democracy as a political system is its supposed responsiveness to the concerns and desires of citizens. The economy must always be understood as being embedded in, and contingent upon, prevailing political norms and processes. The nature and scope of the economy (the arena of markets) are, after all, social constructs. The market economy is not an end in itself but is, instead, merely instrumental to other ends. From this we may infer that if economic calculations were meant to rule collective choice in democratic societies, then we could quite easily dispense with a great deal of the expensive accoutrements of democracy—legislatures, elections, the judicial branch—and turn public policy over to a small council of economic advisers with a very large staff. That this has not happened in any democracy would seem suggestive of how citizens in democracies view the calculations and welfaristic prescriptions of Paretian economists in comparison with the more expansive and inclusive considerations that emerge from the political process.

Obviously, if public policy were in the hands of a dictator, then there would be grounds for concern. But the processes under discussion here cannot logically be called dictatorial, ill-informed, hasty, or any of the other epithets implied by those who denounce public policy as the triumph of politics over "good" Paretian economics. All public policy deliberations are accompanied by extensive discussions, a longtime delay for public comment, protracted hearings and posting of the proposed institutional arrangements for all to see and react to, expert testimony from the executive branch, research results from consultants for industry and public health groups, and endless legislative wrangling (and yes, with a lobbyist or two working the corridors). Despite this, it is not at all uncommon to see environmental economists deploying their simple deductive models to "prove" that political solutions to environmental problems are irrational if they are not made in accord with how these economists insist those choices ought to be decided.

We see this idea reflected in a celebratory issue of the *Journal of Environmental Economics and Management* in recognition of the twenty-fifth year of its publication. The purpose of the special issue was to produce a "policy report card for the profession" (of environmental and resource economics). In one of the main papers we are told that:

> Environmental economics is fundamentally a policy-oriented discipline. Its goal is to promote the efficient use of environmental resources, which, by their open-access nature, are unlikely to be allocated efficiently by private markets. This means that government policies are needed to ensure efficient use of the environment. . . . the goal of this article is to assess whether researchers have developed the tools that environmental managers need to make efficient decisions. Typically, these decisions fall into two categories: (1) how to set goals or standards; and (2) how to achieve stated environmental goals. . . . Efficiency requires that goals (or standards) be set to balance benefits and costs and that stated goals be achieved at least cost. . . . Whether or not economists are always successful in promoting efficiency in environmental regulation, it is appropriate to ask whether they have provided the tools that would enable policymakers to make efficient decisions were they *willing and able to do so*. (Cropper 2000, pp. 328–29; emphasis added)

It would appear that some environmental economists have not yet heard about the fatal circularity of efficiency calculations as a guide to coherent policy. Or perhaps efficiency calculations are so profoundly constitutive and instrumental for this particular branch of economics that to abandon efficiency as a "truth rule" would undermine their prescriptive certitude. Of course, there is a marvelous caveat in the preceding quotation—provided there are policy makers "willing and able" to make allegedly "efficient decisions." In other words, environmental economists have many of the right tools for the job of divining proper (efficient) environmental policy. The only vexing problem is an apparent scarcity of decision makers willing and able to listen.

Just how might the truth rules of environmental economics be deployed to bring about the "efficient use of environmental resources"? How about water quality in urban Delhi, India? In one study we are assured that the research will attempt to estimate the social benefits of cleaning the Ganges River in India, apparently on the conviction that no action can be taken unless it is found that the benefits exceed the costs of cleaning up this foul open sewer (Markandya and Murty 2004). In estimating the "social benefits" of cleaner water in the river, both market and nonmarket valuation of environmental goods is used. The "benefits estimated include user and non-user benefits, health benefits to the poor households living along the river, and agricultural benefits to farmers among other benefits" (Markandya and Murty 2004, p. 61). Even without including benefits to the fishing industry, the program of cleaning the Ganges is reported to have "positive net present social benefits at a 10 percent social rate of discount and an internal rate of return as high as 15 percent" (Markandya and Murty 2004, p. 61). The basis of much of the "benefits" from this cleaning program is the lost wages from workers being sick and morbid during part of the year from their necessary reliance on drinking water from this highly polluted river.

Now one might suppose that if the lost wages of Delhi's poor are sufficient to "rationalize" an investment in cleaning a river that now makes most of them sick enough to stay away from much-needed wage employment, one might be able to find plausible reasons for a cleanup without the extensive (and expensive) research underlying this study. And what would we conclude about the "efficient use of environment resources" if the only persons victimized by the foul river happened to be the many in Delhi without a job of any kind? That is, what might we conclude if the harms (to the environmental economist these are called "damages") from this open sewer fell on those without wages to be forgone because of their general unemployment owing to persistent morbidity? Suddenly it seems that there could be very few social "benefits" from cleaning the Ganges. And it then would seem—at least to the Paretian economist—that the Ganges is optimally polluted.

And there is yet another study to ponder, also in Delhi. This one seeks to "value health damages from water pollution in urban Delhi, India." Specifically, we are assured that:

> The present study conducts an *objective* assessment of the health damages incurred by urban households by adopting a health production function approach. A model for valuing the damages from contaminated water supplies, based on the theory of utility-maximizing consumer behaviour is developed for estimating the probability of illness for a household. An estimate for the predicted probability of observing illness in a household is obtained. This probability measure is subsequently used along with data on illness to derive treatment costs and the wage-loss arising from the illness. Thus, a measure of total costs of illness is obtained. (Dasgupta 2004, p. 83; emphasis added)

One may wonder about the adjective in the first sentence that puts the reader on notice that we are about to discover an "objective" assessment of the health damages. And what, exactly, would a "subjective" assessment of health damages look like? Equally stark is the purpose here to derive a monetized cost of illness for the entire population so that we might be informed of an "objective assessment of the damage caused by water contamination" (Dasgupta 2004, p. 100). The author then assures us that these costs can be interpreted as an "indicator of the (minimum) willingness to accept compensation for the surveyed population. The cost of illness consists of two components, the costs of treatment and the wage-loss arising from absence from work due to ill health" (Dasgupta 2004, pp. 100–1).

The point in both of these studies—as with much of what is written in environmental economics these days—is to discover whether environmental resources are being used, in Cropper's words, "efficiently." A related issue, of course, is to discover whether it would be "efficient" to take steps to reduce the extent to which the residents of Dehli are being poisoned by their only source of drinking water. If it is found that the costs of avoiding this situation of widespread illness and morbidity somehow exceed the very low level of lost wages in an urban economy where there is not much in the way of wages to be "lost" (forgone), then it would seem that the conjured logic of "efficiency" reveals to us that it is not "worth it" to prevent the public health problem that would seem, on mature reflection, to be rather serious. Can it really be that environmental economists find this "logic" compelling?

This larger problem is on stark display in an exchange in the fall 1995 issue of the *Journal of Economic Perspectives*. In an article on environmental regulations and the competitiveness of firms, Michael Porter and Claas van der Linde write that:

> [T]he environmental-competitiveness debate has been framed incorrectly. The notion of an inevitable struggle between ecology and the economy grows out of a static view of environmental regulation, in which technology, products, processes and customer needs are all fixed. In this static world, where firms have already made their cost-minimizing choices, environmental regulations inevitably raise costs and will tend to reduce the market share of domestic companies on global markets. . . . However, . . . the new paradigm of international competitiveness is a dynamic one, based on innovation. . . . internationally competitive companies are not those with the cheapest inputs or the largest scale, but those with the capacity to improve and innovate continually. . . . in this paper we will argue that properly designed environmental standards can trigger innovation that may partially or more than fully offset the costs of complying with them. Such "innovation offsets" . . . can not only lower the net cost of meeting environmental regulations, but can even lead to absolute advantages over firms in foreign countries not subject to similar regulations. Innovation offsets will be

common because reducing pollution is often coincident with improving the productivity with which resources are used. In short, firms can actually benefit from properly crafted environmental regulations that are more stringent (or are imposed earlier) than those faced by their competitors in other countries. By stimulating innovation, strict environmental regulations can actually enhance competitiveness. (Porter and van der Linde 1995, pp. 97–98)

What has come to be called the Porter hypothesis is found in the formula, "strict environmental regulations can actually enhance competitiveness." This hypothesis has been met with profound incredulity by most environmental economists. Indeed, in a companion article, several environmental economists dismissed the Porter hypothesis as "astonishing" (Palmer, Oates, and Portney 1995, p. 119). These economists expressed shock that Porter and van der Linde had "turned their back on a long tradition of benefit-cost analysis" in attempting to determine whether environmental regulations are in the public interest. Their attack on the Porter hypothesis took two forms—a strained (and flawed) appeal to deduction, and a familiar value judgment among environmental economists about how environmental policy ought to be decided.

Those economists attacking the Porter hypothesis developed a simple static model of a competitive firm and then used this naive model to "prove" (their words) that "incentive-based environmental regulation results in reduced profits for the regulated firm" (Palmer, Oates, and Portney 1995, p. 122). The authors acknowledge that theirs is a static model that fails to address the inherent uncertainty in research and development (R&D) decisions. But, curiously, they do not seem to notice that their naive model also fails to treat technical change as endogenous, a serious flaw in the environmental policy realm. They also admit that it is precisely such static models that are criticized by Porter and van der Linde. Yet, they regard their static model as providing a "useful point of entry into the issue" (Palmer, Oates, and Portney 1995, p. 122). We see that such models are "points of entry" but that they also "prove" what the authors wish to have proved. This way the economist has covered all contingencies. If no one notices the flaws in the model, it will soon come to stand as definitive proof. If someone challenges the model, the authors can quickly retreat to the "it's-just-a-point-of-entry" defense. Or the model is said to convey useful "stylized facts."

The static (deductive) model under discussion represents a profit-maximizing firm operating in a competitive industry with R&D expenditures treated as exogenous. The model depicts a simple competitive firm choosing a level of abatement for a production process that is given and unchanging. The new environmental regulation can be met by the firm paying new effluent charges, or by agreeing to undertake new abatement expenditures. In the static model, the firm chooses the profit-maximizing level of abatement where marginal abatement cost equals the effluent charge. The model demonstrates that because the profit-maximizing firm would not freely choose to undertake abatement R&D, it must necessarily follow that profits would thereby be reduced. This deductive program authorizes Palmer, Oates, and Portney to declare that they have "proved" the flaw in the Porter hypothesis. But, of course, as long as technology is constant, the results could not possibly be otherwise. The authors confidently conclude:

> Thus, in this model of innovation in abatement technology, an increase in the stringency of environmental regulations unambiguously makes the polluting firm worse off. Even if the firm can invest and adopt a new, more efficient abatement technology, if that technology wasn't worth investing in before, its benefits won't be enough to raise the company's profits after the environmental standards are raised, either. (Palmer, Oates, and Portney 1995, p. 125)

Notice that the authors do not say "in the *real world* an increase in the stringency of environmental regulations unambiguously makes the polluting firm worse off." Rather, they say, "in this model . . . an increase in the stringency of environmental regulations unambiguously makes the polluting firm worse off." Curiously, there seems little interest here in determining whether the static model of a competitive firm fits the world it presumes to model—a world made up of 3M, Dow, Ciba-Geigy, Monsanto, and the like. Indeed, the authors resisted the opportunity to build a model in which the Porter hypothesis was possible and then to assess the assumptions required to make the hypothesis plausible. Their simple static model was sufficient grounds for them to denounce the Porter hypothesis as "astonishing." Perhaps they wished to believe that the Porter hypothesis was impossible and with but little effort managed to conjure a model that validated their predisposition?

We see that because it was not "worth" it (economically efficient) for the firm to invest in pollution abatement in the absence of the regulation, it cannot possibly be other than harmful to the firm once a regulation is introduced. Regulations must, ipso facto, harm firms and thus reduce their competitiveness. The authors then seem pleased enough with their static model to observe that, "We have little doubt about the general applicability of this conclusion" (p. 127), and they go on to refer to the estimates of pollution abatement and control expenditures in the United States compiled by the Environmental Economics Division of the Commerce Department's Bureau of Economic Analysis. There follows a discussion of how expensive environmental regulations have been in the United States. Despite their observation that environmental regulations have been costly, there is a closing admission that "it is not clear that environmental regulation is harming the competitiveness of U.S. firms (Palmer, Oates, and Portney 1995, p. 130). Interestingly, this ambiguity about whether strict environmental regulations have harmed the international competitiveness of the U.S. economy is reflected in a study by one of the authors so aggressively critical of the Porter hypothesis (Jaffe et al. 1995). One begins to wonder what all of the fuss is about.

We see that the Porter hypothesis is aggressively rejected by its critics because it failed to follow the "accepted tradition" of pronouncing on the wisdom of particular public policies on the basis of a calculation of benefits and costs by economists. Deduction quite easily becomes a normative device in the service of justifying a particular approach to public policy. The authors declare that environmental regulations can only be justified if it can be shown that the economic benefits of an improved environment are greater than the alleged costs of that improvement. Notice that the prior deliberations of the legislature and the executive branch in formulating new environmental standards apparently do not qualify as a legitimate forum for considering and deciding on the benefits and costs of a cleaner environment. To Porter's critics, only monetized benefits and costs as measured by economists seem to count as evidence. That is, credibility resides in estimates of the benefits of a cleaner environment that will be determined by some study showing the aggregate willingness to pay for a cleaner environment.

One curiosity of this line of work is that only rarely is there interest in determining the necessary compensation for citizens to continue to endure a foul environment. But, of course, it matters very much which way the question is put to the citizenry. Usually willingness-to-pay estimates of the "benefits" of improving the environment are three to ten times less than estimates of the required compensation to continue to be denied improvements in environmental conditions (Vatn and Bromley 1994). We see that many individuals may wonder why they should be expected to pay to obtain relief from pollution. The issue here concerns the *presumed* rights structure against which policy judgments are rendered (Bromley 1995). If the citizenry supposes that it has a right to a clean environment, then the idea of paying for it to become clean seems odd. To such individuals, compensation for continuing to endure poor environmental quality seems more appropriate. We see that the results of an empirical approach that is both value laden and theoretically naive are preferred guides to right action compared with the deliberations of legislative and executive bodies created for precisely that purpose. To the committed deductivist, explanation offers compelling justification.

Although economists insist that they do not let their values contaminate their work, Porter's critics are certainly adamant in indicating how environmental policy decisions ought to be made. Interestingly, many economists do not consider it a value judgment to assert that environmental policy should be decided by weighing the social benefits and costs as applied economists choose to calculate them. For environmental economists to argue for this particular decision rule is to insist that the values inherent in our theoretical structure—the two Paretian value judgments—are socially valid and command widespread assent. As Mishan (1980) reminds us, however, in the absence of an ethical consensus for this view it remains a mere assertion by environmental economists and has no more claim to our attention than assertions from others. All such propositions are simply value judgments—normative propositions—and must be seen as such.

ABDUCTION

Let us look at the matter of environmental regulations through the prism of volitional pragmatism. In this instance, we would start with two surprises, not one. The first surprise (a truth claim actually) originates with the Porter hypothesis:

S_1: strict environmental regulations can actually enhance competitiveness.

This is clearly a surprise to environmental economists because they tend to believe—and they can build naive models to "prove" that regulations must, ipso facto, harm the cost structure of firms and therefore stifle their competitiveness. The second surprise is:

S_2: despite years of stringent environmental regulations, the costs of which are estimated to be $102 billion in 1992, the American economy remains one of the most competitive in the world. (Jaffe et al. 1995)

The surprise that would animate the pragmatist would be that these two statements assert very similar positions (claims), despite the oddity that one of the authors of the second "surprise" is also an author of the quite aggressive attack on the first "surprise." What is going on here? Do some environmental economists feel duty-bound—disciplinarily predisposed—to attack regulations while at the same time participating in empirical studies that cannot prove regulations to be harmful to the economy?

The pragmatist would construct the following abductive syllogism:

> The surprising fact, C, is observed.
> But if A were true, C would be a matter of course.
> Hence, there is reason to suspect A is true.

Here, the surprising fact (C) is that regulations can enhance competitiveness (S_1) and that many years of stringent environmental regulations—and claims of "enormous costs" of compliance—seem not to have harmed American competitiveness (S_2). What must be the content of A in the preceding syllogism to render C a "matter of course"? The answer to that question is approached by advancing some assumptions (hypotheses) constituting the content of A (the case) such that their acceptance would render C both plausible and to be expected—that is, not surprising. The content of A is found precisely in the extensive quotation from Porter and van der Linde earlier in this chapter. Specifically, owners and mangers of polluting firms are obviously aware that social attitudes about pollution are changing. That is, these individuals live in a dynamic social setting, and they operate business in a dynamic market setting. Accordingly, they look into the future and, as sapient beings, try to formulate created imaginings with respect to the choice sets they will face in that future. If they are alert, they cannot but conjure imaginings that entail new environmental regulations with respect to particular pollutants. While unsure perhaps about how to move to one of these new futures, they certainly understand that pollution abatement is more sophisticated than the naive models built by the earnest deductivists who are "astonished" at Michael Porter and his hypothesis. In fact, owners and managers understand quite well that technology is both dynamic and endogenous. The imminent threat of regulations triggers discussions of technical change, but most assuredly discussions of the manifold advantages to the early adopters. Not surprisingly, these technological discussions are precisely of the sort that we would expect from basic microeconomics. That is, the firm economizes on those things for which it must pay, and it ignores those things that are now free. As long as firms can freely discharge their wastes into nearby rivers, what manager would bother to worry about effluents?

Only when that free opportunity appears tenuous and threatened do the costs associated with that customary behavior come under managerial scrutiny. Then the firm may suddenly realize that its current "recipe" for making its product entails considerable waste. But, of course, what is considered waste under one cost regime differs from what is considered waste under another regime. Perhaps they are using too much of certain inputs? Perhaps they are not combining those inputs in the least-cost manner under new (and threatened) waste-discharge pricing scenarios? These discussions prompt research, planning, and redesign of the recipe. When that redesign is finished, we should not be surprised to learn that the firm is able to continue to make its product at a significant reduction in cost. After all, the shelf of technology from which the firm will choose new processes and devices is not static but is always changing. That is, the new technology can be expected to offer the firm a distinct cost advantage to its existing (old) technology. The rest of the story is obvious. The early adopters move quickly, they acquire the latest technology, and to no one's surprise they now have a cost advantage over the laggards in that industry. Did the looming regulations cause the cost advantage? Or did the looming regulations provide a sufficient reason for owners and managers to undertake an operational diagnosis of their going concerns? Volitional pragmatism invites us to work from the latter presumption.

IMPLICATIONS

We see that many environmental economists are trapped by their deductive models in which strained efforts at explanation become distorted into justification of those models and the truth claims that emerge there from. Are they merely defending their naive models? Or are they doing something more? Are they defending a particular demarcationist worldview, one in which economists must be consulted before society will know what it wants? The pragmatist would say that they are doing both, and they are doing so without the benefit of understanding the extent to which they are imprisoned by their epistemology.

Obviously, as with endogenous growth theory, intellectual progress will occur as new researchers enter the debate over the Porter hypothesis. Indeed this has already begun, and the results of this work undermine the static deductive approach of those who were so profoundly "astonished" by the Porter hypothesis (Alpay, Buccola, and Kerkvliet 2002; Altman 2001; Gabel and Sinclair-Desgagné 1998; Mohr 2002). From this work, new models will emerge that can produce assumptions (explanations) consistent with the fact that despite years of stringent environmental regulations, said to amount to $102 billion in 1992, the American economy remains one of the most competitive in the world (Jaffe et al. 1995).

As we know, theoretical reconsideration by committed deductivists will only come when they are finally convinced that their simple models—not the data with which they work—are flawed. That is the basis for the interesting dissonance between the two surprises mentioned here. The data associated with the second surprise offered evidence of the plausibility of the first surprise. But because the automatic reaction here was to discredit the implicit model of the Porter hypothesis, the critics ended up contradicting themselves. The aggressive defense of their demarcationist worldview (and the naive models central to that worldview) deluded them about their own contradictions. Of course, abandoning vested positions in particular bundles of knowledge—models and worldviews—is never easy. To quote the German physicist Max Planck: "An important scientific innovation rarely makes its way by gradually winning over and converting its opponents: it rarely happens that Saul becomes Paul. What does happen is that its opponents gradually die out and that the growing generation is familiarized with the idea from the beginning" (Planck 1936). In essence, Planck is suggesting that science progress funeral by funeral.

CHAPTER FOURTEEN

Sufficient Reason

> Belief does not make us act at once, but puts us into such a
> condition that we shall behave in some certain way, when the
> occasion arises. Doubt has not the least such active effect, but
> stimulates us to inquiry until it is destroyed.
> —Charles Sanders Peirce, *Essays in the Philosophy*
> *of Science* (1957)

Driving the Machine from the Mind

My purpose here is to develop the broad outlines of a theory of economic
institutions and of institutional change. I seek to offer an account, a description, of how individuals and groups arrive at decisions about the nature and
structure of those working rules and property relations that will restrain,
liberate, and expand their range of volitional choice and action. This account consists of concepts, relations, and entailments that together constitute a theory of choice and action with respect to economic institutions.
The approach offered here will allow us to determine if indeed there is a
particular logic to a process that is regularly criticized for its resistance
to the optimality prescriptions from welfare economics. Spelling out an
alternative theory of action will allow us to assess if there are indeed logical
flaws in the decision process that somehow lead to wrong decisions in the
absence of welfaristic prescriptions from economists.

The task is, therefore, to offer a description of how public policy actually
proceeds in most democratic market economies. If this description is regarded as reasonably plausible, I will have offered a theory of public policy
and therefore of the evolution of economic institutions. Notice that this
will not be a normative theory about how collective choice and institutional
change ought to proceed. It will be descriptive in that it will provide concepts and relations that offer, in the spirit of the pragmatic theory of action,
an expression of how institutional change seems to unfold. Notice that I
do not presume to offer an account of how it "actually" unfolds. Rather,
I seek to provide a description of the stage on which collective action is
played out. We may think of this as a truth claim or an assertion on my
part—my settled belief. I cannot claim that this account constitutes warranted belief. That benediction must await the judgment of other scholars.

Before going further, I must devote a few moments to the idea of a theory. This is necessary because in economics we have a quite restrictive idea about what constitutes a theory. Indeed, when talking of "theory," it is common for economists immediately to launch into a discussion of their models. A model is not a theory. A model is a structurally dependent analytical engine whose pertinence resides entirely on its internal validity. Models may or may not fit the world they presume to reflect. A theory, on the other hand, is a constellation of concepts and relations offering a plausible structure for thinking about and comprehending particular connections of interest. If one has a theory of the French Revolution, it means that one can advance specific concepts, connections, and logical entailments that offer a plausible explanation of—the reasons for—that event.

What does a theory do for us? A theory allows plausible explanations of past and current events, and it allows plausible predictions of future—and, indeed, of past—events. How do we know we have a good theory? A theory is good if it can withstand internal (disciplinary) challenges to its concepts, to its relational properties, and to its entailments (explanations and predictions). The philosopher William Whewell insisted that a theory, upon formulation, must pass a variety of tests before it can be considered a plausible empirical engine for fixing belief. These tests concern: prediction, consilience, and coherence (Whewell 1858).

Notice that the term *theory* is—and has generally become—a shorthand expression for one or more related hypotheses that seem to address a particular event or situation. Indeed, it would seem much better if we thought of both explanation and prediction as sets of hypotheses about particular events. With respect to prediction, a theory's hypotheses must be able to foretell events that have yet to occur. Or, the hypotheses must be able to predict as-yet-unknown events that have happened in the past. In this latter case, predictions are tested when we are induced to take a more careful look at the past to see if the predicted event did in fact occur. Consilience implies that a theory's hypotheses must be able to explain and determine cases of a kind different from those imagined in the formation of the hypotheses. Coherence implies that the hypotheses of a theory must become more coherent over time. To Whewell, coherence occurs when we can extend our hypotheses to "colligate" (unite) a new class of phenomena without ad hoc modification of those hypotheses. Colligation brings together a number of empirical regularities by "superinducing" upon them a conception that unites these regularities and renders them expressible by a more general law.

So when I say that I am attempting to work out a theory of public policy—of institutional change—it means that I seek an account that will allow me to offer particular hypotheses about an explanation of why and how particular decisions emerge from that process. If I am successful, we may gain an *understanding* of the policy process. The theory should also allow hypotheses that entail predictions of particular aspects of past or future policies (not the specific policies themselves). The theory should permit inferences about other kinds of policy initiatives, and the salience of these inferences should increase with time. Notice that unlike much work in prescriptive economics, I do not offer a theory about how public policy ought to be carried out. Nor am I interested here in demonstrating how the world would be a better place, a more rational place, if only individuals and groups would learn to decide things in the way that prescriptive economics insists they should be decided. Such tendentious accounts are plentiful enough and are now recognized as inherently flawed (Akerlof and Dickens 1982; Brock and Colander 2000; Hahn 1970). Missing from this standard literature is any serious effort to describe how individuals actually decide what is better, at the moment, to do. Pragmatism, with its foundations in psychology, offers insights here. Pragmatism places emphasis on problem solving and on the asking for and the giving of reasons. Why, exactly, do you believe that school vouchers will help public schools and the children in them? Why, exactly, do you believe that the air is now "inefficiently" clean? Why, exactly, do you believe that child labor is good for India and other developing countries (let alone good for the children involved in that work)? Why, exactly, are you certain that globalization and free trade will benefit Rwanda? Why, exactly, do you believe that victims of pollution should be made to pay polluters in order to be liberated from the damages they currently endure? Why, exactly, do you believe that the "worth" of a wetland is revealed by how much individuals indicate they are willing to pay to prevent its destruction? Why, exactly, do the poor residents of Delhi deserve unsafe drinking water unless their lost wages from illness can be found to exceed the costs of bringing about a cleaner river?

The search for a theory of institutional change has been hampered by the deductive bias prevalent in Paretian economics. The quest to make institutional change endogenous has been, ironically, an endeavor geared to render institutional change mechanically deterministic rather than explicable by the search for and apprehension of reasons. As with standard economic stories of individual choice, the idea of endogenous institutional change is simply an endeavor that seeks to remove the human will in action from playing any role at all. In the received story, institutions change—machinelike—when it is efficient for them to change (North and Thomas, 1970, 1971, 1973). And if they do not change, then it is efficient that they not change (Demsetz 1967). Or, in a slight wrinkle on this story, if they do not change, and it can be shown by deductivist logic that these resistant institutions are inefficient ("merely redistributive"), then we must search for the reasons why these pernicious inefficiencies persist (Olson 1996). And here the standard "explanation" is that perverse political entrepreneurs prevent institutional change that would move the economy to its efficiency locus (production possibilities frontier) (North 1990). These stories appear to be descriptive: after all, who would wish for nation-states to be in the grip of perverse political forces that prevent it from achieving, as Olson puts it, their "economic potential"? But there is a prescriptive part as well: if institutional change is efficient, then institutions should change; and if it is not efficient for institutions to change, then they should not change. Such a theory of institutional change is a tautology, and yet its normative presumptions continue to hold a firm grip on many economists. Those who have managed to create such a "theory" may feel exhilaration at the mere thought of it, but it is not much of a theory because its hypotheses are vulnerable to validationism. Moreover, the project to make institutional change endogenous in economic models suffers from the fatal flaw that endogenization brings events into a structured mechanical relation, and this fact necessarily strips away any possibility of actual choice. Endogeneity is just another word for nothing left to choose.

Public policy is collective action in restraint, liberation, and expansion of individual action. Public policy alters the institutional foundations of an economy by altering the realms of choice—fields of action—for individuals. If we can gain clarity about how individuals and groups of individuals decide what is better, at the moment, to do, we will be on our way to an improved understanding of institutional change. What reasons count as explanations for collective action that will redefine individual fields of action? Current approaches fail to offer an understanding of institutional change because they are intent on embedding institutional change in the same mechanistic choice-theoretic algorithms that are thought to explain individual choice. Because we have good evidence of the failure to understand and explain individual choice with such models, it should come as no surprise that the same approach cannot but fail when it is deployed to explain the processes whereby collective action leads to new institutional arrangements. The epistemic turn offered here takes us away from the mechanism of logical positivism and redirects us toward the quest for—and articulation of—reasons that constitutes the core of pragmatism. Interestingly, recent recognition in economics of the profound role of complexity supports the pragmatist's approach to institutional change (Brock and Colander 2000). After all, if economic equilibrium is a convenient fiction, if Pareto optimality is an unknowable state, and if the future is confounded by insurmountable information problems, then mechanical welfaristic prescriptions represent mere wishful thinking instead of plausible accounts (Hahn 1970).

Volitional Pragmatism: The Emergent Theory

Pragmatism asks that individuals reveal the purposes and reasons behind their current belief. And when the answer comes back that a particular belief is firmly held because it is true, the pragmatist will not be surprised because another speaker can soon be found, equally earnest, convinced that just the opposite is true. Pragmatists encounter many people with great certitude about their "true" beliefs. Obviously not all "true" beliefs are true. But there seem to be many individuals who readily and vigorously insist that it is *their* true belief that is really true. It would seem that there are more certain people than there are certain truths. Friedrich Nietzsche suggests that convictions are more dangerous to the truth than lies. While positivists will suggest that this is precisely why we need "good science" to distinguish truth from mere opinion, pragmatists will then ask who shall stand in judgment at that particular tournament? And when a scientific discipline—an epistemic community—speaks with one voice about the veracity and desirability of a particular belief, pragmatists will ask whether or not these widely held scientific truths (warranted belief) constitute valuable belief? That is, can these warranted claims be justified to the widest possible audience of interested and affected individuals? Pragmatists tend to be quite insistent that there be sufficient reason for a particular belief. After all, a belief is the launching pad for action. Are you really prepared to act on your belief? Are you now ready to take your children out of elite suburban (or private) schools so that they (and you) can experience firsthand the allegedly salutary and exhilarating effects of school vouchers on school performance in the hollowed-out urban core where poverty and hopelessness abound? Or is your belief just adequate to inspire you to dictate how others shall contend with the sorry world in which they are situated, but not sufficient to entail a serious change in the behavior of you and others quite favorably insulated from horrible schools? To pragmatists, beliefs are that upon which we are prepared to act. Are you prepared to act on your beliefs?

The approach here is called *volitional* pragmatism. I invoke the adjective to stress that the concern here is with the human will in action, looking to the future, struggling with the perplexing problem of how that future ought to unfold. This is not a plausible domain for mechanistic Paretian truth rules about what is claimed to be socially preferred. It is, instead, a domain for articulating reasons—reasons for various images of plausible ends, and reasons for various images of plausible means. Volitional pragmatism holds that we will know how we wish the future to unfold when we have contemplated that future, and in the course of serious dialogue with others equally situated, manage to fix our belief about what seems better, at this time, to do. From there we must justify our settled belief to others, so that they might understand our reasons and thereby find our settled belief pertinent and valuable to them. Collective action is thus predicated and animated upon the widest possible justification for a particular belief, and for the widest possible justification for specific action for which that particular belief constitutes sufficient reason. I shall reprise the essence of this emergent theory.

Concepts

Abduction: reasoning from effect to cause (or reason). Inferring the existence of a fact quite different from anything observed, from which, according to known laws, something observed would necessarily result. Abduction explains effects.

Belief: that upon which we are prepared to act

Collective action: the rationing transactions of those social entities created for the purpose of redefining the institutional structure of a going concern. For nation-states, this is the essence of public policy.

Created imaginings: our imagined outcomes of actions imagined to be available

Doubt: the irritant that motivates thought in the quest for fixed belief

Epistemic premise: fixed belief that plausibly justifies particular action related to a volitional premise

Expressions: the produced (created) effect of impressions—what we make of our impressions, and therefore what becomes the basis of stories we tell to ourselves and others about our particular situatedness

Final cause: an outcome in the future for the sake of which particular action now seems justified

Fixed belief: The purpose of thought

Impressions: those sensible apprehensions that start with surprise or doubt and that form the raw material of what is, at the moment, thought

Institutions: norms, working rules, and property relations (entitlements) that define realms of choice for individuals in a going concern (usually, though not necessarily) a nation-state

Instrumental valuing: recognition of the usefulness of particular belief for the attainment of particular outcomes

Prospective volition: the human will in action, looking to the future, deciding how that future ought to unfold

Public policy: collective action in restraint, liberation, and expansion of individual action

Rationing transactions: the collective control of individual action wherein the new meaning of "reasonable" working rules and property relations (institutions) is worked out and then decreed

Sufficient reason: thoughts that give us fixed belief that then authorizes action

Surprise: the instigator of thought (see doubt)

Valuable belief: warranted belief that can be justified to the widest possible audience of thinking and reasoning agents

Volitional premise: a want statement, the plausible reaction to doubt or surprise

Warranted belief: the settled deliberations of a community of individuals (usually a professional discipline) constituted to produce belief about specific realms of our existence

Relations

What can we say about these concepts embedded in a structured set of relations? As we saw in the previous chapter, our situatedness is constituted by the constructed impressions and expressions that emerge from our experiences. Onto this stage appears doubt and surprise that immediately create irritation. Irritation represents the motivation for thought whose sole purpose is to fix belief. Why is that fellow angry with me? Why did I not receive an invitation to her dinner party? Why did that spacecraft disintegrate upon reentry into the earth's atmosphere? Why is my dog listless? Abduction is an inferential program that facilitates reasoning from effects to causes or reasons. When we have listened to warranted belief and it has been justified to us, we regard that as valuable belief. With valuable belief in hand, we assess future action. Unfortunately, when doubt and surprise animate us, puzzlement follows because we have never done that before—we have never had to respond to that particular surprise or doubt (otherwise we would know immediately what to think or to do). As we ponder that which we have never done before, we must rely on stories that will form the raw material of our volitional premises and epistemic premises for action. That is, we conjure created imaginings. In essence, we undertake instrumental valuing as we work through the process of fixing what we want by working out what we seem able to have (to get). This thought process is the human will in action, contemplating the future, figuring out how we wish that future to unfold for us. This is prospective volition in the service of human action. Our chosen course of action then becomes the reason for a particular imagined outcome in the future. Abduction gives us the reason for the effect. That reason is the final cause of our action, an outcome in the future for the sake of which we act now. We have acquired sufficient reason.

When we move from individual action to joint action, we observe this same process at work, but now it is necessary that the many disparate individual visions be reconciled. After all, public policy is collective action in restraint, liberation, and expansion of individual action. Collective action is the means whereby new economic institutions are considered, formulated, and implemented. This process of collective action can be thought of as a class of rationing transactions.

Plausible Entailments

Abduction liberates the economist to create propositions about institutional change that constitute plausibly true accounts of the pertinent reasons for the changes under consideration. Allegations of self-interested bureaucrats and politicians, or grand allegorical narratives concerning economic efficiency, cannot possibly comprise such accounts. Self-interest, because it is ubiquitous, cannot possibly comprise a reason for institutional change—unless one is charmed by a "theory" that says institutional change favors those with the ability to get their way. On this account, the circularity of such "theories" ought to be apparent. Similarly, economic efficiency, because it is merely a concept by postulation, cannot logically be a guide to institutional change. To say that the pursuit of economic efficiency is a reason for institutional change is to commit the teleological fallacy. But there is a more serious flaw in the deductive approach to institutional change. Advancing the pursuit of efficiency as a reason for institutional change entraps the economist in a futile search for affirmation, the absence of which comprises grounds not to challenge the dichotomous explanatory project of economics but to reproach politicians for doing the "wrong" thing.

The need to understand institutional change requires that we first understand how individuals and groups think about action. I suggest that individuals employ abduction in their quest for a new (revised) belief. I also suggest that this new belief is then epistemically linked to the existing institutional setup. This linking provides a "theory" about existing outcomes, the plausible explanation (reason) for those outcomes, and clarity about how behaviors and hence outcomes might be modified by novel institutions. Scientific belief is central here. But the truth claims from scientists about what is "right" or "good" carry limited weight unless they resonate with those to whom they are directed. Warranted belief is necessary but not sufficient for the rest of us to change our mind. We will only do that when we have been presented with valuable belief. After all, who among us decides to act on the basis of beliefs they do not believe? Who wishes to act on "false" beliefs?

Plausible descriptions of reasons for particular actions (decisions) bring us immediately to the concept of created imaginings. Because all proposed action regarding the future entails new circumstances beyond the experience of most, if not all, members of the decision-making body, individuals must create their own imaginings of the possible futures. These created imaginings comprise—indeed inform—the volitional premises of those contemplating particular actions. These volitional premises comprise the imagined desired outcomes that constitute the purpose for which a particular decision is contemplated. But recall that created imaginings must be brought onto the stage of extant expressions of present and plausible futures. For it is against these expressions that created imaginings gain—or fail to gain—the requisite traction.

We now come to the task of reconciling the emerged consensus about some created imagining with those defeated imaginings. How shall we regard the chosen path? This entails instrumental valuing—coming to like (prefer) the choice that seems to have become the essence of settled deliberations on instrumental grounds—because it will "deliver the goods." Or, as William James would put it, the solution has "cash value." The classical institutionalists would consider this to be the pragmatic evaluation of truth. Contemporary pragmatists would say that truth is a matter of collective judgment that serves to transform particular conceptual and empirical claims into warranted belief. That is, truth is a term we apply to that which it now seems plausible to believe.

This is seen to concern individual and collective determinations of what seems better, at the time, to do. The key here is that a particular group constituted to make particular decisions—and to justify those decisions to a broader community—can assuredly say that their settled deliberations have now given them valuable belief. And, as noted previously, a belief is that upon which we are prepared to act. In other words, the decision group has finally found sufficient reason to alter specific institutional arrangements in the interest of modifying particular economic outcomes. And that group is prepared to defend and to justify its reasons to others who remain skeptical. That justification will occur in terms of conversations about desired outcomes in the future for the sake of which the proposed action today seems like the best thing to do. Notice that the justification must necessarily entail not only particular outcomes in the future but also the specific means on which those outcomes seem most plausibly reliant.

The practical implications of this final step can be apprehended by a thought experiment. Consider Robert Owen's eventual ability to convince the British Parliament, surely no enemy of the industrial class, to pass several laws concerning the treatment of women and children in factories, such laws having long been bitterly opposed by the captains of industry. What can possibly explain this circumstance? What reasons seem plausibly implicated here? Is clarity gained by the standard explanation that Owen and his reformers suddenly had more "power" than the other side? I suggest not. Rather, volitional pragmatism suggests that such reforms were finally accepted because Owen offered better reasons why such laws were suddenly seen as the right thing to do. Notice the subtlety here. I did not say that it suddenly became right to pass such laws. Nor do I suggest that a majority of the British Parliament one day awoke to its morally superior Kantian obligation. I insist, instead, that a volitional and epistemic transformation had been underway for some time and that finally those in favor of reform were able to marshal the more compelling reasons to favor reform over the status quo ante institutional setup governing factory work. As Joseph Raz would say, deliberation is not a process of discovering what we want but a process of reflecting upon what there is the most reason to want (Raz 1997). If I choose to lie in a hammock rather than weed my garden, I am obviously able to marshal better reasons for doing the former rather than the latter. At the time, it was better to believe that I had the more sufficient reasons to choose the hammock over weeding. Where does "utility" fit in here—except as a rationalization of action predicated on other reasons?

In the case of Robert Owen and the British Parliament, dedicated deductivists will likely insist on knowing why this transformation in definition of the "right" happened at that time rather than twenty years earlier? Or, deductivists will demand to be shown proof that Owen and his reformers had not bribed a few key members of the Parliament. Or there will be any number of other "explanations" not covered in my account. To such protests I can only concur, and quickly add that a good theory is always suggestive of testable hypotheses. Volitional pragmatism, because it is grounded on the asking for and giving of reasons, offers many avenues to a number of testable hypotheses.

We see that understanding institutions and institutional change via volitional pragmatism does not close doors on possible hypotheses, nor does it prejudge institutional change as always in the interest of efficiency or else it is merely redistributive. Volitional pragmatism simply asks that the scientific enterprise approach the study of institutions and institutional change with an open and enabling epistemology. Consider the structure of explanation about some unexpected event. Recall that we proceed as:

> The surprising fact, C, is observed.
> But if A were true, C would be a matter of course.
> Hence, there is reason to suspect A is true.

Assume that the surprising fact C is that the World Health Organization (WHO) suddenly announces that it will now press governments to eliminate the ban on DDT. This surprising move suggests that the medical experts and officials within the WHO suddenly acquired a new fixed belief. We would be surprised by this announcement because hitherto the WHO had been an advocate of a ban on DDT. We are in need of an explanation of this sudden effort to mobilize governments in new collective action to redefine national laws to reconstitute the structures of correlated restraint and liberation concerning the use of DDT. We are now in need of the constituents of A such that C suddenly became the expected (rational) thing to do. Plausible constituents of A might include:

- New epidemiological research suggesting that malaria has suddenly become a very serious threat to millions of poor people
- New research suggesting that the reigning epistemic premise about DDT and the fate of bird's eggs and hatchling survival was mistaken
- New research suggesting that the original demise of bald eagles and other birds was caused by the prevalence of chlorofluorcarbons in the atmosphere, such compounds having recently been banned to forestall the depletion of atmospheric ozone
- A change in the leadership of WHO from the former prime minister of Norway to the former head of an aggressive NGO from Bangladesh, said NGO having been at the forefront of action to fight childhood malaria in poor countries
- Evidence suggesting that the manufacturers of DDT had launched an aggressive information and lobbying campaign to discredit current warranted and valuable belief regarding DDT residues and the survival of bald eagles and other birds

We see that an explanation for the new official position of the WHO might have more than one component. Volitional pragmatism asks that we seek reasons for new fixed belief on the part of WHO, and the explanatory hypotheses provide one plausible starting point for that quest of sufficient reason. Notice that the issue here is not necessarily to prove that one particular hypothesis is the right one. Rather, the task is to find plausible reasons—explanations—for this pronounced change in the fixed belief of the WHO.

Of course, volitional pragmatism reminds us that we cannot stop with the WHO. For the next step in this process of institutional change is for the WHO to pressure a number of governments to change their laws (institutions) regarding the use of DDT. Here we will encounter the asking for and giving of reasons. That is, the officials of WHO will need to devote time and financial resources to the giving of good reasons for their new belief, and justifying that new belief to others who still remain committed to the old belief about DDT and birds. Notice that the process of abduction would start anew with the issue now focusing on the ability of WHO officials to justify their new belief to disparate national governments. It is not hard to imagine that this justification will be easier (come more quickly) in those countries with millions of poor people living in swamp-infested lowlands, in areas where national environmental organizations are weak or nonexistent, and in those nations in which the WHO has a long history of constructive and helpful programmatic interaction.

Notice that the process of following the mooted hypotheses (the plausible conjectures) back to their necessary grounding engages us in a new round of either abduction or deduction. That is, if a hypothesis is to survive as having explanatory power, then we must keep "digging down" to investigate whether the necessary conditions for its existence in the present setting have been met. We enter into a new sequence of "if-then" chains in search for evidence that particular hypotheses can be sustained—or must be discarded.

Notice that this process necessarily brings us into the domain of prediction. If a particular hypothesis cannot be sustained in the absence of clear evidence of some other settings or circumstances, then we have here the basis for offering predictions about past circumstances—the test of which could be carried out. Or, we have predictions of future events that can be expected. Notice that these activities include following the entailments of our mooted hypotheses that we expect to light the way toward an explanation.

Coherence implies that the hypotheses of a theory must become more coherent over time. Coherence occurs when we can extend our hypotheses to colligate (unite) a new class of phenomena without ad hoc modification of those hypotheses. Colligation brings together a number of empirical facts by "superinducing" upon them a conception that unites the "facts" and renders them expressible by a more general law.

IMPLICATIONS

A credible theory of institutional change requires, first, recognition that individuals undertake those actions for which they can, at the moment, marshal the most compelling reasons. This process conflates both the volitional and epistemic premises in a process of getting in touch with what we want by coming to grips with what we imagine we can get (have). Wanting is not some abstract and dreamlike lunging toward the infeasible. It is, instead, a process of reasoned construction of created imaginings that are informed and constituted by their very feasibility. From this constructed realm of plausible futures, we then reflect on—and usually argue about—the various reasons why these plausible futures make more or less sense to us. We reason about what we want predicated on reasoning about what we come to believe we can have. We may want all manner of grand things—a villa in the South of France, a Bentley automobile, a quiet neighborhood, a successful career as a concert violinist—but these wants are, for most of us, the stuff of daydreams, not feasible plans of action. We may correctly regard them as contingent wants.

However, our daily life, embedded as it is in democratic market economies, is not about contingent wants. It is, instead, about coping with doubt and surprise, with impressions and expressions, and with prevalent behaviors and outcomes that please us, or that fail to do so. When we are not pleased with those outcomes, we seek, through democratic structures and processes, relief. It is often tedious, and it can be contentious. But the process of seeking relief forces us, on all sides of suddenly contentious issues, to create imaginings about what constitutes relief. More important, we are forced to confront the reality of what constitutes plausible relief. The very act of accepting the adjective *plausible* brings us, as individuals, or as members of decision-making bodies, in direct contact with the pragmatic evaluation of truth. That is, what is better than what we now have? What would move us in an agreeable direction? What will it take to move us? Is it worth it? What will others seek?

We are, the pragmatist would point out, searching for new belief— those things upon which, once we have them, we are quite prepared to act. That is all there is.

Bibliography

Adler, Matthew D., and Eric A. Posner (eds.). 2001. *Cost-Benefit Analysis: Legal, Economic and Philosophical Perspectives*. Chicago: University of Chicago Press.

Akerlof, George, and William T. Dickens. 1982. "The Economic Consequences of Cognitive Dissonance." *American Economic Review* 72 (3): 307–19.

Allen, Julia C., and Douglas F. Barnes. 1985. "The Causes of Deforestation in Developing Countries." *Annals of the Association of American Geographers* 75 (2): 163–84.

Alpay, E., Steven Buccola, and Joe Kerkvliet. 2002. "Productivity Growth and Environmental Regulation in Mexican and U.S. Food Manufacturing." *American Journal of Agricultural Economics* 84 (4): 887–901.

Altman, Morris. 2001. "When Green Isn't Mean: Economic Theory and the Heuristics of the Impacts of Environmental Regulations on Competitiveness and Opportunity Cost." *Ecological Economics* 36 (1): 31–44.

Arrow, Kenneth J., Maureen J. Cropper, George C. Eads, Robert W. Hahn, Lester B. Lave, Roger G. Noll, Paul R. Portney, Milton Russell, Richard Schmalensee, V. Kerry Smith, and Robert N. Stavins. 1996. "Is There a Role for Benefit-Cost Analysis in Environmental, Health, and Safety Regulation?" *Science* 272: (12 April) 221–22.

Ascher, William. 1999. *Why Governments Waste Natural Resources*. Baltimore: Johns Hopkins University Press.

Barbier, E. T., J. C. Burgess, and A. Markandya. 1991. "The Economics of Tropical Deforestation." *Ambio* 20 (2): 55–58.

Bator, Francis M. 1958. "The Anatomy of Market Failure." *Quarterly Journal of Economics* 72: 351–79.

Baumol, William J. 1972. "On Taxation and the Control of Externalities." *American Economic Review* 62: 307–22.

Baumol, William J., and Wallace E. Oates. 1988. *The Theory of Environmental Policy*. Cambridge: Cambridge University Press.

Bazelon, Coleman, and Kent Smetters. 1999. "Discounting inside the Washington, D.C. Beltway." *Journal of Economic Perspectives* 13 (4): 213–28.

Becker, Lawrence C. 1977. *Property Rights*. London: Routledge and Kegan Paul.

Bernstein, Richard. 1983. *Beyond Objectivism and Relativism: Science, Hermeneutics, and Praxis*. Philadelphia: University of Pennsylvania Press.

Besley, Timothy. 1995. "Property Rights and Investment Incentives: Theory and Evidence from Ghana." *Journal of Political Economy* 103 (5): 903–37.

Blackorby, Charles, and David Donaldson. 1990. "A Review Article: The Case against the Use of the Sum of Compensating Variations in Cost-Benefit Analysis." *Canadian Economics Journal* 3 (August): 471–94.

Boadway, Robin W. 1974. "The Welfare Foundations of Cost-Benefit Analysis." *Economic Journal* 84: 926–39.

————. 1976. "Integrating Equity and Efficiency in Applied Welfare Economics." *Quarterly Journal of Economics* 90: 541–56.

Boadway, Robin W., and Neil Bruce. 1984. *Welfare Economics.* Oxford: Blackwell.

Bowles, Samuel. 1998. "Endogenous Preferences: The Cultural Consequences of Markets and Other Economic Institutions." *Journal of Economic Literature* 36 (March): 75–111.

Brandom, Robert B. 1994. *Making It Explicit: Reasoning, Representing, and Discursive Commitment.* Cambridge, MA: Harvard University Press.

————. 2000. *Articulating Reasons.* Cambridge, MA: Harvard University Press.

Broberg, Gunnar. 1992. *Carl Linnaeus.* Stockholm: Swedish Institute.

Brock, William A., and David Colander. 2000. "Complexity and Policy." In David Colander (ed.), *The Complexity Vision and the Teaching of Economics*, pp. 73–96. Cheltenham: Edward Elgar.

Bromley, Daniel W. 1989. *Economic Interests and Institutions: The Conceptual Foundations of Public Policy.* Oxford: Blackwell.

————. 1990. "The Ideology of Efficiency: Searching for a Theory of Policy Analysis." *Journal of Environmental Economics and Management* 19: 86–107.

————. 1991. *Environment and Economy: Property Rights and Public Policy.* Oxford: Blackwell.

————. 1993. "Regulatory Takings: Coherent Concept or Logical Contradiction?" 17 *Vermont Law Review* (3): 647–82.

————. 1995. "Property Rights and Natural Resource Damage Assessment." *Ecological Economics* 14: 129–35.

————. 1997. "Rethinking Markets." *American Journal of Agricultural Economics* 79 (5): 1383–93.

————. 1998. "Expectations, Incentives, and Performance in America's Schools." *Daedalus* 127 (4): 41–66.

————. 2004. "Property Rights: Locke, Kant, Peirce and the Logic of Volitional Pragmatism." In Harvey M. Jacobs (ed.), *Private Property in the 21st Century*, pp. 19–30. Cheltenham: Edward Elgar.

Bromley, Daniel W., and Jouni Paavola (eds). 2002. *Economics, Ethics, and Environmental Policy: Contested Choices.* Oxford: Blackwell.

Buchanan, James M. 1972. "Politics, Property, and the Law: An Alternative Interpretation of *Miller et al. v. Schoene.*" *Journal of Law and Economics* (October) 15: 439–52.

Buchanan, James M., and W. C. Stubblebine. 1962. "Externality." *Economica* 29 (November): 371–84.

Burrows, Paul. 1980. *The Economic Theory of Pollution Control.* Cambridge, MA: MIT Press.

Checkland, S. G. 1964. *The Rise of Industrial Society in England: 1815–1885.* London: Longmans.

Chipman, John S., and James C. Moore. 1978. "The New Welfare Economics: 1939–1974." *International Economic Review* 19 (3): 547–84.

Christman, John. 1994. *The Myth of Property.* Oxford: Oxford University Press.

Coase, Ronald. 1937. "The Nature of the Firm." *Economica* 4: 386–405.

———. 1960. "The Problem of Social Cost." *Journal of Law and Economics* 3: 1–44.

Coate, Stephen. 2000. "An Efficiency Approach to the Evaluation of Policy Changes." *The Economic Journal* (April) 110: 437–55.

Cohen, Morris R., and Ernest Nagel. 1934. *An Introduction to Logic and Scientific Method.* New York: Harcourt and Brace.

Commons, John R. 1924. *Legal Foundations of Capitalism.* London: Macmillan.

———. 1931. "Institutional Economics." *American Economic Review* 21 (December): 648–57.

———. 1934. *Institutional Economics: Its Place in Political Economy.* London: Macmillan.

Cooter, Robert, and Peter Rappoport. 1984. "Were the Ordinalists Wrong about Welfare Economics?" *Journal of Economic Literature* 22 (June): 507–30.

Cropper, Maureen L. 2000. "Has Economic Research Answered the Needs of Environmental Policy?" *Journal of Environmental Economics and Management* 39 (3): 328–50.

Dahlman, Carl J. 1979. "The Problem of Externality." *Journal of Law and Economics* 22 (April): 141–62.

Damasio, Antonio. 1999. *The Feeling of What Happens.* New York: Harcourt Brace.

Dasgupta, Purnamita. 2004. "Valuing Health Damages from Water Pollution in Urban Delhi, India: A Health Production Function Approach." *Environment and Development Economics* 9: 83–106.

Davidson, Donald. 1963. "Actions, Reasons, and Causes." *Journal of Philosophy* 60 (23): 685–700.

Deacon, Robert T. 1994. "Deforestation and the Rule of Law in a Cross-Section of Countries." *Land Economics* 70 (4): 414–30.

———. 1995. "Assessing the Relationship between Government Policy and Deforestation." *Journal of Environmental Economics and Management* 28 (1): 1–18.

Deacon, Robert T., and Paul Murphy. 1997. "The Structure of an Environmental Transaction: The Debt-for-Nature Swap." *Land Economics* 73 (1): 1–24.

Demsetz, Harold. 1967. "Toward a Theory of Property Rights." *American Economic Review* (May) 57: 347–59.

Dewey, John. 1916. *Democracy and Education.* New York: Macmillan.

Diamond, Peter A., and Jerry A. Hausman. 1994. "Contingent Valuation: Is Some Number Better than No Number?" *Journal of Economic Perspectives* 8 (4): 45–64.

Ducasse, C. J. 1925. "Explanation, Mechanism, and Teleology." *Journal of Philosophy* 22: 150–55.

Ellickson, Robert C. 1991. *Order without Law: How Neighbors Settle Disputes.* Cambridge, MA: Harvard University Press.

Epstein, Richard. 1985. *Takings.* Cambridge, MA: Harvard University Press.

Feder, Gershon, and David Feeny. 1991. "Land Tenure and Property Rights: Theory and Implications for Development Policy." *World Bank Economic Review* 5 (1): 135–53.

Field, Alexander J. 1979. "On the Explanation of Rules Using Rational Choice Models." *Journal of Economic Issues* (March) 13: 49–72.

———. 1981. "The Problem with Neoclassical Institutional Economics: A Critique with Special Reference to the North/Thomas Model of Pre–1500 Europe." *Explorations in Economic History* 18: 174–98.

Fish, Stanley. 1989. *Doing What Comes Naturally.* Oxford: Clarendon Press.

Fisher, Anthony C. 1990. *Resource and Environmental Economics.* Cambridge: Cambridge University Press.

Gabel, H. Landis, and Bernard Sinclair-Desgagné. 1998. "The Firm, Its Routines and the Environment." In Tom Tietenberg and Henk Folmer (eds.), *The International Yearbook of Environmental Economics: 1998–1999*, chap. 3. Cheltenham: Edward Elgar.

George, Henry. 1955 [1905]. *Progress and Poverty.* New York: Doubleday, Page.

Gillroy, John Martin. 1992. "The Ethical Poverty of Cost-Benefit Methods: Autonomy, Efficiency, and Public Policy Choice." *Policy Science* 25: 83–102.

Gorman, William M. 1955. "The Intransitivity of Certain Criteria Used in Welfare Economics." *Oxford Economic Papers*, n.s., 7 (1): 25–35.

Graaff, J. de V. 1957. *Theoretical Welfare Economics.* Cambridge: Cambridge University Press.

Hahn, Frank H. 1970. "Some Adjustment Problems." *Econometrica* 38 (January): 1–17.

Hallowell, A. Irving. 1943. "The Nature and Function of Property as a Social Institution." *Journal of Legal and Political Sociology* (April) 1: 115–38.

Hands, D. Wade. 2001. *Reflection without Rules: Economic Methodology and Contemporary Science Theory.* Cambridge: Cambridge University Press.

Hardin, Russell. 2003. *Indeterminacy and Society.* Princeton: Princeton University Press.

Hartwick, J. M., and Nancy D. Oleweiler. 1986. *The Economics of Natural Resource Use.* New York: HarperCollins.

Hausman, Daniel M. 2001. "Explanation and Diagnosis in Economics." *Revue Internationale de Philosophie* 217: 11–26.

Hausman, D. M., and M. S. McPherson. 1996. *Economic Analysis and Moral Philosophy.* Cambridge: Cambridge University Press.

Hayek, F. 1960. *The Constitution of Liberty.* London: Routledge and Kegan Paul.

Hodgson, Geoffrey. 1988. *Economics and Institutions.* Cambridge: Polity Press.

———. 1998. "The Approach of Institutional Economics." *Journal of Economic Literature* 36 (March): 166–92.

Hoebel, E. Adamson. 1942. "Fundamental Legal Concepts as Applied in the Study of Primitive Law." 51 *Yale Law Journal* 951–66.

Hohfeld, Wesley N. 1913. "Some Fundamental Legal Conceptions as Applied in Judicial Reasoning." 23 *Yale Law Journal* 16–59.

———. 1917. "Fundamental Legal Conceptions as Applied in Judicial Reasoning." 26 *Yale Law Journal* 710–70.

Hoover, Kevin D. 1994. "Pragmatism, Pragmaticism, and Economic Method." In Roger Backhouse (ed.), *Contemporary Issues in Economic Methodology*, pp. 286–315. London: Routledge.

Hulswit, Menno. 2002. *From Cause to Causation: A Peircean Perspective*. Dordrecht: Kluwer.

Jaffe, Adam B., S. R. Peterson, Paul R. Portney, and Robert N. Stavins. 1995. "Environmental Regulations and the Competitiveness of U.S. Manufacturing: What Does the Evidence Tell Us?" *Journal of Economic Literature* 33 (March): 132–63.

James, William. 1907. *Pragmatism*. New York: World Publishing.

Joas, Hans. 1993. *Pragmatism and Social Theory*. Chicago: University of Chicago Press.

———. 1997. *The Creativity of Action*. Chicago: University of Chicago Press.

———. 2000. *The Genesis of Values*. Chicago: University of Chicago Press.

Kahneman, Daniel, and Amos Tversky. 1979. "Prospect Theory: An Analysis of Decision under Risk." *Econometrica* 47: 263–91.

Kaimowitz, David, and Arild Angelsen. 1998. *Economic Models of Tropical Deforestation*. Bogor, Indonesia: Center for International Forestry Research.

Kelman, Steve. 2002. Review of Matthew D. Adler, and Eric. A. Posner (eds.), *Cost-Benefit Analysis: Legal, Economic and Philosophical Perspectives* (Chicago: University of Chicago Press, 2001). *Journal of Economic Literature* 60 (December): 1241–42.

Krueckeberg, Donald A. 1999. "Private Property in Africa: Creation Stories of Economy, State, and Culture." *Journal of Planning Education and Research* 19 (Winter): 176–82.

Kuhn, Thomas S. 1989. "Objectivity, Value Judgment, and Theory Choice." In B. A. Brody and R. E. Grandy (eds.), *Readings in the Philosophy of Science*, pp. 356–68. Englewood Cliffs, NJ: Prentice-Hall.

Lancaster, Kelvin J. 1966. "A New Approach to Consumer Theory." *Journal of Political Economy* 74 (2): 132–57.

Lawson, Tony. 1997. *Economics and Reality*. London: Routledge.

Lewin, Shira B. 1996. "Economics and Psychology: Lessons for Our Own Day from the Early Twentieth Century." *Journal of Economic Perspectives* 34 (September): 1293–1323.

Little, I.M.D. 1949. "A Reformulation of the Theory of Consumer's Behaviour." *Oxford Economic Papers* 1: 90–102.

———. 1950. *A Critique of Welfare Economics*. London: Oxford University Press.

McCloskey, Donald. 1983. "The Rhetoric of Economics." *Journal of Economic Literature* 21: 481–517.

Macpherson, C. B. 1973. *Democratic Theory: Essays in Retrieval*. Oxford: Clarendon Press.

Macpherson, C.B. 1978. *Property: Mainstream and Critical Positions*. Toronto: University of Toronto Press.

Mäler, Karl-Göran. 1974. *Environmental Economics: A Theoretical Inquiry*. Baltimore: Johns Hopkins University Press.

Markandya, Anil, and M. N. Murty. 2004. "Cost-Benefit Analysis of Cleaning the Ganges: Some Emerging Environmental and Development Issues." *Environment and Development Economics* 9: 61–81.

Menand, Louis. 2001. *The Metaphysical Club*. New York: Farrar, Straus, and Giroux.

Mishan, E. J. 1969. *Welfare Economics: An Assessment*. Amsterdam: North-Holland.

———. 1971. "The Postwar Literature on Externalities: An Interpretive Essay." *Journal of Economic Literature* 9: 1–28.

———. 1980. "How Valid Are Economic Evaluations of Allocative Changes?" *Journal of Economic Issues* 14 (March): 143–61.

Mohr, Robert D. 2002. "Technical Change, External Economies, and the Porter Hypothesis." *Journal of Environmental Economics and Management* 43 (1): 158–68.

Nelson, Richard R., and Bhaven N. Sampat. 2001. "Making Sense of Economic Institutions as a Factor Shaping Economic Performance." *Journal of Economic Behavior and Organization* 44: 31–54.

Nietzsche, Friedrich. 1966. *Beyond Good and Evil: Prelude to a Philosophy of the Future*. New York: Random House.

———. 1984. *Human, All Too Human: A Book for Free Spirits*. Lincoln: University of Nebraska Press.

North, Douglass C. 1990. *Institutions, Institutional Change and Economic Performance*. Cambridge: Cambridge University Press.

North, Douglass C., and Robert P. Thomas. 1970. "An Economic Theory of the Growth of the Western World." *Economic History Review* 23 (1): 1–17.

———. 1971. "The Rise and Fall of the Manorial System: A Theoretical Model." *Journal of Economic History* 31: 777–803.

———. 1973. *The Rise of the Western World: A New Economic History*. Cambridge: Cambridge University Press.

Northrop, F.S.C. 1967. *The Logic of the Sciences and the Humanities*. New York: Meridian Books.

Olson, Mancur, Jr. 1965. *The Logic of Collective Action*. Cambridge, MA: Harvard University Press.

———. 1996. "Big Bills Left on the Sidewalk: Why Some Nations Are Rich, and Others Poor." *Journal of Economic Perspectives* 10 (Spring): 3–24.

Palmer, Karen, Wallace Oates, and Paul R. Portney. 1995. "Tightening Environmental Standards: The Benefit-Cost or the No-Cost Paradigm?" *Journal of Economic Perspectives* 9 (Fall): 119–32.

Pearce, David W., 1997. "Benefit-Cost Analysis, Environment, and Health in the Developed and Developing World." *Environment and Development Economics* 2: 210–14.

Pearce, David W., and R. Kerry Turner. 1990. *Economics of Natural Resources and the Environment*. Baltimore: Johns Hopkins University Press.

Peirce, Charles Sanders. 1877 [1997]. "The Fixation of Belief." In Louis Menand (ed.), *Pragmatism*, pp. 7–25. New York: Vintage Books.

———. 1878 [1997]. "How to Make Our Ideas Clear." In Louis Menand (ed.), *Pragmatism*. New York: Vintage Books.

———. 1934. *Collected Papers*. Vol. 5. Cambridge, MA: Harvard University Press.

———. 1957. *Essays in the Philosophy of Science.* Ed. Vincent Tomas. New York: Liberal Arts Press.

Planck, Max. 1936. *The Philosophy of Physics.* New York: Norton. Accessed at http://hypertextbook.com/physics/modern/planck/.

Porter, Michael E., and Claas van der Linde. 1995. "Toward a New Conception of the Environment-Competitiveness Relationship." *Journal of Economic Perspectives* (Fall) 9: 97–118.

Posner, Richard A. 2003. *Law, Pragmatism, and Democracy.* Cambridge, MA: Harvard University Press.

Rabin, Matthew. 1998. "Psychology and Economics." *Journal of Economic Literature* (March) 36: 11–46.

Ramstad, Yngve. 1990. "The Institutionalism of John R. Commons: Theoretical Foundations of a Volitional Economics." In Warren Samuels (ed.), *Research in the History of Economic Thought and Methodology*, pp. 53–104. Boston: JAI Press.

———. 2001. "John R. Commons' Reasonable Value and the Problem of Just Price." *Journal of Economic Issues* 35 (2): 253–77.

Raz, Joseph. 1997. "Incommensurability and Agency." In Ruth Chang (ed.), *Incommensurability, Incomparability, and Practical Reason*, pp. 110–28. Cambridge, MA: Harvard University Press.

Reder, Melvin W. 1982. "Chicago Economics: Permanence and Change." *Journal of Economic Literature* 35: 1–38.

Renouvier, Charles. 1859. *Essais de critique générale: Deuxième essai: L'homme.* Paris: Ladrange.

Robbins, Lionel. 1932. *An Essay on the Nature and Significance of Economic Science.* London: Macmillan.

Romer, Paul M. 1994. "The Origins of Endogenous Growth." *Journal of Economic Perspectives* 8 (1): 3–22.

Rorty, Richard. 1979. *Philosophy and the Mirror of Nature.* Princeton: Princeton University Press.

———. 1982. *Consequences of Pragmatism.* Minneapolis: University of Minnesota Press.

———. 1999. *Philosophy and Social Hope.* London: Penguin Books.

Rosenberg, Alexander. 1995. *Philosophy of Social Science.* Boulder, CO: Westview Press.

Runes, D. D. 1983. *Dictionary of Philosophy.* Savage, MD: Littlefield, Adams.

Russell, Bertrand. 1945. *A History of Western Philosophy.* New York: Simon and Schuster.

Samuels, Warren J. 1971. "The Interrelations between Legal and Economic Processes." *Journal of Law and Economics* 14 (October): 435–50.

———. 1974. "The Coase Theorem and the Study of Law and Economics." *Natural Resources Journal* 14 (January): 1–33.

———. 1989. "The Legal-Economic Nexus." 57 *George Washington Law Review* (6): 1556–78.

Samuelson, Paul A. 1950. "Evaluation of Real National Income." *Oxford Economic Papers*, n.s., 2 (1): 1–29.

Sanchez, Nicolas, and Jeffrey B. Nugent. 2000. "Fence Laws vs. Herd Laws: A Nineteenth-Century Kansas Paradox." *Land Economics* 76 (4): 518–33.

Sandler, Todd. 1993. "Tropical Deforestation: Markets and Market Failures." *Land Economics* 69 (3): 225–33.

Satz, Debra, and John Ferejohn. 1994. "Rational Choice and Social Theory." *Journal of Philosophy* 91 (2): 71–87.

Schmid, A. Allan. 1978. *Property, Power and Public Choice.* New York: Praeger.

———. 1986. "Neo-Institutional Economic Theory: Issues of Landlord and Tenant Law." In Terence Daintith and Gunther Teubner (eds.), *Contract and Organization: Legal Analysis in the light of Economic and Social Theory,* pp. 132–41. New York: Walter deGruyter.

Schumpeter, Joseph. 1961. *The Theory of Economic Development.* New York: Oxford University Press.

Selden, Thomas M., and Daqing Song. 1994. "Environmental Quality and Development: Is There a Kuznets Curve for Air Pollution Emissions?" *Journal of Environmental Economics and Management* 27 (2): 147–62.

Sen, Amartya. 1977. "Rational Fools: A Critique of the Behavioral Foundations of Economic Theory." *Philosophy and Public Affairs* 6: 317–44.

———. 1982. *Choice, Welfare, and Measurement.* Oxford: Backwell.

———. 1993. "Markets and Freedoms: Achievements and Limitations of the Market Mechanism in Promoting Individual Freedoms." *Oxford Economic Papers* 45: 519–41.

Shackle, G.L.S. 1961. *Decision, Order and Time in Human Affairs.* Cambridge: Cambridge University Press.

———. 1992. *Epistemics and Economics.* New Brunswick, NJ: Transaction Publishers.

Shapin, Steven. 1994. *A Social History of Truth.* Chicago: University of Chicago Press.

Simon, Herbert A. 1987. "Rationality in Psychology and Economics." In Robin Hogarth and Melvin W. Reder (eds.), *Rational Choice,* pp. 25–40. Chicago: University of Chicago Press.

———. 1991. "Organizations and Markets." *Journal of Economic Perspectives* 5 (Spring): 25–44.

Southgate, Douglas, Rodrigo Sierra, and Lawrence Brown. 1991. "The Causes of Tropical Deforestation in Ecuador: A Statistical Analysis." *World Development* 19 (9): 1145–51.

Stiglitz, Joseph E. 2002. *Globalization and Its Discontents.* New York: W. W. Norton.

Stone, Deborah. 1989. "Causal Stories and the Formation of Policy Agendas." *Political Science Quarterly* 104 (2): 281–300.

Tawney, R. H. 1978. "Property and Creative Work." In C. B. Macpherson (ed.), *Property: Mainstream and Critical Positions,* pp. 135–51. Toronto: University of Toronto Press.

Taylor, Lance. 1997. "The Revival of the Liberal Creed: The IMF and the World Bank in a Globalized Economy." *World Development* 25 (2): 145–52.

Tribe, Laurence H. 1972. "Policy Science: Analysis or Ideology?" *Philosophy & Public Affairs* 2 (1): 66–110.

Tversky, Amos, and Daniel Kahneman. 1987. "Rational Choice and the Framing of Decisions." In Robin Hogarth and Melvin W. Reder (eds.), *Rational Choice*, Chicago: University of Chicago Press.

Uchitelle, Louis. 1999. "A Real-World Economist: Kreuger and the Empiricists Challenge the Theorists." *New York Times*, April 20, C1.

Vatn, Arild. 2005. *Institutions and the Environment*. Cheltenham: Edward Elgar.

Vatn, Arild, and Daniel W. Bromley. 1994. "Choices without Prices without Apologies." *Journal of Environmental Economics and Management* 26 (2): 129–48.

———. 1997. "Externalities: A Market Model Failure." *Environmental and Resource Economics* 9: 135–51.

Veblen, Thorstein. 1898. "Why Is Economics not an Evolutionary Science?" *Quarterly Journal of Economics* 12 (4): 373–97. Reprinted in Thorstein Veblen, *The Place of Science in Modern Civilization*, pp. 56–81. (New Brunswick, NJ: Transaction Publishers, 1990).

Vincent, J. R. 1990. "Rent Capture and the Feasibility of Tropical Forest Management." *Land Economics* 66 (2): 212–23.

Viner, Jacob. 1961. "Hayek on Freedom and Coercion." *Southern Economic Journal* 27: 230–36.

von Wright, Georg Henrik. 1971. *Explanation and Understanding*. Ithaca: Cornell University Press.

———. 1983. *Practical Reason*. Ithaca: Cornell University Press.

Whewell, William. 1858. In Edward N. Zalta (ed.), *The Stanford Encyclopedia of Philosophy* (Spring ed.). Accessed at http://plato.stanford.edu/archives/spr2004/entries/whewell/.

Williams, Howard. 1977. "Kant's Concept of Property." *Philosophical Quarterly* 27: 32–40.

Index

abduction: applicability postulates and, 96–100; belief and, 23–24, 96–100, 127; cause and, 218–23; defined, 217; environmental issues and, 170, 178–79, 209–11; explanation and, 104; mad cow disease and, 160–61; neoclassical growth theory and, 168–69; plausible descriptions and, 218–23; prescription and, 127; property relations and, 192–94; public smoking and, 155–59; sufficient reason and, 110–14; truth and, 219–20; volitional pragmatism and, 137–38

Adler, Matthew D., 132

age requirements, 37–38

Agins v. City of Tiburon, 192

agriculture, 65–66, 82–83; deforestation and, 169–79; GMOs and, 164

Akerlof, George, 214

Allen, Julia C., 170

Alpay, E., 211

Altman, Morris, 211

American Cancer Society, 156

analytical engines, 90–96

Angelsen, Arild, 170, 173

antirealism, 20

Archimedean point, 21

architecture, 46

Arrow, Kenneth J., 5, 9, 118, 120, 201

Ascher, William, 175, 178

autobiographical self, 130

Barbier, E. T., 170

Barnes, Douglas F., 170

Bator, Francis M., 118

Baumol, William J., 118, 121

Bazelon, Coleman, 16

Beaux-Arts architecture, 46

Becker, Lawrence, 63

belief, 1, 165; abduction and, 23–24, 96–100, 127; applicability postulates and, 87; assumptions and, 92–96, 99; as benediction, 133; consensus and, 143–44, 148–49; deduction and, 88–96, 126–27; defined, 217; deforestation and, 169–79; desire and, 136–44; empirical testing and, 95–96; epistemic community and, 88; fixed, 166–79, 188, 217; GMOs and, 163–64; inductive, 100–102; internal acceptance and, 133; Pareto optimality and, 87, 131; plausible descriptions and, 218–23; predictive, 126–27; preferences and, 89; prescriptive, 126–27; primitive axioms and, 87–88, 92–101; scientific method and, 27, 87–88; settled, 27–28, 144–48; skepticism and, 133–34; surprise and, 139–40, 151; utility and, 89; valuable, 28, 133–36, 149, 218; warranted, 27, 130–32, 218

benefit-cost analysis: British fox hunts and, 4–5; DDT and, 3–4; environmental issues and, 205–11 (*see also* environmental issues); epistemic premise and, 15–16; European Union and, 14; national parks and, 5; Swedish traffic law and, 3; volitional pragmatism and, 132

Bernstein, Richard J., 20–21

Besley, Timothy, 119

Beyond Objectivism and Relativism (Bernstein), 20

Blackorby, Charles, 132

Boadway, Robin, 132

bovine spongiform encephalopathy (BSE), 159–61

Bowles, Samuel, 68, 149

Brandom, Robert B., 142

British Parliament, 4–5, 8, 220–21

Broberg, Gunnar, 101

Brock, William A., 125, 131, 214–15

Bromley, Daniel W., 16, 73, 132; economic regulations and, 202, 208; institutional content and, 56, 63–64; institutional evolution and, 186, 190, 194–95; prescription and, 119

Brown, Lawrence, 170

Bruce, Neil, 132

Buccola, Steven, 211

Buchanan, James M., 118, 120–21, 124

Bureau of Economic Analysis, 207–8

Burgess, J. C., 170

Burrows, Paul, 121

stituted personality and, 49; property relations and, 54–64; provisioning and, 33–34, 43; rationing transactions and, 72; religion and, 44, 46; spontaneous, 43–44; Swedish traffic and, 3, 47; working rules and, 43–54 (*see also* working rules)

organized provisioning, 33–34, 43

Origins of Endogenous Growth, The (Romer), 166

Owen, Robert, 4, 8, 220–21

ownership, 38–39; deforestation and, 169–79; *Just v. Marinette County* and, 186; Kant and, 188–89; *Penn Central Transportation Co. v. New York City* and, 184–88, 192; *possessio phenomenon* and, 189; property relations and, 54–64, 78–79, 180–98 (*see also* property relations); wetlands and, 185–86

Paavola, Jouni, 132

Palazzolo v. State of Rhode Island, 192

Palmer, Karen, 118, 120, 201–2, 206–8

Pareto optimality, 4–5, 81; belief and, 87; consequentialist welfarism and, 13; DDT and, 10–11; deductive bias and, 214–15; environmental issues and, 200, 202–3, 209; policy and, 6, 9–11; political economy and, 202; prescription and, 118–19, 122–26; property relations and, 182; sufficient reason and, 215; volitional pragmatism and, 150; warranted belief and, 131

Pearce, David W., 121, 201

Peirce, Charles Sanders, 19, 23–24, 139, 163; abduction and, 96; belief and, 87; deforestation and, 178; essence and, 195–96; induction and, 102; institutional content and, 45, 62–63; property relations and, 195; sufficient reason and, 212; volitional pragmatism and, 141, 146

Penn Central Transportation Co. v. New York City, 184–88, 192

Pennsylvania Coal Co. v. Mahon, 192

Pigovian tax, 126–27

Planck, Max, 211

Plato, 21, 72

political economy, 199, 202

politics: economic effects and, 199; environmental issues and, 199–211 (*see also* en-

vironmental issues); intertemporal choice and, 16–17. *See also* government

population growth, 170–71

Porter, Michael, 205–10

Portney, Paul R., 118, 120, 201–2, 206–8

positivism, 67–71, 215

Posner, Eric A., 132

Posner, Richard A., 197

Possessio phenomenon, 189

pragmatism: abduction and, 23–24; consequentialism and, 20–21; epistemic premise and, 15–16; explanation and, 103–14; human action and, 24–27; inference and, 13–19; institutional change and, 22–23 (*see also* institutional change); policy and, 23; prediction and, 115–28; settled belief and, 27–28; volitional, 14–18, 28, 129–51 (*see also* volitional pragmatism)

Pragmatism and Social Theory (Joas), 155

prediction: belief and, 126–27; cause and, 115–28; welfare calculation and, 121

premise, 217; epistemic, 15–16, volitional, 14–18, 144–48, 218

prescription: abduction and, 127; belief and, 126–27; Coase and, 121, 126–27; cognitive conjecture and, 125; comparative advantage precepts and, 127–28; dimwit conjecture and, 124; efficiency and, 123–24; institutional change and, 117–26; Pareto optimality and, 118–19, 122–26; public policy and, 118–19, 125; scientific method and, 123–24; working rules and, 122

Princip, Gavrilo, 116

property relations, 54–55; abduction and, 193–94; benefit stream and, 56–57; cause and, 183–84; Coase and, 58; common law and, 64, 196–97; compensation and, 59–61; contested, 180–88; costs of, 57–58; deforestation and, 169–79; endowments and, 182–83; essential aspect and, 195–96; institutional change and, 78–79; intelligible possession and, 189; *Just v. Marinette County* and, 186; Kant and, 188–90; *Penn Central Transportation Co. v. New York City* and, 184–88, 192; private, 64; property rights and, 61–64; social content of, 57; state, 64; surprise and, 193; wetlands and, 185–86

prospective volition, 25, 217

provisioning, 33–34, 43